MW01681283

Turkey

Turkey

The Middle Kingdom

Tor K. Birkeland

Copyright © 2024 Tor K. Birkeland
All rights reserved. No part of this publication may be reproduced, distributed, or transmitted in any form or by any means without the prior written permission of the publisher, except in the case of brief quotations embodied in critical reviews and certain other noncommercial uses permitted by copyright law.

Photo credits:
Cover photo: Benjamin Goetzinger,
https://commons.wikimedia.org/wiki/File:Istanbul_-_Hagia_Sophia.jpg, cropped.
All other photos: Tor K. Birkeland.

Birkeland, Tor K.
Turkey: the middle kingdom

ISBN: 978-82-303-6593-9

Contents

Preface

The question I had when I first moved to Turkey and which I have tried to answer in this book, is: "Why is Turkey the way it is?" When reading about Turkey in the newspapers it is hard not to scratch one's head. On the one hand, Turkey appears to be a relatively well-functioning democracy where elections are held and there are mainly peaceful changes of government. It also seems that humanism stands strong. Turkey, for example, has taken in more Syrian refugees than any other country.

On the other hand, some aspects of the country are associated with brutal dictatorships. For many years, Turkey has imprisoned more journalists than any other country and there are reports of torture in Turkish prisons. In addition, the country relates to Europe, NATO, and its surrounding countries in a confusing way. Recently, Turkey, a NATO member, acquired a Russian missile system, which has caused some concern in NATO about whether Russia will gain access to important information about NATO's defense systems. Turkish authorities dismiss the plea of the Kurds for more autonomy as justification for terror. The then leader of the party with the most Kurdish votes, the HDP, has been in prison since 2016 on (baseless) charges of terrorist sympathies. Turkey's constitution is crystal clear that the state is secular, but (the Turkish version of) Sunni Islam has a privileged position at the expense of other religions, beliefs, and ways of life.

Why is it so difficult for Turkey to safeguard freedom of expression, freedom of belief and other basic freedoms and rights for the entire population? What can explain Turkey's behavior in the international realm? How legitimate is the Turkish "fight against terrorism"? And not least: How is this experienced by the citizens of the country?

I arrived in Ankara in the summer of 2017, a year after the coup attempt against President Erdoğan. I met people who had experienced the fighter jets flying close by their balconies, and people who, from their living room windows, had seen the attack on the buildings of the government broadcasting agency TRT. I eventually got to know some of the many thousands who, after the coup attempt, had lost their jobs due to very vague or potential connections to the alleged coup plotters, and who therefore had to change careers. Apart from the excessive presence of security forces and the many ID checkpoints in the city center, and some absurd measures such as fencing off a human rights statue in downtown Ankara, there were not many signs of the drama that had taken place in the summer of 2016.

The fact that no one could explain who was behind the coup attempt did not reduce my curiosity about the country. The books I found about Turkey were mainly written by academics, they were often quite comprehensive, with a narrow focus or written for an academic audience. I wanted a book that gave me the main historical events and explanations while being entertaining and with personal stories from some of the people who had experienced those events. That I could not find. And since I assumed that there were more people than me who would be interested in such a book, I decided to write one.

This book is therefore mainly intended for people who want an introduction to Turkey, including historical events, whether the topic is new, one spends one's holiday there every now and then, or one has lived in the country for several years without familiarizing oneself with relevant literature. I also have a small hope that the occasional citizen of Turkey will pick it up and read it and perhaps get the history they know, presented in a slightly different way. Would such an outside perspective be useful for someone from Turkey? Many other conflict-ridden contexts show that such exposure could be useful. A third party's perspectives and analyses often make it easier for those who are in the middle of the situation to take a step back, breathe deeply, see the situation from several sides and think of new and creative solutions.

Some readers may find that I have been excessively diligent with source references in parts of the text. I have been careful with references because what is fact and what is propaganda, conspiracy theories, or fairy tales are not always easy to distinguish in Turkey. Some of the content in the book will probably seem controversial, perhaps even directly provocative. It has not been written to provoke or untimely criticize. It has been written in an attempt to convey relevant facts as objectively and neutrally as possible, in a context filled with politicized and populist portrayals and propaganda. In such a context one must have one's source references in order. The sources I have used are mainly academic books or non-fiction written by renowned academics and journalists as well as peer-reviewed articles.

Let me nevertheless underscore that I do not think that I have in fact managed to separate myself from my own values and normative attitudes. I have written from a conviction that human rights are in fact universal, and that all societies should strive to safeguard them as much as possible. An important part of that safeguarding is to ensure actual people's rule and the individual, physical integrity of each person, i.e. that no one should be exposed to violence without they themselves being an immediate violent threat.

I have tried to draw the long historical lines and describe the patterns which I believe can explain why Turkey is the way it is. In other words, I have tried to highlight the aspects of Turkey that will continue to be relevant for explaining the country long after the book is published. I have therefore tried to avoid placing too much emphasis on the most recent events, as it is too early to say whether those events are part of a pattern that will have great significance in the future.

Terminology and Spelling

Turkey's territory largely coincides with the Anatolian Peninsula, or Anatolia, also known as Asia Minor. Anatolia is the peninsula between the Black Sea and the Mediterranean, and the reader will become quite familiar with this name.

Pasha was a high-ranking official title, not a name. It is therefore capitalized when referring to a specific pasha (including his name) and lowercased when referring to pashas in general.

I mainly use English spellings for words and places where I have found English spellings. For well-known cities such as Istanbul and Izmir, I use English spellings, although in Turkish they are written with the first letter İ, i.e. İstanbul and İzmir. For lesser-known places, I use Turkish spellings, such as İznik and Aydın. The difference between I/ı and İ/i in Turkish is that İ/i is pronounced like the 'i' in the English *still*, while the pronunciation of Turkish I/ı resembles the sound of the final 'e' in *teacher, baker* or *roses*.

In addition to I/ı and İ/i, there are a few more Turkish letters that are pronounced differently than - or that do not exist - in English:

C/c is pronounced like 'j' in most English words, like the first sound of the English word *journey*. *Cep* (pocket) is pronounced 'jep.'

Ç/ç is pronounced 'ch,' like the start of the English word *cherry*. *Çin* (China) is pronounced 'chin.'

Ğ/ğ is silent and usually lengthens the preceding vowel. The Turkish name for Ararat, the mountain, is *Ağrı* and is pronounced with a long 'A' sound, something like 'A-ar-uh.'

I/ı and İ/i: See above paragraph.

J/j is pronounced like a voiced 'sh' sound, like the end of the French word *plage* or the 's' in the English word *treasure*. *Plaj* (beach) is pronounced like the French word for the same thing, *plage*.

Ö/ö is pronounced like the German 'ö' and does not have an equivalent sound in English. The last sound of the French words *adieu* and *milieu* is the same sound as the Turkish 'ö.'

R/r is pronounced like in Spanish and Italian.

U/u is pronounced like the German 'u' and does not have an equivalent sound in English. *Mutlu* (happy) is pronounced something like 'mootloo' but where the 'oo' sound is short.

Ü/ü resembles the German ü, like in *über*, and does not have an exact equivalent sound in English, although the last sound of *new* is very close. *Süt* (milk) is pronounced somewhat similarly to the English word *suit*.

The rest of the Turkish letters are pronounced similarly to the English pronunciation.

Acknowledgements

This book would be quite different, and probably far more boring, if it were not for everyone who has been willing to talk to me, knowing that what they said could end up in my book. In particular, I would like to mention my main interviewees who have shared their stories: Jihad, "Engin," Senem Deniz, "Mehmet," Fethiye Çetin and Damla Umut Uzun. They have breathed life into this narrative about Turkey.

When the book is published, it is unclear whether it will be perceived as controversial or provocative. I therefore choose not to mention by name all those whom I have not asked for permission to name, or who otherwise have not explicitly given me that permission, but who have shared their experiences and stories with me. I have also spoken to journalists, academics and other professionals in Turkey who have shared their experiences of writing about conditions in the country, who have explained political power dynamics to me or advised me on or lent me books or articles I should read. They know who they are, and I am deeply grateful to them.

I would especially like to thank Ceylan Akça, Özcan Öğüt, Ahmet Doğan at Sigma Insight Turkey, the Hrant Dink Foundation, Esteban Refshauge and Reidun Nesvik Birkeland for invaluable feedback on the script and tips for interviewees and sources. Others who have helped me with this have asked to be anonymous. Any errors that may remain are my sole responsibility.

1. Before Turkey

Places mentioned in this chapter.

Yet another child. Dead. God, where is your mercy? Where is your justice?

The year was probably 1911 and young Ummuhan lived in the village of Akyazı near Amasya, in the north of today's Turkey. She was a devout Muslim, there was no reason for God to let her children die. But now it had happened again. This time she had been pregnant with twin sons. The first was named Sabri before he died. It is unclear how long Sabri lived, but it is said that the parents were given a document equivalent to a birth certificate, and thus he must have lived long enough for this to have happened. According to Ummuhan's grandnephews, who live in the same village today, Sabri's twin brother, Mustafa, was born much later. It may have been weeks, perhaps even months, a rare but medically possible occurrence. When Sabri died Ummuhan made a promise - a *nazir* - to God; If he let Mustafa live, she would move to Medina, the City of the Prophet, and become a *mujaveer*, neighbor of the Prophet.

Mustafa grew and became strong and healthy, and Ummuhan realized that the time had come to fulfill her part of the *nazir*. She negotiated with her husband to move to the Hijaz, the area along the west coast of modern-day Saudi Arabia, which includes the holy cities of Mecca and Medina. She promised that she would find him a beautiful second wife there. Her husband could live with that arrangement. After arriving in Mecca, Ummuhan kept her promise of finding a second wife, but her husband and the new wife was not a good match, so he sent her away. It was probably an unfortunate turn of events to become a rejected second wife, but it did not, as it turned out, become a complete disaster for her. She eventually ended up as a tailor for Queen Iffat of Saudi Arabia. After Ummuhan and her family had spent one year in Mecca, they moved to Medina.

Almost thirty kilometers south of Ummuhan's hometown in Turkey is a town called Zile. From there another Turk, Moussa Kazim, moved to Medina for unknown reasons. Moussa Kazim must have been a respectable man, because in 1910 he was appointed director of one of Medina's many charitable foundations (*vakif*), founded by the black chief eunuch[1] Hacı Beşir Ağa under Sultan Ahmed III, in the 18th century. It was not uncommon for the dignitaries of the Ottoman Empire to ensure their legacies by establishing charitable foundations that would outlive them. During the lifetime of the Ottoman Empire, it was the Ministry of Divinity and Foundations that was responsible for appointing the directors of these foundations. However, the ministry was shut down together with the abolishment of the caliphate in March 1924. How would the new directors of the foundations be appointed now? The directors ended up taking over as the owners of the foundations, and the director's title became a matter of inheritance. The foundations were usually in possession of much wealth and many properties. Being born into a foundation family meant that one's future was secured.

When Moussa Kazim died in 1945, his son took over the foundation. When the son died in 1974, Moussa Kazim's grandson was too young to take over and the Saudi authorities appropriated the foundation temporarily, promising to return it to Moussa Kazim's grandson upon his coming of age. This promise was never kept, and the grandson is still trying, after more than 40 years, to get the foundation back to the family.

Ummuhan from Akyazı and Moussa Kazim from Zile belonged to the same generation and came from the same area of the Ottoman

Empire, and both ended up in Medina. They probably knew about each other since the Turkish community in Medina was rather small, but there is no indication that they were acquaintances or friends. Their grandchildren, however, ended up marrying each other. Moussa Kazim's granddaughter married Ummuhan's grandson, and the couple had a son and a daughter.

The son, Jihad, does not protrude from his immediate surroundings and has a somewhat cautious appearance. When he opens his mouth, however, one quickly understands that this is a man with a lot to offer. In his fluent and perfect English, he explains that while studying at the University of Ankara he is trying to document his Turkish ancestry. He is a Saudi Arabian citizen but believes Turkish citizenship would give him more opportunities and greater freedom.

"I have the old Ottoman document that my great-grandfather, Moussa Kazim, received from the Ministry of Foundations when he was appointed director of the Beşir Ağa Foundation. But I haven't found any document linking him to Zile or the Ottoman census records. If I find it, my mother can apply for Turkish citizenship, and then I can apply," he explains. He has visited the archives of both Amasya, Zile, Istanbul, and Ankara to find documents that may be helpful, but in the sea of documents you need more than a name of the person you are looking for. Jihad's mother visited the archive in Zile, but almost all the original documents had disappeared during a fire. In the Amasya archive, a flood had destroyed most documents. The local census records had been restored by registering locals who turned up at a public office for that purpose, but only people still living in the area were registered. His best bet now is the Ottoman census records in Ankara, but the archives are not open to just anybody to come and look through old documents. Jihad needs specific information about exactly which document he is looking for, and then ask the archive staff to find it.

Jihad's story is by no means unique. The Ottoman Empire was enormous, and officials were sent out from Istanbul to serve in the provinces. Most of the cities having a large Ottoman presence at that time, such as Baghdad, Cairo, Tripoli in Libya, Akkar and Tripoli in Lebanon, Tunis, and Algiers, today still have a significant group of Turks who are descendants of the Ottomans. Jihad's father grew up in a home where both Turkish and Arabic were still spoken, but Jihad's father was the youngest and never learned Turkish like his older brothers. Jihad grew up in an Arabic speaking home and learned Turkish as an adult. The scheme that grants Turkish citizenship to anyone who can trace their ancestry directly back to current Turkey, makes the Ottoman Empire still have tangible consequences for people's lives far beyond Turkey's borders.

The Turkey of today, however, is something completely different from a mini version of the Ottoman Empire. Although the Ottomans have left their clear mark on current Turkey, Anatolia (also known as Asia Minor, or *Anadolu* in Turkish), the peninsula between the Black Sea and the Mediterranean Sea, which makes up most of today's Turkey, has always been populated by many different peoples. Only separated from Europe by the narrow Bosporus Strait and the Dardanelles, the peninsula has bound together north, south, east, and west for a very long time. 'Anatolia' means 'where the sun rises' and originates from Greek.

This chapter is about the time in Anatolia before Turkey became a country. There are two aspects in particular that it is important to convey regarding this time period. Firstly, Anatolia has been the arena for the migration of people groups for a very long time. Many people groups have migrated through or by the peninsula, or they have warred to create their own space on it until they have been conquered themselves. People groups have had to relate to Anatolia in one way or the other when they have migrated between Africa and Europe, or between Europe and Asia. In many ways, Anatolia is in the middle of everything. The population of Anatolia today - that is, the population of Turkey - is a result of this.

Secondly, the Ottoman Empire played a major role for how Turkey turned out. A significant part of the political elite that established the Republic of Turkey in 1923 had many years of experience from the Ottoman state apparatus. Furthermore, the Islamic nature of the Ottoman state was the reason why the population in Anatolia in the 1920s was predominantly Muslim. The tension between the religious groups - mainly between Muslims and Christians - had enormous and horrible consequences right before the foundation of the republic. Also, the greatness of the Ottoman era plays an important role in Turkish political rhetoric. Many Turks appreciate being reminded of the fact that they are "actually" Ottoman, and some politicians are eager to tie this into their political arguments. Understanding the Ottoman greatness is important for understanding Turkish political rhetoric.

We will start from the beginning of human settlement right after the ice age and move swiftly through time and the powerful kings who ruled in their pockets of the world until we get to the Romans. We will see how the Roman presence became the Byzantine Empire, which was then defeated, slowly but surely, by the Turks. We will then look at the strengthening and growth of the Ottoman Empire and explore some of the aspects that may have caused its downfall.

In the Beginning

The earliest traces of human settlement, from 13,000 to 7,000 B.C., have been found in Belbaşı and Beldibi, southwest of modern Antalya. If you travel a little north, about an hour's drive from Konya, you reach Çatalhöyük, the largest settlement from the late Stone Age found in the Middle East. Only small parts of the two large mounds have been excavated and there is still much to explore, but archaeologists say that people began settling there around 7,400 B.C., and it is estimated that between 3,500 and 8,000 people lived in the town at most.[2]

Many of the findings that have been made in connection with the excavations have been transported to the well-renowned Museum of Anatolian Civilizations in Ankara.[3] In the east, close to Diyarbakır, is Çayönü, an archaeological site where there have been several significant findings of early civilization, including what is probably the earliest known production of copper.[4]

Moving forward in time, we arrive at two well-known Anatolian civilizations from ancient times: the Trojans and the Hittites. The first findings from the fabled city of Troy are from the year 2,920 B.C., and after that year the city was destroyed several times by fire, earthquakes, and war. The ruins of Troy are two miles south of Çanakkale at the Aegean coast. Since no texts have been found in the city, we do not know what language the population spoke. The war that destroyed the city around 1,200 B.C. may have been the one described by Homer in his Iliad if that is based on actual events. Later, both the Persian King Xerxes and the Macedonian Alexander the Great visited the city, in 480 and 334 B.C., respectively, before it was conquered by the Romans in 85 B.C. The Romans liked the city especially well because of a myth that linked their ancestors to Troy. This can be seen, among other things, through the aqueduct, the beautiful buildings, and the theater. After the sixth century A.D. the city was gradually forgotten.[5]

The other ancient civilization that is known outside of the academic world is the Hittites, who are repeatedly mentioned in the Tanakh, the holy scriptures of the Jews (the Old Testament for Christians). The Hittites, according to Scripture, were the descendants of Heth, Canaan's son and Noah's great-grandchild. According to archeology, it is unclear where the Hittites came from, but they spoke an Indo-European language and entered Anatolia around 2000 B.C. They took the capital of the Hatties, Hattuşa, in 1700 B.C. and made it their own capital. The city had already existed at that time as the mighty city of the Hatties for 700 years, i.e. since 2500 B.C., and its ruins can today be seen some 180 km east of Ankara.

In a remarkably short time, the Hittites conquered large areas of land. The kingdom has been called the "fourth great power" of the time (where the three others were Egypt, Babylonia, and Assyria). The core area of the Hittites stretched approximately from today's Ankara and northeast to approximately today's Amasya (but not all the way to the Black Sea) and southeast to today's Kayseri. In addition, the area west, south (to the Mediterranean), and east of this is also considered to have been part of the realm of the Hittites, although it is unclear how far away from Hattuşa the Hittites had some form of control.

The Hittites dominated most of Anatolia for 400 years and it is unclear why they lost their power. It may have been the Phrygians, a third Anatolian civilization, who became too strong for them. The power of the Phrygians grew from the year 1200 B.C. until they dominated almost the entire Anatolian peninsula in the 8th century B.C. Several of Phrygia's kings were named Midas, and the tomb of one of them can today be visited near Polatlı, southwest of Ankara. There you can also see the ruins of Gordium, the Phrygian capital, known for its famous knot. According to legend, the yoke of a bull cart in the palace in Gordium had been tied with a very complicated and tight knot. An oracle had predicted that the man who was able to untie the Gordian knot would rule over all of Asia. Alexander the Great arrived in Gordium in the winter of 334-33 B.C., and he wanted to try his hand on the knot. The most popular version of how he solved the task is the following: He first tried to loosen the knot in the conventional way, but after a while without luck he declared that it did not matter how the knot was loosened. He took his sword and cut the knot in two with a single stroke.

Besides the Trojans, the Hittites, the Phrygians, and the Macedonian Alexander the Great, Anatolia has been dominated by Persian and more local kings and chiefs. Around the year 200 B.C. the Romans arrived and subdued much of Anatolia over the next centuries. About a hundred years before the Romans came, the Galatians[6] came from Europe and conquered an area which came to be known as Galatia. Galatia was later made into a Roman province, with Ancyra (modern day Ankara) as its capital.

The Roman Empire declined simultaneously with the increasing popularity of Christianity. Emperor Constantine the Great (272-337 A.D) also embraced the new faith, and in the year 330 A.D. he decided that a new capital should be established in the ancient Greek city of Byzantium. The city was first called New Rome (*Nova Roma*) and then became known as Constantinople, the capital of the Eastern Roman Empire. The city has been known to different people by different names. The local Jews used the first two syllables of the Greek name Konstantinoupolis to form the name Kushta. Armenians picked the last part of the Greek name and called it Bolis. Slavs called it Tsarigrad. The Vikings called it Miklagard, "the great city." Interestingly, the Greek *eis tēn polin* - "to the city" - is similar to "Istanbul."[7]

Initially, Constantinople was only supposed to ease the burden on Rome and manage the eastern part of the Roman Empire. In 395, however, they became two separate empires, and the Eastern Roman Empire, now known as the Byzantine Empire, became the dominant one. The "Byzantine Empire" name, however, is a fairly modern invention. It first appeared in English in 1794, and the people running the empire never thought of it as something politically separate from the Roman Empire.[8]

There was a close connection between church and state, and it was unclear what was what. Greek became the administrative language. At its largest, the Byzantine Empire covered much of Europe, the Middle East, and North Africa but the territory was under constant pressure. For example, Arab tribes became a force to be reckoned with after the death of the Prophet Muhammad in 632 A.D., and they fought their way all the way to Constantinople, which they besieged for five years before the Byzantines managed to drive them away in 678.

The Byzantine Empire had its heyday in the 10th and 11th centuries before its decline began. After Constantinople fell under the fourth crusade in 1204, a result of Venetian power politics,[9] the Latin Empire was established in Constantinople. The rest of the empire disintegrated into various feudal states, where the Byzantine kingdoms Nicaea (headquartered in the city of Nicaea,[10] today's İznik) and Trebizond (with headquarters in the town of Trabzon along the Black Sea) were the most powerful.

The Turks

As events would have it, it was the Turks who in the end destroyed the Byzantine Empire. The Turks, however, were not native to Anatolia. They originally came from Asia, where archaeological findings and Chinese texts reveal some of their history. At the end of the 19th century, archaeological findings in Mongolia and Siberia showed that the Turks had their own epic poetry in the 8th century. The contents of the epic corresponded with historical events described in Chinese sources. It is in Chinese sources that the earliest use of the word "Turk" is found, referring to a nomadic tribe that was at the foot of a mountain that was reminiscent of a helmet. "Turk" is said to have been a Turkish word that meant helmet (it does not in modern Turkey-Turkish). The Turks and the Uighurs[11] probably have the same origin as the Huns.[12]

A man by the name of Asena is said to have led a tribe in an area that is today part of the Chinese province Gansu. Asena and his people were driven away by the Wei Dynasty in the 400s, and they fled west.[13] A few generations later, in the mid-500s, Notur was the leader of the tribe, and he is to have been the first to use the word "Turk" about his people. The power of the Turks had to be reckoned with, and several Turkish kingdoms came and went in Asia and Central Asia.

The large and sustained migration from the steppes to the Middle East began in the 10th century when Turkish tribes in Central Asia crossed the Jaxartes River.[14] The Turkish chief Seljuk and his descendants moved ever further westwards, and they had vassal states[15] in the late 11th century from Kashgar in modern China to Palestine. The great realm of the Seljuks had several power centers, including Merv in modern-day Turkmenistan, Ray (near Teheran), Isfahan/Esfahan and Hamadan in Iran, and Baghdad in modern-day Iraq. Some of the Seljuk sultans moved between these cities based on season. Several branches of the Seljuk dynasty controlled areas in the periphery of the empire, if one can call a realm with so little concentration of power an empire. The most important of these "peripheral branches" was the Süleyman branch which ruled over much of Anatolia from 1071 to 1308.[16]

No one understands precisely why the existing kingdoms collapsed in the face of the Seljuks. It appears to be a mixture of luck and good timing that the Seljuks would go on the offensive at a time when the local kings and chiefs of the area were weak.[17] In 1071, they went up against the Byzantines near Manzikert[18] and won. This caused a power vacuum in Anatolia that different groups tried to fill. Autonomous Turkmen tribes moved far into Anatolia, often bypassing Byzantine fortifications standing as Byzantine islands in a sea of Turkmen tribes. All the violence made it difficult to cultivate the land, and this led to widespread hunger in 1079-80. The power struggles that went on at the top of the Byzantine hierarchy, where aspiring leaders used Turkish mercenaries in exchange for land, largely caused the Byzantines to lose control of Anatolia. The population of Anatolia at this point in time was a mixture of mainly Kurds, Arabs, Greeks, Armenians and Jews, as well as Turkmen.[19]

The Seljuks, however, were not the only Turks in Anatolia. Although the nomadic Turkmen and the Seljuks in Anatolia were not one political entity, they were portrayed as such in several crusader documents. It has nonetheless been difficult to determine the relationship between the Turkmen and the Seljuks due to the lack and insufficiency of source material. What historians know is that there were Turks who led a nomadic lifestyle, referred to as Turkmen in the literature, and Turks who claimed sovereignty over the former Byzantine possessions (towns and territories). The latter are referred to as Seljuks or Seljuk Turks.

The Seljuks were passionate, but pragmatic, Sunni Muslims. There were many Shiites high up in the Seljuk administration, and several Shiite dynasties were allowed to keep their local power upon becoming vassals. The Seljuk leader was called sultan by the Seljuks, which would indicate that they were the sole rulers in the area they saw themselves as controlling. Nevertheless, there is much to suggest that many of the Turkmen did not consider the Seljuk leaders as anything more than warrior chiefs.

Anatolia has attracted warriors from the east and west, and even the Normans from the far north were at one time a power element on the peninsula. The Normans initially came as Vikings from Scandinavia to Northern France with the chief Rollo in 911. They conquered the area, which became known as Normandy. Some of them moved further south, and conquered areas in southern Italy and in Sicily. Normans from there were hired as mercenaries by the Byzantine Empire (and later by the Crusades). They acted with a great deal of autonomy, sometimes in a treacherous manner. The Norman Roussel de Bailleul was on the Byzantine side at the Battle of Manzikert but withdrew when defeat seemed inevitable. Despite the betrayal, he was retained as a general for the Byzantines, who needed all the help they could get. He established his own independent state in Galatia, with Ankara as its capital, in 1073. On several occasions, he had disputes with the emperor because of his obstinacy. Finally, the emperor had had enough and entered into an agreement with the Seljuks to capture Roussel. The Seljuks succeeded, and he was handed over to the Byzantines and executed in 1077.[20]

This was not the beginning of a long and happy friendship between the Seljuks and the Byzantines. In the period between 1071 and the arrival of the First Crusade in 1097, who had power over which areas and cities fluctuated. Occasionally, Turkmen warrior tribes operated without Seljuk influence, or to escape Seljuk dominance, further and further into Byzantine area. Both these Turkmen tribes and the Seljuks increasingly became a threat to the Byzantine Empire, and in the end, Emperor Alexander asked the Pope in Rome to come to his aid. Pope Urban II was not dumbfounded and initiated the First Crusade. When the crusaders arrived in 1097, they helped recover much of the lost territories along the coast of Anatolia before they fought their way onward and conquered Jerusalem. After the crusaders defeated the Seljuks at their headquarters in Nicaea, many Turks withdrew to the inlands. A number of Turks entered the city of Iconium (modern Konya) which eventually became the Seljuk capital of Rum. The Byzantine Empire lasted for another several centuries, but it is doubtful whether the Byzantines had any meaningful control over the Anatolian inlands after 1071.

The Seljuks were in control of most of Anatolia until the Mongols became interested in the territory in the mid-13th century. The Mongolian chief Genghis Khan, possibly history's greatest military genius, had by then established a vast empire stretching from the Pacific to the Black Sea. After he died in 1227, his descendants continued the conquests and expanded Mongolian Empire. Although the Mongols defeated the Seljuks in an important battle in 1243 and introduced direct administration of the Seljuk realm in the late 13th century, the degree of control was not very high. The Mongols were also engulfed in their own internal strifes and were mostly interested in controlling the trade routes from India to Europe which went through North-East Anatolia. Western Anatolia was not monitored as closely.

The Ottoman Empire

In the early 14th century, Anatolia was dominated by a number of Muslim Turkmen emirates. One of them was Osman's emirate in Anatolia's northwest. It is unclear when and why Osman began to behave like a sultan and conqueror, but 150 years after his death, the myth that would justify the Ottomans' supremacy was recorded. According to legend, Osman one night stayed in the house of a holy man, and that night he had a dream:

> He saw that a moon arose from the holy man's breast and came to sink in his own breast. A tree then sprouted from his navel and its shade compassed the world. Beneath this shade there were mountains, and streams flowed forth from the foot of each mountain. Some people drank from these running waters, others watered gardens, while yet others caused fountains to flow. When Osman awoke he told the story to the holy man, who said 'Osman, my son, congratulations, for God has given the imperial office to you and your descendants and my daughter Malhun shall be your wife'.[21]

Thus began Osman's God-given mission and the seed of the Ottoman Empire had been sown.

The Ottomans were first mentioned by a Byzantine historian in 1301, when the first military encounter between Osman's men and Byzantine soldiers took place. It would be another century and a half before Osman's descendants managed to put an end to the Byzantine Empire. The historians have still not found a very good explanation for why it was precisely Osman's dynasty that would conquer the surrounding dynasties. However, it is clear that Osman and his descendants had found a key to military superiority, and they continued to refine this advantage. Already in the 14th century, long before the Europeans did so, the Ottomans established their strong, permanent, central army. The core of the army was the Janissaries (in Ottoman Turkish *yeni çeri*, new army/soldier). Europe did not establish comparable armies until the mid-17th century. Until then, European kings and princes fought their wars with mercenary armies and seasonal soldiers. For example, in 1558, 70% of the French army were German and Swiss soldiers. The Europeans only had a core of the army as salaried soldiers - the rest were hired based on need in wartime.

Although the Ottoman leader was sultan, that is, Islamic emperor/king, coexistence and compromise with other religious groups always signified the Ottomans. Their own historians, however, have placed great emphasis on the Holy War and the spread of Islam as a driving force for the sultans' conquests. Nonetheless, there is reason to believe that the pursuit of wealth and power was the main driving force, as it was in the later "Christian" European colonization of America, Africa, and Asia.

In the Ottomans' own historical justification of the conquests, it is made clear that the Christian states (mainly to the west, that is, the Balkans and Europe) could justifiably be conquered at will, and that it was only a matter of time before they would be incorporated into "Islamic land." It was more challenging to justify the conquests of other Muslim territories, which were often portrayed as peaceful conjugations with the Ottoman Empire. Alternatively, they were artfully justified in other ways by religious authorities.[22] In addition to the open and public role that Islam played in the empire, the mystical Muslim brotherhoods (*tarikat* in Turkish) have also always played a role. For example, the Bektaşi Order, initially an insignificant sect, was to be closely linked to the Janissaries, the core of the Ottoman military.

The Ottomans continued expanding their realm and exploited the weaknesses and internal strife of both the Byzantines and other rulers, and also made use of strategic marriages. In 1333, the first diplomatic meeting was held between the Byzantine emperor and the head of the Ottomans, Osman's son Orhan. The emperor agreed with Orhan that the Byzantines would keep the few areas in Anatolia of which they were still in control in exchange for payment to Orhan.

The progress of the Ottomans was noticed in Europe. Orhan's son Murat invaded Serbia in 1389, and although the Ottomans defeated the Serbs, Murat died in the Battle of Kosovo. France's King Charles VI went to Notre Dame to thank God when he heard the news of Murat's death.[23]

Murat's son, Bayezid, took over the throne. He made sure his brother was killed to remove any threats to his own power. It is possible that previous takeovers in the Ottoman dynasty also involved killing close male family members, but Bayezid's killing of his brother is the first documented murder. It was not to be the last. The Ottomans followed the Mongolian practice, which also the Seljuks had followed, letting it be up to God to decide who would inherit the throne. This meant that it was the one who *de facto* sat on the throne who was the legitimate leader. To be the one who sat on the throne, the Sultan had to have the backing of his soldiers and officials. In other words, the Sultan's legitimacy suffered from circular logic; It was God's will for him to have the power if he actually had power, and if he had the power, it was God's will.

This succession arrangement resulted in the acceptance - and normality - of the eldest son killing his younger brothers when the sultan died. The gravest examples of this happened towards the end of the 16th century when Murat III was to take over the throne after his father, and when Murat III's son Mehmet III was to take over from his father. Murat III got his nine brothers - several of them small children - strangled. (The brothers had to be strangled so as not to commit a sin by shedding royal blood.)[24] Mehmet III did the same with his younger brothers. The justification for the killings was that the choice was to either kill them while one had the chance or wait for them to try to seize power by going to war at a later date.

But even though the theory was that it was the most qualified son of the sultan (or, exceptionally, another qualified male family member) who were to take over the throne, the reality was that the leaders of the sultan's military power, the Janissaries, had to agree with the assessment. If the Janissaries believed that a son other than the sultan's favorite should become the new sultan, it was ultimately the Janissaries who had their way.

The succession arrangement made the empire vulnerable to external manipulation. For example, the Byzantine Empire on occasion played the Ottoman princes up against each other, something they themselves were subjected to in the opposite direction. Enemies could also capture a prince during a battle and hold him until an opportune moment came to create a power struggle within the Ottoman Empire by releasing him. Alternatively, one could demand money from the sultan to keep him in captivity.

Ottoman Women

As elsewhere in the world, it was the men who had the power in the Ottoman Empire, but in some cases the women of the sultan's harem[25] took advantage of the opportunities they had for influence. A wife or concubine who had born the sultan a son could ally with like-minded officials to get her son to become the next sultan. One of the most famous is Hürrem Sultan (c. 1502-1558). (The sultan's wife was also called sultan.)

There was a lot about Hürrem that was new and different. She was a slave girl from Ruthenia[26] who ended up being Sultan Süleyman's favorite concubine (*haseki*). After she had given birth to six children, five of whom were sons, Süleyman married her in 1534 at a spectacular wedding. A European witness wrote about what he had seen during the wedding:

> In the old Hippodrome a great tribune is set up, the place reserved for the Empress and her ladies screened with a gilt lattice. Here Roxelana and the Court attended a great tournament in which both Christian and Moslem Knights were engaged and tumblers and jugglers and a procession of wild beasts and giraffes with necks so long they as it were touched the sky.[27]

Until then it was unheard of for a sultan to marry a concubine. It was also unheard of to get more than one son with the same woman in the harem, as this would necessarily cause the sons' mother to ally with one of them in the inevitable succession struggle. After the wedding, Hürrem moved with the children from the old palace, where the harem was, to the sultan's Topkapı Palace, another breach of convention. If the sultan was away, she would write passionate letters to him, and she was accused of enchanting him. Considering what the sultan allowed of Hürrem's innovations, it is evident that the Sultan was very enthusiastic about her. Who wouldn't be, at the recipient end of the passion that Hürrem exuded, for instance in these lines from one of her letters:

> My Sultan, there is no limit to the burning anguish of separation. Now spare this miserable one and do not withhold your noble letters. Let my soul gain at least some comfort from a letter.[28]

Hürrem knew the art of conspiracy and was able to rid herself of enemies and people who might threaten her future position. It was probably because of her conspiring that her greatest enemy, Grand Vizier Ibrahim (the sultan's right hand and head of government), was executed. The next grand vizier was easier for Hürrem to work with in order to secure her position. An example of this is how the two are supposed to have got rid of the sultan's oldest son, Mustafa, whose mother was another concubine. Mustafa grew up and became a popular man, and rumors arose that he planned to take over the throne (which the sultan's father had done to his father). The rumors developed into suspicions, and Mustafa was executed in 1553 when he was in his late 30s. Sultan Süleyman I thus took the life of his own son, and Mustafa was the second adult son of a sultan to be executed in the history of the Ottoman Empire.

Half a century later, another woman, Kösem Sultan (c. 1589-1651), was to go down in the history books as one of the most powerful Ottoman women. In her case as in Hürrem's, it was her ability to play the power game that secured her position. She became Sultan Ahmed's favorite concubine and later wife, and when Ahmed died in 1617 it was his 26-year-old brother, Mustafa (I), instead of his eldest, but only 14-year-old son, Osman, who became the sultan. It is believed that Kösem played a crucial role in preventing Osman - who was not her son - from becoming the sultan. Kösem had ambitions for her own, younger, sons. She succeeded in first getting her eldest but very young son Murat (IV) on the throne in 1623, and she served as regent until Murat grew up. Murat died in 1640, before reaching the age of 30, upon which Kösem's second oldest son, Ibrahim, took over the throne. He was considered mad and was executed in 1648, when his seven-year-old son Mehmet (IV) - Kösem's grandson - was made sultan. Kösem had great influence over her young sons and her young grandchild, and in the beginning acted as regent for all three until they were old enough to govern.

Things went south for Kösem when she participated in the plan of the Janissaries to get rid of her daughter-in-law, Turhan, Sultan Mehmet's mother. It had been decided that her daughter-in-law was too young to become regent for her son Mehmet, and that was why the grandmother, Kösem, had assumed the position. But as Turhan grew older, Kösem considered her a threat. Kösem was suspected, with good reason, of planning to poison Mehmet so that his younger half-brother, whose mother was less ambitious, would be sultan. But

Turhan was not caught off guard; She moved preemptively and sent someone to kill Kösem one night in September 1651. Kösem was then nearly 70 years old and had greatly influenced the governing of the Ottoman Empire for half a century.

Thus, there were some women who ended up with a substantial amount of real power in the Ottoman Empire. But most women in the harem, especially the sultan's daughters, did not have much say and were married off according to what was best for building alliances and strengthening the sultan's power. Sultan Ahmed III (sultan in the period 1703-1730) brought this strategy to new heights. He had a total of 30 daughters, and those who did not die at a young age - which was quite normal - were married to mighty men in the empire to ensure their loyalty. If a husband died, the sultan's daughter had to expect getting married again. "Six of Ahmed's daughters contracted seventeen marriages between them: the most-married was Saliha Sultan, who had five husbands."[29]

State or Mafia?

When exploring the history of the Ottoman Empire, one will find that there is a strong similarity between a sultan and a mafia boss. This is of course not unique to the Ottoman Empire; the concept of gathering all the power in a few hands (kings, sultans, emperors, tsars, and so on) has always been similar to what we today see as mafia behavior or organized crime. You take over an area, demand tax or protection money, and do whatever you assume will make you richer and more powerful. Providing something for the population, such as health care or education, is not so important unless it will make you popular - and therefore protected - in certain areas. In some cases, it seems that the difference between a mafia boss and a supreme ruler is mainly about semantics; if actors who are not part of the state carry out organized crime, it is referred to as mafia activity. If it is the state that does it, it is referred to by other names. Corruption, power abuse, nepotism, police state, and so on.

For the Ottoman Empire, the state-enacted mafia business manifested itself in its own way. An early example of mafia-like lies, deception and backstabbing is from the 15th century, after a rebellion against Sultan Murat II (r. 1421-1444 and 1446-1451). Murat did away with the main antagonist and promised his co-conspirator Cüneyd of

Aydın safe passage home to Aydın.[30] The passage turned out not to be so safe. Cüneyd and his family were murdered, and Murat took over Aydın. A few years later, in 1463, Bosnia's king, Stephen Tomašević, surrendered in battle against the Ottomans, against a promise that he would not be harmed. Sultan Mehmet II made Bosnia an Ottoman province (Bosnia had been a vassal state until then), and despite his promises gave orders to have King Stephen executed.

The Japanese Yakuza mafia is known for its practice of ordering members who make mistakes to cut off a finger joint. In the Ottoman Empire, a mistake or a failed mission could be significantly worse for one's health. Towards the end of the 15th century, Sultan Bayezid II had to pursue his brother Cem after the latter had made claims to the throne. Cem managed to get away and fled west, to France. Bayezid placed the responsibility for Cem's escape on Gedik Ahmed Pasha, former grand vizier, and had him murdered. In addition, Cem's young son was killed in Istanbul. Losing control of some of the empire's territory could also be an unforgivable mistake. When the commander-in-chief Arab Receb Pasha failed to hold Nis in Serbia when a Habsburg army came to take the city in September 1689, he was executed.

"Never go against the family" became a very well-known Don Carleone quote from the Godfather movies. That instruction also applied in practice to the vassals and provincial governors of the Ottoman Empire. The Druse chief Fakhr al-Din controlled a territory that covered modern Lebanon and Northern Israel. He was not completely satisfied with his subordinate position in the Ottoman Empire. In 1608, he entered into an agreement with the Duke of Tuscany, a clear "go against the family" maneuver. The Ottoman grand vizier decided to put an end to Fakhr al-Dins growing power. The latter had to seek refuge at his duke friend's in 1613 but returned five years later when his brother had come to an agreement with the sultan. Fakhr al-Din, however, maintained his defiant behavior. He continued trying to expand his territories, which in 1635 resulted in his execution.

The Legitimacy of the Ottoman Empire

Like other countries and empires, the Ottoman Empire was a state system that was fundamentally unjust. An elite was awash in wealth and abundance, while many were vulnerable to war, drought and other disasters and therefore in constant danger of ending up in life-threatening poverty. Those adhering to the correct religion had privileges, while those with the wrong faith had to compensate for this.[31] On this point, however, the Ottoman Empire was better than in many European countries. For example, when the Jews were banned from Spain in 1492, it was with the Ottomans they sought refuge. The latent injustice led to several rebellions throughout the centuries. The poor endured poverty up to a certain limit, whereupon a rebellion could result in a temporary reduction of the injustice.

From the end of the 17th century, the number of people living in poverty in Istanbul increased because the Ottoman wars from that time on were fought on their own territory. When the Ottomans lost control of a territory, many local Muslims left their homes and traveled to Istanbul. This led to a growing subclass in the capital, sometimes letting out its frustration. In 1726, the population stoned Sultan Ahmed's palace for ten nights, causing him to move to another residence. Again in 1730, there was a part of Istanbul's population that had had enough. The political protests often took place after the Friday prayer, a custom still held by many of the world's Muslims. A Friday in the autumn of 1730, a protest was started which eventually gained great support among the city's *misérables*. The protest lasted for several weeks and has become known as the Patrona Halil Rebellion, after its Albanian leader. On November 5, the sultan invited the protest leaders to the palace. They believed that the sultan would comply with their demands and appoint them to various important positions. Instead, everyone was killed, about 30 men. When their bloody bodies were carried out of the palace, the crowd lost its courage. Many of the rebels tried to escape the city, but the sultan gave orders for all those fleeing to be arrested. According to the then French ambassador, about a thousand people were arrested and killed during the following four days.[32]

However, the sultan's legitimacy was not just based on fear. The Ottoman Empire eventually encompassed many languages and several religions, and it had to be able to point to some form of legitimacy other than the fact that the sultan's soldiers were superior at inflicting violence. The dream that Osman was said to have had was well-known and useful in that respect, but more was needed. If it could be proven that Osman was a descendant of a former great ruler, that would strengthen the legitimacy of the sultans who came after him. At the end of the 15th century, 200 years after Osman began his conquests, a story spread that Osman's father had been granted the family's original land by the then Seljuk sultan in Rum (Konya). Later, the link to the Seljuks was strengthened by a story that Osman had received formal insignia[33] from the Seljuk sultan as a sign that he was the right leader to "inherit" the power of the Seljuks. A hundred years after this, in 1575, an Ottoman official falsified a document intended to be the historical record that such a handover had indeed taken place. Other attempts were made to point to a kind of predetermined, elevated position for Osman's descendants, including putting the Ottoman dynasty into the family tree of the Prophet Noah. In reality, it is unclear where Osman's family came from. There are historical documents that hint to the family simply being ordinary peasants.[34]

In addition to showing the sultan's legitimacy by generating kinship to former rulers, it also became important to show his legitimacy in religious terms. Until the Mongols in 1258 in Baghdad killed the Muslim supreme leader, the Caliph al-Musta of the Abbasid dynasty, the Abbasid family had had the caliph for five hundred years. A Mamluk general[35] had in 1260 transferred an Abbasid heir to Cairo to make him a caliph and thus save the caliphate. The caliph's real power was, however, weakened for good. When the Ottoman Sultan Selim conquered Cairo and hence the Mamluk Empire in 1517, he sent the last caliph, al-Mutawakkil, to Istanbul. Only much later, when the Russians in the 18th century claimed they were patrons of the Ottoman Christians, Ottoman intellectuals began to take an interest in the caliphate. The Ottomans then claimed, in response, that the caliphate had been transferred to the Ottoman sultan when Selim took Cairo, and that the sultan was thus caliph and head of all Russian Muslims.[36]

Even the Janissaries, despite having substantial real power over who would hold the most important positions in the Ottoman Empire, needed religious justifications for their interventions. They were all well-educated in Islam from childhood, and their need for religious justifications of their behavior is thus not very surprising. From the outset they were to be the sultan's elite forces, but the creature that was the Janissary corps was increasingly taking on a life of its own. The Janissaries gradually began to consider themselves the high protectors of the Ottoman dynasty, not unlike the way in which Turkish generals would later consider themselves regarding the protection of Mustafa Kemal Atatürk's ideas of the Turkish republic.

If the Janissaries considered it necessary to dethrone a sultan to protect the dynasty, they did just that, but never without it being in accordance with the legal assessment of the *şeyhülislam*, the supreme leader of the religious scholars of the Ottoman Empire. After receiving the *şeyhülislam*'s blessing, they performed the necessary actions to safeguard the Ottoman dynasty. Coincidentally, these actions never went against the self-interest of the Janissaries, namely, to preserve and strengthen their own position. If they (thought they) had reason to believe the sultan would make reforms or changes that would weaken the position of the Janissaries, they would be eager to get a religious assessment ruling in their favor and acting upon it.

This "selfless" form of military intervention never died off completely and was, to some extent, continued into the Turkish Republic. The military coups or "interventions" in 1960, 1971, 1980 and 1997 were all justified by the fact that the military saw it as their duty to protect Turkey's constitution. As we will see in later chapters, the military leaders of these interventions miraculously were better off on a personal level after having led the intervention.

The Sick Man of Europe

The end of the 17th century was the beginning of the Ottoman Empire's persistent decline, and more and more territory was lost to the enemies. There was obviously something - many things - that was not working properly in the state administration. The European powers began in the 19th century to refer to the empire as "the sick man of Europe,"[37] but by then the disease had advanced quite far. However, it was unclear what kind of illness it could be. Several explanations have pointed to cultural aspects of the Ottomans, suggesting that they were simply unable to modernize as quickly as Europe. These explanations that the Ottoman culture was inferior are at best inadequate, at worst racist. A more convincing explanation is this: The Ottoman institutions - and especially the military ones - were organized in such a way that it was very difficult, and in some cases dangerous, for the sultan and his officials to reform them.[38]

For a long time, the Ottomans had been militarily far ahead of Europe. In the 16th century, the Ottoman military apparatus was still more sophisticated than anything that could be seen in Europe. The Ottoman war machine consisted of several parts, where the provincial troops and the Janissaries constituted the most important elements during new conquests. The Janissaries were an institution that gained a lot of power in the empire. Several factors contributed to this. For example, the Janissaries had the important task of controlling militant elements within the empire. After Mehmet II (r. 1451-1481) conquered Constantinople and made the city his new capital, he placed the bulk of the Janissary corps inside the city, where they could effectively protect his power. However, it also made the distance between the sultan and Janissaries very short. Simply the physical proximity increased the influence of the Janissaries. In Europe, the kings usually preferred to have the fighting forces a little further away to avoid having them too close to themselves.

Another factor contributing to the exaggerated power of the Janissaries was the succession arrangement of the sultans. As it was not the regent's oldest son, as in Europe, but the most "appropriate" son that would take over the throne, this became an opportunity for the Janissaries to ensure that the (to them) right son ended up on the throne. What was "right" for the Janissaries would, among other things, mean someone who would not restrict their power and privileges.

A third factor was the way in which soldiers were recruited to the Janissary corps. From 1380 onward, a scheme was established (called *devshirme*), which in practice was a kind of taxation of Christian boys aged eight to fifteen. Every three to five years, one boy per 40 families in occupied Christian territories was taken to join the Janissaries as a slave soldier. After a long period of being taught culture, Islam, and military skills, they became part of the Janissary corps. This indoctrination cut the ties between the boys and their home districts and ensured loyalty to the sultan. However, it also greatly contributed to internal loyalty among the Janissaries, and this internal loyalty became so strong that it was not uncommon that it came before the loyalty to the incumbent sultan.[39] The European armies were, to a much greater extent, heterogeneous, both in terms of language, national affiliation and religion. Consequently, the internal loyalty never became equally strong. Moreover, the European officers were noblemen and had more common interests with the king than with their foot soldiers. The Janissary officers, on the other hand, had risen through the ranks and to a larger extent shared interests and identity with the lower ranked Janissaries.

The French Revolution brought with it the introduction of universal conscription, nationalist indoctrination, and a merit-based military system. An important point is that before this happened, the civilian institutions had gained a solid enough authority and capacity to limit the ability of the military to dictate how the government should relate to the military. In the Ottoman Empire, the power relationship between the civilian and military institutions was different. In the face of less developed civilian institutions, the Janissaries were able to demand ever greater rewards for lesser efforts. As the European armies became more effective, the Ottoman response was to increase its military quantity, not the quality. Increased quality would have meant reforms that the Janissaries opposed. This became an expensive and inefficient solution. When Osman II became sultan in 1618, it was obvious that the Ottoman military had to be reformed if the sultan were to keep his lead on the European kings. The Janissaries conspired to prevent Osman's military reform plans, and it culminated in the murder of the sultan. This was the first time an incumbent sultan was killed. Later, when a grand vizier under Sultan Ibrahim I tried to reform the military, the sultan in 1644 agreed to have him executed.[40]

In 1697, the Ottomans suffered a humiliating defeat in the Battle of Zenta (in modern Serbia) against the Habsburg army. Although the Ottomans were twice as many, the Habsburgs were victorious. Thirty thousand Ottoman soldiers were killed while the Habsburgs lost 2,100. It would get worse. In 1770, the Russian army - in a matter of four hours and with sick and tired soldiers - defeated an Ottoman force five times as large.

At the same time as the military clout declined, costs grew. The Janissaries were good at keeping dead or otherwise inactive soldiers on the payrolls and thus enrich themselves. At the end of the 18th century, the Ottomans had 400,000 Janissaries on their payrolls, while in reality there were only between 20,000 and 50,000 of them.

The need for reform became clearer and clearer, but Sultan Selim III (r. 1789-1807), too, had to pay with his life when he tried to reform the military. From 1794 he hired foreign, mainly French, officers who helped him create the New Order Corps (*Nizam-ı Cedid*). In 1807, this new corps had close to 30,000 men.[41] The Janissaries refused to accept this, caused Selim to reverse the reforms, and also forced him to allow them to massacre the New Order soldiers. Selim was then forced to abdicate and was shortly thereafter murdered. To make sure they were in the right, the Janissaries went once again to the *şeyhülislam* and made him declare that the proposed military reforms were not according to Islamic law.

A few years later, Selim's successor Mahmud II (r. 1808-1839) was horrified at how badly his soldiers performed during the Greek War of Independence (1821). He revived the New Order Corps, but under a more strategic name: Muhammad's Trained Victory Soldiers. The name made the reform less vulnerable to religious criticism. Meanwhile, divisions had arisen among the Janissaries, making them vulnerable. Mahmud II had, by 1826, allied himself with enough supporters to order his Victorious Soldiers to annihilate the Janissaries in their barracks in Istanbul. Many Janissaries were killed, and the sultan was able to implement the much-needed reforms.

Although the Janissaries - or at least the way in which the Janissary institution was set up - must take a substantial part of the blame for the lack of military reform, they can't be blamed for the lack of progress in military technology. It is possible (but not very likely) that a technician and inventor around the year 1630 was able to fly across the Bosphorus, gliding on the wind and using "eagle wings" that he had made for the occasion. His name was Hezarfen Ahmed Çelebi[42]. According to Evliya Çelebi, a 17th century writer, the fearless Ahmed, after having practiced a few times, "flew from the very top of the Galata Tower [in contemporary Karaköy on the European side of the Bosphorus] and landed in the Doğancılar Square in Üsküdar [on the Anatolian side], with the help of the south-west wind." Sultan Murat IV had witnessed the event but did not recognize the major technological advantage military aviation could have given the Ottomans. Instead, he gave Ahmed "a sack of golden coins, and said: 'This is a scary man. He is capable of doing anything he wishes. It is not right to keep such people,' and thus sent him to Algeria on exile. He died there."[43]

Can this have happened? There are two aspects of the story that make it unlikely. Firstly, the incident has only been mentioned in one contemporary source, that of Evliya Çelebi, and in that source, the whole accomplishment is conveyed in three sentences out of a ten-volume work. Secondly, the laws of physics make it practically a miracle if the story is true. The difference in altitude between the top of the Galata Tower and the Doğancılar Square is 77 meters, and the distance is more than 3.3 kilometers. The glide ratio required for that trip is 44:1 (that is, 44 meters forward per meter down). A modern competition hang glider may reach a glide ratio of 20:1.[44] In other words, today's best hang glider can fly less than half the distance of the flight that is to have taken place 400 years ago. Nevertheless, the story is well liked in Turkey, and Hezarfen Ahmed Çelebi's incredible flight was depicted in the 1996 movie "Istanbul Beneath My Wings" (*İstanbul Kanatlarımın Altında*).

If we disregard the lack of investment in technological research; By the time the sultan was able to reform his military in terms of organization and training, it was too late to save the Ottoman greatness. The Ottomans had missed the military revolution that had taken place in Europe in the 16th and 17th centuries and lacked the technological and institutional preconditions to keep up with the Europeans. European kings, in turn, had encountered little opposition when introducing military innovations. They had systematically improved their armies since the mid-16th century, including the introduction of military drills and practicing complex military maneuvers.

In this way it was true that the Ottoman Empire was the sick man of Europe. The Janissaries, initially the sultan's key to ever increasing power and wealth, had become a tumor. But removing this tumor was not nearly enough. Although it might have slowed down the empire's demise, the state had major structural problems that were not resolved in time to preserve the empire. Two central problems were related to each other; Firstly, the state, with its growing bureaucracy, did not get enough money into its coffins. Secondly, the economic elite was dominated by Christians, which in the 1800s strengthened the tendency for nationalism and separatism among the Christian groups.

There were two important reasons why the Christians dominated the business sector. First, the bureaucracy was reserved for Muslims, so there were no sector other than the private one that was open to Christians. Secondly, European traders had their own special rights in the Ottoman Empire, which they had gained through a series of "capitulations," that is, concessions given in different treaties between the Ottomans and the Europeans. Limitations had been put on how much taxes and fees the Ottomans could charge for traded goods, and separate rules had been created for the legal status of Europeans. Also, many of the Greek traders and Armenian bankers (i.e., from the two largest Christian groups in the empire) had been classified as foreigners, which made them powerful. These capitulations were one of the reasons why the state did not get enough revenue for the infrastructure that was necessary for economic development, which also meant that the Ottomans lagged behind in the industrial arms race.

A separate reason for the insufficient revenue was that the taxes that were collected largely ended up other places than in state coffins. According to some estimates, only between 10 and 20 percent of the taxes collected actually reached the state. The rest disappeared in the hands of intermediaries on the long journey from taxpayer to sultan.[45] Over time, this had major consequences; In 1900, Russia - at that time the Ottomans' biggest rival - had seven times more government revenue than the Ottomans.[46]

However, for there to be any tax revenue, there must be something to tax. While the European powers had experienced major economic development during the Industrial Revolution, the Ottomans lagged behind. The Ottoman coal production was just a fraction of that of the Europeans, and the Ottomans had not prioritized railway construction. Prior to World War I, each of Britain, France, Germany and Russia had on average ten times more railroad than the Ottomans.[47] This had major implications for both economic capacity and military capacity (i.e. the capacity to move troops and materiel).

The Empire Approaches an End

The Crimean War (1854-56) not only (again) revealed the military, but also the institutional, inferiority of the Ottomans. Although, thanks to France and Britain, they were on the winning side of the war, it was obvious that the state and the military had to be reformed. The Ottoman dignitaries out in the provinces had always had to ensure an income in addition to the state's salary, which was often months and even years delayed. They also had to make sure that they were appointed to their positions from year to year. In addition, there was always a danger that, if they fell into the sultan's disfavor, they would be deprived of all their possessions. In Europe, the bureaucrats had, to a much greater extent, wages that came on time, and they held safe jobs defined by regulations.[48] The sultan in 1856 issued a reform statement called *Hatt-i Humayun,* which aimed at transforming the empire into a state that looked more like the European ones. Everyone in the realm would get citizenship, and everyone would be equal under the law. This was something new. Earlier, Christians and

Muslims had dealt with different laws, legal systems, and taxation. The army was opened to all (until then only for Muslims), the tax system was to be reformed, torture was banned. The widespread corruption among state officials was to be combated.

Sincere attempts to implement these changes lasted for 20 years, but there were too few officials with the right expertise and experience to make it happen. Moreover, the reforms came from above. They did not come as a result of popular pressure, and the wider society had no ownership of them, unlike in Europe. In addition, the reforms bore the traits of being half-hearted, as old regulations often remained in parallel with the new.[49]

The reforms were an expensive venture, and Sultan Abdul Aziz (r. 1861-1876) had taken up loans from Europe. However, he spent the money a little too freely, including on his harem. In 1874, the government had to inform its creditors that half of the empire's debt would not be repaid. A new reform minister was appointed, Midhat Pasha, who had Sultan Abdul Aziz deposed and replaced with Abdul's nephew, who was deposed after just three months and replaced with Abdülhamid II, the reign of whom became known as the Hamidian Era (1876-1909).

Abdülhamid II first gave the impression of passionately wanting to carry on with the reforms, and, among other things, introduced a constitution in 1876. A number of freedoms and rights were promised to all the inhabitants of the empire, and the parliament met for the first time in 1877. But the sultan suddenly made a U-turn and deposed the reform minister - who later suffered a violent death[50] - dissolved the parliament and got rid of the constitution. Reform had once again been prevented.

The Ottoman Empire had grown steadily from the late 13th century to the end of the 17th century. At that time, the entire Balkan Peninsula, Anatolia, much of the Middle East and the Arabian Peninsula as well as Egypt were subject to Ottoman rule. In addition, the Ottomans had vassal states along almost all of Africa's Mediterranean coast, in the north along the Black Sea, and in the east all the way to the Caspian Sea. On two occasions with 150 years between them (1529 and 1683), even Vienna had been targeted for conquest, without success. Then the empire slowly but surely deteriorated, caused by both internal and external factors.

2. Turkey Becomes a Country

Places mentioned in this chapter.

"I don't understand why the family was given only 24 hours to leave."[51] Prince Bayezid was interviewed in 2015, at that time the oldest in the Osmanoğlu family and thus heir to the throne - had there been a throne to inherit. The journalist who interviewed him had pressed him as to what he thought about how his family had been treated by the government of Mustafa Kemal Atatürk in 1924. The only criticism he had was that 24 hours was slightly insufficient for the sultan family to pack up and leave their country. Generally, there has been very little pouting from the sultan family that was sent into exile. Although they only had a day to leave their tremendous wealth in Istanbul, most of the family members, especially the heads of the family, have been cautious about criticizing the treatment they received from the Ankara government when they suddenly had to leave their wealth and privilege and establish normal lives abroad. For some of them, life in exile became a life in poverty. Members of the sultan family were scattered throughout Europe, the United States, and the Middle East.

Bayezid was the first heir to the throne born in exile, just months after his parents' arrival in Paris. He was known for his kindness, generosity, humility and humor. "At least I am fortunate to be conceived in my homeland," he said. After starting life in Paris, he ended up as a New York librarian in 1954. He was able to speak and write in six languages and worked at the Foreign Languages section of the New York Library for over forty years. There he wrote descriptions of books in foreign languages, held puppet shows with homemade dolls, and read for the blind. When he died in 2017 at the age of 92, the role of head of family went to 85-year-old Dundar Efendi in Damascus, Syria.[52]

Family members further down the hierarchy have been less frequently sought out by journalists. In England, however, one of them has become a comedian and uses his royal identity in his material. Nazim Osmanoğlu (b. 1985), when he was interviewed in 2016, was the seventeenth in succession. That same year, he visited Istanbul for the first time in his life and did three stand-up performances. "My granddad was born in Dolmabahçe palace, in a golden crib," he told the audience. "Now I'm paying 30 lira to see it."[53] Unlike his father, Nazim did not experience being banished from Turkey and therefore to a lesser extent has mixed feelings about the country. His father's first visit to Turkey had been difficult, but not so difficult that he, in 2016, declined the Turkish citizenship that was offered him (and Nazim). After the family's protracted exile, Nazim's sultan family origin is not something he goes around thinking about. "I'm proud of my family's rich history but I'm a regular guy doing my thing," he told the journalist. And his "thing" includes telling jokes about his identity in his performances. "All I need to do is kill 16 other guys to become sultan of Turkey," he told a roaring audience in Istanbul.[54]

Ethnic and Religious Tension and Mass Killings

Before the sultan family was banished from the new Turkey in 1924, the head of the family was only caliph, not sultan, and his power had become very limited as a result of processes that had started long ago. One of these processes related to the tensions between the various ethnic groups in the empire, which had gradually increased over the previous decades. Violent episodes in one place could increase the tension between groups elsewhere, and this became a vicious circle. One early event that received much attention was the Jeddah Massacre in 1858, with the ensuing revenge attacks. The incident is an example of how religion, politics and economic change has affected each other.[55] It is also an example of how religious perceptions can have very specific political, even violent, consequences.

All religions have among their followers people who have quite rigid opinions regarding how certain things should or should not be. Or more precisely; Almost all religious people are quite rigid about a few key aspects of their faith, but among these people there are also some who are very rigid regarding a number of less key, more practical issues. For instance, according to some Muslims, the city of Jeddah, as part of Islam's holy land Hijaz, was to be reserved for Muslims. The presence of non-Muslims desecrated the land. Yet, since the capture of Hijaz in 1517, the Ottoman sultans had allowed the presence of Christian traders in the city, as it was the port of Mecca and the main economic hub of the Red Sea.

This in itself caused a certain amount of hostility towards the Christians in Jeddah. The negative view of Christians increased as the Ottomans introduced reforms that, to the Muslims of Hijaz, were an imitation of the (European) Christian ways. In 1855 there were riots in Mecca protesting the restrictions of the slave trade, another Christian invention. What kind of justice was there to Christians being able to sell liquor in Jeddah while slavery was to be forbidden? The God of Islam was crystal clear that alcohol was forbidden, while slavery was allowed. When, in 1858, disagreements arose over which flag the ship *Irani* was going to sail under, the conflict quickly escalated into violence. British marine soldiers had at one point lowered the Ottoman flag of the ship and hoisted the British one. In the process, they were said to have stepped on the Ottoman flag. This could not be tolerated. That night, 22 foreigners were killed: British, French, Ottomans, a Russian and a Greek.

The British and French immediately demanded that those responsible be arrested and executed, but that kind of decision had to be taken by the sultan's envoy, who was not present. The communication lines were slow, and no killers were arrested by local authorities. The British lost patience and began bombarding Jeddah. This got the local authorities moving and soon the accused were arrested. When the sultan's envoy finally arrived, 50 days after the massacre, eleven men were found guilty and executed. Some time after this, the British apologized to the sultan for bombarding Jeddah, and relatively normal relations were restored.

However, the incident had caused lasting damage to the relationship between Muslims and Christians (which in many places was already characterized by tension and mistrust). The Jeddah bombardment was to be remembered among Muslims as a collective trauma. In 1860, Muslims in Damascus and Lebanon attacked Christians and Jews, only to be severely beaten back by European forces. It turned out that fighting the Christian, European presence with direct violence did not work. The Muslims had to accept, bitterly, that the Christians would remain while becoming ever richer, protected by superior European military power.

Over the next decades, a pattern developed of mass killings of, respectively, Christian and Muslim groups in and around the Ottoman Empire. A major cause of the deterioration was a famine in Anatolia in 1873-74, caused by floods and droughts. People had to slaughter their animals and moved to where there was food. This reduced tax revenues, and the state responded by raising taxes for those who were able to pay. Christian peasants in the Balkans tolerated this badly and rebelled. Many Muslims were killed, and the sultan solved the problem by the use of brutal violence. In Bulgaria, Ottoman troops killed between 12,000 and 15,000 people, shocking Europe.[56]

Just a few years later, in 1877-78, the Ottoman Empire for the first time lost territory with a substantial Muslim population. As many as 260,000 were killed or died of disease and starvation, and about a million people fled. Many ended up in Istanbul, but many more were resettled in Anatolia, the Ottoman Balkans, Crete and even Syria. The difficulties they experienced contributed to the anti-Christian feeling that became such a force in the late nineteenth century.[57]

The subsequent fear of "the other" (between Christians and Muslims) was based on these and other traumatic experiences, and the mass killings that occurred toward the end of the empire were justified by this fear. Killings of members of a group in one location led to killings of members of the other group somewhere else. Unfortunately, this is not a unique phenomenon for the Ottoman Empire at the end of the 1800s and the beginning of the 1900s; It is a normal and predictable human dynamic.[58]

The author Louis de Bernières - writing about the Greek-Turkish relationship - has summarized this dynamic well in his novel "Birds

Without Wings" with the following sentence: "We haven't done anything to you that you haven't done to us already."[59] No matter what cruelties one inflicted on "the other" it was always possible to point to something worse, or at least as bad, that the other had done to members of one's own group, at one time or another, at some place or another.

The Jews fell between a rock and a hard place towards the end of the 1800s. While the relationship between the Greeks and the Armenians - the large Christian minorities - on the one hand, and the Muslims on the other, became more tense, the situation became very complex for the Jews. They were a small minority that did not constitute a majority anywhere in the empire - except in very local neighborhoods. Zionism had not started properly, so even in Palestine the Jews were a small minority. They therefore had to be careful about how they related to the violence that was taking place around them.[60]

In August 1896, massacres of Armenians took place in Istanbul in response to a group of Armenians carrying out terrorist activities in the city. They had set off a number of bombs and robbed a bank, killing dozens of people. The purpose was to make Armenian political demands known to the outside world. Within hours, large gangs armed with sticks and knives attacked and killed many Armenians. It is unclear who participated in the massacres, but Kurds, Laz and religious extremists probably made up a significant proportion. In addition, some witness statements indicate that the police were involved. After two days of killing, the authorities intervened and stopped the violence. According to diplomatic sources, several thousand Armenians were killed, while the authorities set the number of killed closer to one thousand.

Conflicting versions soon emerged of what role the Jews had played during the massacres. The Hasköy district was (and is) a place where many Jews lived, and many Armenians were killed there. On the one hand, the Jews were said to have helped the Armenians by, among other things, lending them Jewish religious artifacts so that they would appear Jewish. They were also said to have helped them with hiding places in their homes or helped them aboard merchant ships. On the other hand, the Jews were said to have helped the killers in attacking Armenians, and also to have participated in the looting of Armenian homes. After the massacre, the Jews had to navigate among the different versions vis-à-vis the different actors in the way that seemed the least dangerous in any given situation.

The Jews thus played a more complex role than the larger minorities. Although there surely were both Christians and Muslims calling for peace and brotherhood, the Jewish situation was to a larger extent characterized by the complexity and need for balance, for their own survival. When war broke out in the spring of 1897 between Greece and the Ottoman Empire due to disagreements over Crete, violence also erupted between Christians and Muslims in cities scattered throughout the Ottoman Empire. The Jews had to be very careful about how they related to this. For example, when Jews in Izmir participated in Ottoman celebrations of military victories, they incurred anger from the local Greek Orthodox Christians who boycotted their businesses and threatened them if they entered the wrong neighborhoods of the city (at the time there were more Greeks in Izmir than in Athens). The Jews, in other words, had to make an effort to be regarded as friends of all parties. If not, they could quickly and unpredictably be considered enemies, in a context that was very tense, polarized, and violent.

The Sultan Who Didn't Want to Reform[61]

Sultan Abdülhamid II refused to let go of the old ways of doing things and remained an absolute monarch for 30 years, from 1876 to 1909. However, it was clear to all who paid attention that modernization was absolutely necessary. Furthermore, enough people with sufficient power and influence knew - partly because of the way Europe was governed - that it was possible to distribute power in a way that would empower themselves. Diligent work was done in secret political groups to take the Ottoman Empire facing forward into the future. At the end of the 19th century, four students at the Military Medical College in Istanbul formed a group which would eventually be called the Unity and Progress Association (*İttihat ve Terakki Cemiyeti - İTC)*. The group grew over the next few years, and while some members were arrested, others managed to flee abroad, mainly to Paris, Cairo and Athens. In France, the group called itself *Jeunes Turcs* (the Young Turks), much like another similar group, otherwise known as the Young Ottomans, had done 30 years earlier. The goal of İTC/the Young Turks was to get the constitution and parliament reinstated (it had been cancelled by Abdülhamid II in 1878). Among the four original members of the group were an Albanian, a Kurd, and a Circassian,[62] and the word "unity" was to reflect on the various ethnic groups in the empire. But the Young Turks was not a movement for the masses; it was an elite project. Their allies in France represented the conservative political right. None of the members of the Young Turks were particularly interested in socialism and the labor movement that was emerging in Europe.[63] And this set the standard for the next century of Turkish politics - socialism was (violently) never allowed a stage in Turkey.

Several opposition groups established themselves, based on ethnicity among other things, and Sultan Abdülhamid did what he could to repress them. However, they continued their business underground and abroad. In 1902 and 1907 congresses were held in Paris that included the entire breadth of the opposition. The majority in 1902 was of the opinion that it was legitimate to use violence against the sultan, and although the Young Turks opposed it then, they agreed in 1907. Several Ottoman officers were secretly members of the Young Turks, and in a coordinated campaign they rebelled and demanded the constitution reinstated. The sultan sent loyal officers to take care of the rebels, but the troops were in solidarity with the Young Turks and refused to fight them. The sultan was forced to yield and reintroduced the constitution and parliament in the summer of 1908.[64]

A year of unrest followed, where conservative forces took back power in Istanbul, only to lose it again in a coup organized by the Young Turks, who finally deposed Sultan Abdülhamid and replaced him with his younger brother Mehmet V. The turmoil generally did not spread to Anatolia, with the exception of a riot in the city of Adana in the east, where as many as 20,000 Armenians may have been massacred.[65] The Young Turks changed the constitution, further weakening the sultan. They went on to remove more than 10,000 military officers from their posts.

In October 1912, an alliance of Balkan countries - Montenegro, Serbia, Greece and Bulgaria, all of which had won their independence from the Ottomans during the previous 100 years - declared war on the Ottoman Empire. The pretext was that the Ottomans did not comply with the demand for reform in Macedonia, but in reality, they wanted to drive the Ottomans out of Europe. This they almost succeeded in doing, had they not started fighting each other. The Ottomans had lost practically all of Thrace,[66] their last remnant of European soil, but were able to win back the territory going up to the city of Edirne, which is where the border currently goes.

The Balkan War was a disaster for the Ottomans. Almost the entire European territory - home to nearly four million people - was lost. The area had been the core territory of the Ottoman Empire for over 500 years. Istanbul was flooded (again) by Muslim refugees and the overcrowding brought with it typhoid and cholera. A demographically very important consequence was that ethnic Turks were now in the majority for the first time in the history of the empire.

After the Balkan War, in 1913, the Ottomans realized that they should not stay diplomatically isolated. International tension increased, and the Ottomans needed someone to stand with if things were to blow up again. At first the government approached Paris to see if the French were interested in strengthening the ties but was blankly rejected. Both France and the United Kingdom were interested in good relations with Russia and could not then ally with the Ottomans. This made Germany the best option. Secretly, a small group from the Ottoman government negotiated an agreement of alliance with the Germans. The agreement was mainly about joining forces against Russia. France and the United Kingdom were not mentioned. What the Ottomans did not know was that the Germans planned to go after Russia's alliance partner France first, before an attack on Russia would come into question. Germany knew that the Ottomans did not have much military power but hoped that they would be able to get the Muslims of the colonies of France and Britain to rise up against their colonial rulers. In addition, the Ottomans could stop Russian ships from exiting the Black Sea, the Bosphorus Strait being the only way out.

When Russia entered the war in August 1914, the Ottoman Empire had committed itself to declare war against Russia according to the agreement with Germany but had neither the economy nor the arms to do so. After pressure and financial guarantees from Germany, the Ottomans decided to attack the Russian navy in the Black Sea. By doing so, France and Great Britain became their enemies as well.

The war against Russia in the Caucasus went very badly, and the Ottomans eventually lost large areas of eastern Anatolia. This was of great importance to the Armenians. An estimate of the Armenian population indicates that they made up about ten percent of the population of Anatolia, around 1.5 million. Following recent violent incidents and massacres, they had a strained relationship with the Muslims, and especially with the Kurds. When the war broke out, nationalist Armenians saw it as a golden opportunity to finally establish their own Armenian state in eastern Anatolia. Several thousand Armenians signed up to serve in the Russian military. The Ottomans could not tolerate this treachery and what has subsequently been called the Armenian Genocide began in full force in May 1915. During the summer of that year, eastern and central Anatolia was cleansed of Armenians. During the following year, the Armenians of western Anatolia suffered the same fate. This topic will be discussed in more detail in the chapter on the Armenians.

Çanakkale/Gallipoli - March 18, 1915

Another - for Turkey - major event during the First World War is the battles of Çanakkale, better known to Europeans as the Gallipoli campaign (Gallipoli, *Gelibolu* in Turkish, is the peninsula on the west side of the Dardanelles, while Çanakkale is a city on the east side). Britain led on, well assisted by its alliance partner France and soldiers from different parts of the British Empire. The goal was to take control of the Dardanelles and the Bosporus to gain free access to its alliance partner Russia, and to cut off the sea route for German aid to Istanbul. However, the Turks were prepared to provide considerable resistance. The campaign was a major failure for the British, and the First Lord of the Admiralty, Winston Churchill, had to step down.[67]

To begin with, in February and March 1915, the British aimed at a purely naval attack. They bombarded fortifications at the entrance of the Dardanelles and wanted to try to sweep the minefields in the strait. But on March 18, the Turks succeeded in sinking several ships at Çanakkale, and the British side suffered heavy losses. They changed strategy and decided to combine combat on land on both sides of the strait, with bombardment from the sea. The first landing took place on April 25, but the invading soldiers did not get much further than the beaches before the Turks stopped them. It was bitterly fought trench warfare with heavy losses on both sides.

In a letter to his wife, an Ottoman captain in the infantry wrote:

> Ayesha, angel of beauty, we are bombarded here by the English. No rest we receive and very little food and our men are dying by hundreds from disease. Discontent is also beginning to show itself among the men, and I pray God to bring this all to an end. I can see lovely Constantinople in ruins and our children put to the sword and nothing but some great

> favor from God can stop it. . . . Oh, why did we join in this wicked war?[68]

The letter was found on the dead soldier's body.

The British sent reinforcements in August, but to no avail. In January 1916, they gave up and withdrew. Although it ended in victory for the Ottomans, the Çanakkale battles undoubtedly were the war's most costly in terms of human loss. At least 86,000 Ottoman soldiers died, while at least 164,000 were injured (a total of at least 250,000). There may have been as many as 300,000 casualties. On the "European" side, over 44,000 were killed and over 97,000 injured. These soldiers were from the following countries: Great Britain and Ireland (21,255), France (10,000), Australia (8709), New Zealand (2779), India (1358), Newfoundland (49).[69]

The victory at Çanakkale became a source of national pride after a war that was otherwise a massive defeat for the Ottomans. If you visit the Museum of Military History in Istanbul, or the Atatürk Mausoleum in Ankara, much attention is paid to the heroic struggle of the Turks against the attacking Europeans. The battle scenes are illustrated on a 10-15-meter-long mural with accompanying sound effects. In addition to the brilliant officer Mustafa Kemal (later Atatürk), you see in the mural another important figure who is also honored with a large statue outside the Museum of Military History. All Turks know his name because they have learned about him since childhood: Kahraman Nefer Seyyid. His name was initially just the common first name Seyyid (this was before surnames were introduced in Turkey), but after his supernatural achievements at Çanakkale, he was given the title Kahraman Nefer, meaning "hero" and "private" or "soldier," i.e., Hero Soldier Seyyid.

What made him deserve such an honorable name? The plaque by his statue explains: He manned one of the cannons to defend the Dardanelles at Çanakkale. The cannon was supplied by the German weapons manufacturer Krupp, ordered by Sultan Abdülhamid II. Normally, a winch would have hoisted the projectile into the cannon for firing, but the winch had been destroyed in the heat of battle, and Seyyid's fellow soldiers were injured or killed. Seyyid - probably filled to the brim by adrenaline - on his own lifted the 276 kg projectile, placed it in the cannon and fired. Incredibly, he managed to do this four times, and he hit and sunk the British warship *HMS Ocean*. Both the images and the statue show Seyyid as he carries the projectile on his back towards the cannon.

How the *HMS Ocean* was *actually* sunk is somewhat unclear. At the Atatürk mausoleum in Ankara we are informed that it was sunk by Seyyid's cannon, but also that it was sunk by mines laid out by the Ottoman minelayer *Nusret*. The most important aspect here may not be what actually happened, but to have a hero narrative to convey to future soldiers and their families. How would politicians be able to sell wars if they didn't have heroes?

The victory in 1915-16 is still commemorated each year in Turkey with "Martyrs' Day" on March 18. After the abolition of the caliphate in 1924, the secular Turkish state never stopped calling its soldiers killed in battle martyrs. That the Ottoman authorities appealed to their soldiers' religious sense of duty by calling them martyrs if they were killed is understandable. After all, they went to war for the sultan, who was also caliph and thus God's supreme authority on earth. It is more difficult to understand that Atatürk's secular Turkey continued this custom. In a sense, the custom illustrates the schizophrenic balancing act Turkey has been doing, between a very rigid understanding of secularism on the one hand, and very conservative Islam on the other.

However, Turkey is not alone in remembering the human tragedy that took place along the Dardanelles. Every year, Australia and New Zealand hold a commemoration on the Gallipoli Peninsula, in collaboration with Turkish authorities. The commemoration takes place on Anzac Day, April 25, the day in 1915 when the first Australian and New Zealand soldiers were set ashore. (Anzac is the abbreviation for the Australia and New Zealand Army Corps, the name of the military collaboration established between the two countries during the First World War, which has been repeated on various occasions since.) Atatürk's consoling words from 1934 are observed every time:

> Those heroes that shed their blood and lost their lives (in Gallipoli). You are now lying in the soil of a friendly country. Therefore rest in peace. There is no difference between the Johnnies and the Mehmets to us where they lie side by side here in this country of ours. You the mothers who sent their sons from far away countries wipe away your tears. Your sons are now living in our bosom and are in peace. Having lost their lives on this land they have become our sons as well.[70]

The commemoration gathers, every year, around two thousand participants from Australia, New Zealand and Turkey, in addition to dignitaries from various countries.

The Great Loss Followed by the Great Victory[71]

When the Ottomans finally agreed on a ceasefire in the fall of 1918, they had nothing with which to negotiate. They had entered an industrial war with an agricultural economy.[72] They signed the terms of the armistice on board a British ship, the peace agreement to be negotiated at a later date. British, French, and Italian forces occupied Istanbul, and by May 1919 the French had occupied Adana, the British had taken Kilis, Urfa (now: Şanliurfa), Maraş (now: Kahramanmaraş), Antep (now: Gaziantep),[73] the Italians occupied Antalya and the Greeks Izmir. When the victors finally had negotiated a peace treaty with the Ottomans in the French city of Sèvres in August 1920, not much regarding the Ottoman Empire was reminiscent of an empire. However, the Ottomans had no choice but to sign the Sèvres Treaty. Thrace was to be part of Greece, which would also gain sovereignty over Izmir and the surrounding area for five years, after which the League of Nations would decide whether the area was to become a permanent part of Greece. US President Woodrow Wilson was to decide the boundaries of an independent Armenian state. The Ottomans were to retain sovereignty over the Kurdish areas of southeastern Anatolia, until the League of Nations had decided whether the Kurds should have their own independent state. The Ottoman Empire was reduced to Istanbul and northern Anatolia.

While the Ottoman government after the war focused on restoring peace and order in collaboration with the victors, many were very dissatisfied with the outcome. A senior officer and war hero, Mustafa Kemal, was one of them. He had been a member of the Young Turks for several years but had not been tainted by the war crimes against the Armenians many of the Young Turks were held responsible for after the war.[74] Together with his closest allies, from the end of 1918 he laid plans for military resistance against the ambitions of the Europeans to enforce the eventual peace treaty. Through secret alliance building and planning, Mustafa Kemal and his associates built up a resistance movement, and people from all social classes and walks of life responded positively.

In the summer of 1919, the resistance movement had adopted its goals. Among other things, the Ottoman territory was to remain as it had been at the time of the armistice, and the Greeks and Armenians were not to be able to claim any Ottoman territory (this was a year before the Treaty of Sèvres was signed). Since the Christian Greeks and Armenians could not be trusted, the resistance movement appealed to the Muslims, i.e. mainly Turks and Kurds.

The resistance movement called itself nationalists and influenced the parliament in Istanbul. In February 1920, the parliament adoptet a "national pact" which demanded that the areas of Ottoman Muslim majority should be Ottoman territory. The British in Istanbul did not particularly like this, arrested a handful of nationalists in parliament and deported them to Malta. The other members of parliament protested by dissolving it and 84 of them fled far inland on the Anatolian plateau, to the small town of Ankara that had become the main seat of the nationalists.[75]

In April 1920, a "national assembly" was held there, of which Mustafa Kemal was elected president. Having no proper alternative to the regime in Istanbul, they still pledged allegiance to the sultan and caliph. Twelve days earlier, the *şeyhülislam* in Istanbul had made a legal assessment declaring that the nationalists were non-believers and urged the faithful to kill them. Mustafa Kemal and his close circle were sentenced to death *in absentia.*[76] The nationalists, on their part, responded by getting the mufti of Ankara to issue a counter fatwa, signed by 250 muftis in Anatolia.[77] According to one source the counter fatwa declared the members of the Istanbul government traitors.[78] Two other sources state that the counter fatwa declared that the caliph had been captured by infidels and that it was the duty of all believers to try to free him.[79] In any case, the will of God almighty, the creator of the universe, was quite different in Istanbul from what it was in Ankara.

The Greeks continued from the west to penetrate further into Anatolia, and on July 2, Mustafa Kemal asked the people to engage in holy war against them. In the east was the Russian threat, now having become the Soviet Union. The Russians wanted to make the eastern provinces of Van and Bitlis part of an Armenian Soviet state. In October 1920, Mustafa Kemal sent a capable commander, Kazım Karabekir, to fight the Russians and the Armenians. Karabekir managed to take back the city of Kars, which had been lost to Russia in 1878, and continued forward until the enemy surrendered. The

Soviet Union took control of what is today Armenia, declared it a Soviet Republic in December 1920, and entered into a friendship agreement - in which the borders were set - with the national assembly in Ankara in 1921.[80]

The really big threat was Greece. Since the invasion began in May 1919, the Greeks had slowly but surely taken territory in Anatolia, far beyond what they were entitled to according to the Sèvres Treaty. In March 1921, they suffered their first significant defeat against the Turks north of the city of Eskişehir. The war was to become known to the Turks as the War of Independence. Britain, France and Italy had more important things to spend their limited resources on after the First World War than enforcing the Sèvres Treaty. In April 1921, they declared themselves neutral in the war between the Greeks and the nationalists in Ankara. Italy and France were concerned that Britain would have too much influence in the Mediterranean and were willing to negotiate with the nationalists. In June 1921, Italy left its last base in Antalya, and in the autumn, France left its bases, albeit after persistent attacks by nationalist forces.

After many excruciating battles, the Greeks in August 1922 realized they were losing and retreated to Izmir. The Turks came after them, took the city on September 9 and showed little mercy. It is estimated that thirty thousand civilian Greeks and Armenians were killed in Izmir.[81] The Turkish commander Nurettin Pasha had a personal score to settle with the Orthodox Archbishop of Izmir. Three years earlier, the archbishop had been able to have Nurettin dismissed from Izmir. Now, Nurettin accused the archbishop of treason and handed him over to a mob who - in front of a French patrol - tore the beard off his face, gouged out his eyes and cut off his ears, nose and hands.[82] This part of the story, of course, receives little attention at the Atatürk Mausoleum in Ankara. There, the audio guide rather emphasizes the following: "On the following day [after the "liberation" of the city], Mustafa Kemal Pasha and the general staff entered Izmir and were given a hero's welcome by the people."

The atrocities that had occurred during the Balkan Wars in 1912-13 had had consequences elsewhere in the Ottoman Empire. About 200,000 Ottoman Greeks had fled from western Anatolia to Greece. When Greece began its invasion of Anatolia in 1919, many of them had returned home, including to Izmir. Then, when the Turks took Izmir in September 1922, both the returning Greeks and many of the Greeks who had remained throughout the turmoil of recent years feared - with good reason - the consequences. People fled all along the coast, and just under half a million Ottoman Greeks whose countless generations of ancestors had lived there, left Anatolia for good.[83]

Ethnic Cleansing and Ethnic Repair

The nationalists in Ankara had set out on their own course after the First World War, while the sultan's government in Istanbul tried to cooperate with the European victors. "Istanbul was the capital of a country that still existed on paper but in reality seemed to have blown away like an Anatolian dust storm."[84] While Ankara and Istanbul played their power game, which lasted until the nationalists won their victory over the Greeks in September 1922, Anatolia was filled with people of different ethnicities and religions, being chased here and there by the chaos of war. In addition to the people who left their homes to save their lives, there were also many in the Ottoman Empire who had been moved by force by the authorities because the risk of treason was considered too great. The consequence was that areas were cleansed of certain ethnic groups.

Historically speaking, such ethnic cleansing is neither new nor sensational. Moving a "politically unreliable" group of people by force was (probably) first done by the Assyrian ruler Tiglath-Pileser III in the eighth century B.C. When he conquered new territory, he relocated about half the population, which was then replaced by people from other regions. Later this was repeated by several rulers and conquerors, first the Babylonians, then the Greeks and Romans.[85]

It was a relocation of people for strategic reasons (which, in the case of the Armenians in particular, also meant a great number of killings) the Ottomans carried out during the First World War. However, the authorities realized, come winter of 1917-18, the catastrophic consequences this had for the economy. Both agriculture and trade were greatly reduced. Although the return of forced migrants was already underway before the Ottomans threw in the towel in World War I, they were also required by the victorious Europeans to return them.[86]

The forced relocation is well documented in official Ottoman documents. When preparing for the peace conference in Paris (which resulted in the Sèvres Treaty in 1920), detailed statistics on the size of the different ethnic groups in the different districts were compiled with figures showing the difference before and after the war. Many of those who had been deported from their hometowns had been sent to Istanbul, where they remained until the end of the War of Independence (late October 1922), at first because of lack of transport options, then because of the lawlessness prevailing in western Anatolia.[87]

When returning the migrants to their hometowns, one of the problems that caused the most headache was the Christian women and children who had received protection in Muslim homes during the war. Many of the women had married Muslim men and converted to Islam and had Muslim children. Some had been forced to convert, but many had done so voluntarily (although what is voluntary and not in an extremely violent context is a hopeless assessment). Young children who had been cared for by Muslim families often did not know what religion they came from and accepted their new family's religion. In Europe, the propaganda went like this: All Christian women and children in the Ottoman Empire had been kidnapped into Muslim harems and wanted to return to their original homes. The reality was of course more complex, but this did not matter much to the victors. Ottoman authorities were ordered to surrender all Christian women and children to missionaries or churches to be converted back to Christianity. It was the missionaries and church leaders who were given the responsibility to identify these women and children in Muslim homes.

Many women and children who were returned to their Armenian and Greek families experienced being ostracized and punished for their Muslim upbringing. The authorities therefore changed the scheme so that only those under the age of twenty were automatically returned. Later, this age limit was reduced to ten. The returned children who could not endure life in "their" Christian families - whether they were their original families or not - often escaped from home, only to be picked up on the street by local authorities and returned once more.

If women and children who had originally been Christian refused to leave their new Muslim homes, the Armenian and Greek church authorities could complain to the Allied local authorities, who would then force them to leave their Muslim families. In September 1919, the French High Commissioner in Cilicia (the southeastern coastal region of Anatolia) ordered all originally Christian women and children in Muslim homes to move into Christian homes within a week unless they requested permission from the High Commission to remain where they were. Those who sought out the High Commission for such permission were met by missionaries who tried to persuade them into reassessing their plans.[88]

Problems also arose when whole families came home to their houses after the war. This has always been a problem after every war, everywhere: Problems arise when refugees return to their homes. In Anatolia, this could be especially true of Armenians returning to their homes, only to find their houses taken over by Turks or Jews who had been deported from Greece, Bulgaria, Serbia, Armenia, or Georgia. In cases where the houses were intact and empty, problems with the Turks in the local community often arose. They had heard about the treacherous behavior of the Armenians, including joining the French soldiers against Turks in Cilicia, and did not want traitors in their midst. The hostility could also go in the opposite direction; Armenians and Greeks who returned to their homes could be burning with vengeance after all that had been done to relatives and friends. Those who returned to areas occupied by European/Allied forces had the opportunity to vent their anger, since the occupying forces protected them. They might have kept their anger hidden all their lives as second-class citizens of the Ottoman Empire[89], and finally had the opportunity to speak their minds.

The Allied forces didn't exactly contribute to laying the foundations for local reconciliation between the various groups. The Allies saw part of their mission to be liberating Christians from "the Muslim yoke."[90] In those instances where Turks would not move out of an Armenian or Greek house, the returning refugees might solve the problem by using the weapons they had been given by Armenian and Greek priests. The priests traveled around Anatolia protected by Allied forces, under the pretext of inspecting the condition of local churches. In the cases where Armenians and Greeks returned to ruined houses, Allied forces might throw Turkish families out of neighboring houses so that the returning refugees could take them over. If there was a dispute over house ownership, the Allied forces usually decided in favor of returning Christians, often based solely on their word. If the Christians complained that the distribution of food was unfair, the occupying forces were quick to make the Christians satisfied, much to the dismay of the Muslims.[91]

As if this was not sufficiently destructive behavior on the part of the Allies, they let two ships with over two hundred Armenian warriors from southern Russia dock in Izmit and Izmir, respectively, in March 1919. The Armenians came under the cover of being returning refugees. One of the ships had been leased by American Armenians for that purpose. The Armenian fighters killed a large number of Muslims in the villages along the west coast of Anatolia and further contributed to the chaos already caused by Greek, Armenian and Turkish bandits.[92] (As the reader will remember, this happened three years before the Turkish nationalists expelled the Greeks and "liberated" Izmir.)

In addition to the Christian refugees, there were almost a million Muslim refugees in the Ottoman Empire after the First World War. Thousands lived in tents around Anatolia. They had fled Russia's occupation in the east of Batum[93], Kars and Ardahan[94] in 1878, the Russian invasion of Lazistan and the rest of northeastern Anatolia in 1916-17, and the massacres of Muslims in Armenia. Circassians had fled Georgia, Chechens, Azeris,[95] and Crimean Tatars had fled their homelands because of Russian occupation; Arabs had fled from the British and French in the Middle East and North Africa. Even Indians who were Muslims had fled their service in British and French occupation forces because they had refused to mistreat their Turkish brothers of faith.[96]

The conflicts and unrest in Anatolia became part of a political game that went over the heads of the local population. Greece was interested in further strengthening its position and justified its occupation - which was steadily expanding - by claiming only to offer protection in a country that appeared chaotic and violent. The Ottoman authorities tried to warn the Turks that they should not give the Europeans an excuse for tearing the country apart. In a few places this led to local Turks not taking things into their own hands. But probably it also caused further frustration among the Turks toward their own government which did not stand up for what was right and did not provide peace and order.

The need for precisely peace and order was enormous in Anatolia. Bandits of all ethnicities had ravaged Anatolia during World War I, while many of the local villagers were fighting in the war and unable to look after their homes and families. After the war, the bandits became more numerous because of all the demobilized soldiers who found no other means of supporting themselves. For the bandits, religion did not matter much; everybody was a legitimate target, Christian as well as Muslim. The bandit business also spread to the

Black Sea coast, where even local fishermen - like Vikings - used their boats to travel to coastal cities to plunder. They did this both along the Anatolian coast and on the Crimean Peninsula, in Bulgaria and Romania. It didn't calm down until the Ankara government finally took over.

The Art of Moving a People

The economic lessons learned by the Ottomans after the forced relocation of people during the First World War proved to be quickly forgotten. Or maybe the thinking was that if the forced relocation happened in a different way, things would go well. In any case, on October 16, 1922, the Greek prime minister sent a letter to the League of Nations suggesting an exchange of the Turkish population in Greece with the Greek population in the Ottoman Empire. The warring of recent years had taught him that ethnic diversity did not work so well combined with nationalist violence. The Ottoman government had drawn similar conclusions. Moreover, they had seen the treacherous nature of the Ottoman Greeks. For instance, when the Allied forces had entered Istanbul in 1918, the Greek Orthodox population had been in a celebratory mood. A Muslim observer wrote that the Greek Orthodox "were in an ecstasy of excitement" when Allied warship upon warship docked in Istanbul whereas the Muslims "looked on dazed . . . their empire broken."[97] Moreover, when Greece in 1919 seized Izmir, the streets of Pera in Istanbul were draped with the Greek blue-and-white colors, and a huge portrait of Greek Prime Minister Venizelos was unveiled in Taksim Square.[98]

The Allied High Commissioners in Istanbul (the British, French, Italian and Japanese) agreed with the assessment of the Greek prime minister and urged the High Commissioner for Refugees of the League of Nations, the Norwegian Fridtjof Nansen, to find a solution. Nansen too was convinced that exchanging the "Greeks" in the Ottoman Empire with the "Turks" in Greece would be beneficial for both countries. In addition, he assumed that many Greeks in Anatolia wanted to move to Greece and, conversely, that many Turks in Greece wanted to move to Anatolia.

When the negotiations to revise the (1920) Sèvres Treaty began in November 1922, population exchange was among the first issues on the agenda. Out of the negotiations came - in addition to the Lausanne

Treaty (1923) - a convention concluded between Greece and the government in Ankara to exchange Greeks and Turks. Article 1 of the convention reads: "As from the 1st May, 1923, there shall take place a compulsory exchange of Turkish nationals of the Greek Orthodox religion established in Turkish territory, and of Greek nationals of the Moslem religion established in Greek territory."[99] In other words, it was to be religion that determined whether one was a Greek or a Turk. Half a million "Turks" - who did not speak Turkish but Greek - were forced to relocate to Anatolia, and 1.5 million "Greeks" - who mainly did not speak Greek but Turkish - were forced to move to Greece.[100] "Greeks" in Istanbul were excluded, as were "Turks" in western Thrace.

The nationalism that had spawned the countries of Europe, and also Greece and the soon to be Republic of Turkey, did not correspond well with the reality in and around the Aegean Sea, namely the ethnic and religious diversity that had characterized the coastal areas and islands since before the Roman Empire. Until 1912, for example, Thessaloniki (incorporated into Greece that year) was an Ottoman city with a linguistic diversity quite out of the ordinary. Shoe shiners in the city could often talk to their customers in 6-7 languages. The linguistic, religious, and cultural wealth of similar international (or rather: interethnic and inter-religious) cities in the area had to surrender to the new, artificial monoculture that had been envisioned by smart and powerful men at the top. Lost was also the local ability to navigate in very complex communities.

The idea of "one country, one people" became a nationalist straitjacket. Land areas that in reality had accommodated different groups of people for many centuries did not fit into the worldview of nationalism. Instead of changing the worldview, it seemed like the best solution for both Greece, Turkey, and the League of Nations to change the reality. The result was a form of ethnic cleansing that affected two million people. The trauma that this inflicted on those who were thrown out of their homes and sent across the ocean to their new "homeland," has been described in a number of oral history projects and reports by NGOs. The book "Twice a Stranger" by Bruce Clark (2006) contains many such testimonials. For example, when "Turks" from Greece were to create a life for themselves in Turkey, they were - over several generations - subjected to suspicion and discrimination from the "real" Turks. This dynamic is well portrayed in the movie "My Grandfather's People" (*Dedemin İnsanları*) from 2011.

The New Republic and Its All-Powerful President

Around 2016-17, there was a very popular YouTube phenomenon called the 'mannequin challenge.' People from all over the world uploaded their videos to contribute to the international video library of the mannequin challenge. The idea was for a number of people in a given location - a classroom, the store, at a party - to be completely still as if they suddenly froze (to mannequins) while doing something, and the person with the camera would move around among them, filming. The result would be a video that made it seem like the viewer was moving around inside a photograph. That was similar to how it felt to walk on the sidewalk in Kızılay in downtown Ankara on November 10, 2017, at 9:05 in the morning. Nobody had told me that at precisely 9:05, everything would stop. People on the sidewalk would stop walking and stand still, the cars on the heavily trafficked street would stop and the drivers would get out and stand as if at attention beside their cars. Store owners would come out and stand outside their stores. I soon found out what this was; the commemoration of the death of Mustafa Kemal Atatürk, the first president of Turkey. His contribution to Turkey is seen as having been so magnificent that it is still deserving of such a display of respect. On the same day that I experienced this remarkable commemoration of Atatürk for the first time, as many as 920,000 people visited his mausoleum in Ankara.[101]

Before Mustafa Kemal became Atatürk, he showed his superb military skills in the First World War and then the War of Independence. At the time there still was no Republic of Turkey, but there hardly was an Ottoman Empire either. Sultan Mehmet VI gradually realized that he had no real power in what used to be his empire. When the nationalists in Ankara managed to kick Greece by force out of Anatolia, he became increasingly worried that they would come after him next. They abolished the sultanate on November 1, 1922,[102] but would they stop there? Fearing for his life, he contacted the general of the British occupying forces in Istanbul and asked to be abducted and transported to a safe place. It was - to put it mildly - an unusual request from a sultan. But these were unusual times, and the general complied. Early in the morning on November 17, the sultan went for a walk in the garden of his Yıldız Palace together with his son and a few servants. British soldiers, in cooperation with the servants, were able to get the sultan out through a back gate and transported him in an ambulance to the harbor, whence the voyage began to exile in San Remo in Italy.[103] The following week the Grand National Assembly in Ankara gave the title of caliph (but not sultan) to the oldest male member of the Ottoman dynasty, Abdülmecid. He was the cousin of the newly self-exiled sultan.

By making the Sèvres Treaty unenforceable the nationalists in Ankara had made the occupying Europeans accept negotiations for a new peace deal. These negotiations started in Lausanne in Switzerland a few days after Mehmet VI had fled Istanbul. Turkey was represented by Mustafa Kemal's trusted supporter İsmet Pasha (later İnönü). On the other side of the table sat Britain, France, Italy and Greece, whereas the Soviet Union, Ukraine, Georgia, Romania and Bulgaria were included when the matter at hand concerned them.[104] The negotiations were difficult and slow, and only on July 24, 1923, was the Lausanne Treaty signed. A few months later, on October 2, 1923, the Allies evacuated Istanbul. Ten days later, the nationalists declared Ankara capital, and on October 29, they finally declared Turkey a republic and made Mustafa Kemal president. Another few months went by before on March 3, 1924, the Ankara government abolished the caliphate and expelled the caliph from Turkey together with 120 members of the Ottoman dynasty.[105]

The Ottoman princes were given ten days to pack up and leave, but the caliph himself had to leave immediately. As soon as the law abolishing the caliphate was passed, the Istanbul governor and police chief "went to Dolmabahçe palace and told Abdülmecid to prepare to leave immediately. Outraged, the caliph ordered the governor out. The police chief thereupon announced that he had orders to remove the caliph, by force if necessary."[106] Abdülmecid realized he had no choice in the matter and complied. In the early morning of March 4, the caliph left the palace, "accompanied by two of his four wives, by his son and daughter, and by his chief chamberlain, private physician and secretary."[107] At the train station, the governor of Istanbul handed them an envelope containing £ 2000 in British banknotes and a visa for Switzerland. As the train arrived the border of Switzerland, the party had to wait for the Swiss authorities to make an exception from the law barring polygamous immigrants. Finding Switzerland too expensive to live in, Abdülmecid soon move to France. In 1944, he died in Paris.[108] The descendants of Abdülmecid were banned from entering Turkey, a ban that was upheld for 50 years.[109]

It was not given that, after World War I, Mustafa Kemal was to become the undisputed leader of the new Turkey. It was İCT, the Young Turks, that had organized the resistance struggle after the First World War, and Mustafa Kemal was not among the İCT leaders at that time. The victory over the Greeks in 1922, however, greatly strengthened his position, and on the way up the hierarchy he played his cards so that all who threatened his power in different ways were removed from their positions.[110] It is true that he played a significant role in the victory over the Greeks and the replacement of the Sèvres Treaty by the Treaty of Lausanne, but this was the result of many influential people pulling in the same direction. The elevated position he received, being referred to as *Halaskar Gazi* (Savior and Conqueror),[111] was put to good use to secure his future power.

Opinions were mixed in the National Assembly in Ankara regarding the future of the caliphate. That Mustafa Kemal was able to abolish it was an important sign confirming what those who had voted against his presidency had feared: He might turn Turkey into a dictatorship, only this time it would be a republican and not a monarchical one. The abolition of the caliphate made the already tense relationship between Mustafa Kemal and more moderate members of the National Assembly even more tense.[112]

The decision was furthermore immensely unpopular among Muslims both in Turkey and countries as far away as India. In the Kurdish areas in eastern Turkey, it was particularly unpopular. What had connected (most of) the Kurds and Turks was precisely their common religion, united by the caliph. A Kurdish sheik in 1925 started a rebellion, which was harshly struck down by the well trained and experienced government army. In response to the Kurdish rebellion, Mustafa Kemal's government introduced a law to "maintain peace and order." Many newspapers were closed down, and martial law governed the east. An opposition party consisting of less radical people who had broken away from Mustafa Kemal's Republican People's Party (*CHP - Cumhuriet Halk Partisi*) in 1924, was closed down. The government also revived the "independence tribunals" that had been used in 1920 to convict those who had criticized the nationalist agenda. The tribunals were set up in Diyarbakır and Ankara, and many dissidents, between 2,500 and 7500, were tried. Of these, as many as 660 people may have been hanged.[113] Although Mustafa Kemal was not quite as brutal as

Stalin, he made it clear that there was only one right way to conduct politics.

Nutuk/The Speech

Between October 15 and 20, 1927, Mustafa Kemal gave a 36-hour speech to the congress of his CHP party, three hours in the morning and three hours in the afternoon, in which he recounted his version - soon to be the only allowed version - of the events that had taken place from 1919 to 1927. An English translation of the speech is 724 pages. In the speech, he settled the score with those who had been critical of his way of doing things (and journalists who had let critical voices be heard). He also criticized his formerly close colleagues who had established the alternative party in 1924 that had been shut down within a year. In the speech Mustafa Kemal justified his power to limit the political discourse.[114]

Mustafa Kemal also justified the extreme measures - such as the law for the maintenance of peace and order and the "independence tribunals" - which had been put in place after the rebellion in 1925. By putting these measures in place, the government did not put itself above the law, he claimed. On the contrary, it was done precisely to restore peace and order. Once these "exceptional" measures were no longer needed, they would be abandoned, he explained.[115] It is not very difficult to draw the lines back to the way the Janissaries justified their "exceptional" interventions in government matters. The military coups that were to take place a few decades later made use of very similar rhetoric.

The speech was seen as tremendously significant from the beginning, and it is simply known as The Speech - *Nutuk*. It remained completely unchallenged for 25 years. In the 1950s, the restrictions on expressing oneself were slightly relaxed, and alternative, albeit not directly challenging, versions of the events just before and after the creation of the Turkish Republic were published. By then, *Nutuk* had already settled into the collective consciousness. It says a lot about the fear of questioning the accepted *Nutuk* truth that the documents from the Turkish nationalist movement have never been systematically published.[116] Since that week in 1927 when Mustafa Kemal gave his speech, those who have criticized his actions and performance as president have almost exclusively been extremists and conspiracy theorists.[117]

One example that only Mustafa Kemal's version of the events was welcome was what happened to the memoirs of Kazım Karabekir, the commander sent by Mustafa Kemal to fight the Russians and the Armenians of Eastern Anatolia in 1920, and who succeeded at this. As described above, he had been a central figure in the events after the First World War, and he wrote about his experiences and opinions in several books, where the most influential one was Our Liberation War (*İstiklal Harbimiz*). It was written between 1926 and 1933 and was in many ways a response to the *Nutuk*. It contains criticism of Mustafa Kemal, including his authoritarian leadership style which created distrust among the nationalists. An attempt was made to publish a summary of the book in 1933, but it was stopped by the government. After the first multiparty elections were held in 1950, in which the new Democratic Party won the election, a new attempt was made to publish the summary, this time successfully (this was after Karabekir's death). In 1960, the book was published in its entirety and was first sold without problems, but then a lawsuit was brought against the publisher in January 1961 for violating a 1951 law that made it a criminal offense to disgrace Mustafa Kemal Atatürk's memory. The case was dropped because the publisher was elected to parliament and thus became immune from prosecution. When the case was brought up again in 1965, the publisher won the case on a technicality. The book was then published in 1968,[118] 35 years after it was finished.

A story that has become an anecdote illustrates Mustafa Kemal's status well. There had been a meeting where Mustafa Kemal and several other important people were present. A waiter came and took orders for coffee. All the meeting participants gave specific instructions as to how much sugar they wanted in their coffee, something one always must do when ordering Turkish coffee. People noticed that the waiter didn't write anything down as he left to prepare the coffee. When he returned, Mustafa Kemal was astonished that the waiter had given him a coffee with precisely the amount of sugar he had ordered. He asked the waiter how he had managed to prepare all those cups of coffee without writing anything down. "I remembered what you ordered," the waiter replied to Mustafa Kemal. "I didn't care about the others."

3. Democracy, Turkey Style

Places mentioned in this chapter.

"How is life in Turkey?"
"We can't complain."
"That's good to hear!"
"No, you don't understand... We *can't*."

Thus goes an old joke about life in Turkey, a joke which may have been adapted from its original Soviet version. Depending on which Soviet period one compares to, complaining about life and government in Turkey has generally been safer than doing the same in the Soviet Union. It has, however, depended on who one is and what one complains about, more than the complaint itself. Historically speaking, complaining while Kurdish or communist should be avoided. So should complaining about corrupt politicians, especially if the corruption can be proven.

Why is it still so difficult to have a free and frank public debate about politics and government in Turkey? The way Mustafa Kemal and his close circle shaped Turkey during the first years of the republic explains quite a bit. In addition to the culture of political obedience that Atatürk created, his CHP party agreed on a set of six principles, or "arrows," by which the country should be governed. They are: Secularism, nationalism, populism, revolutionism, statism and republicanism. These are the main elements of what has been called Kemalism. It takes some goodwill to accept that all of these can be called principles. Most of them cannot be readily understood without some explanation. Furthermore, if the aim is democracy, which Atatürk claimed it was, most of them should be replaced by actual principles, like rule of law, freedom of the press, freedom of speech and assembly, distribution of power and other fundamental pillars of democracy.

After a very turbulent start of the 20th century, the world to Atatürk was a place where one should be careful about whom to call friends and which governing practices to learn from. Turkey had to find its own way. Atatürk really wanted to pull the Turkish society towards the West, but could the West be trusted? To Atatürk it seemed prudent to copy the aspects of European culture that in his mind would lead to "modernization," but at the same time be careful about certain freedoms which might spin the country out of control. Control was key. Atatürk's attempt to modernize Turkey is characterized by a lack of understanding of what caused modernization in Europe, perhaps because both he and his close associates were soldiers and not statesmen. They were used to giving and taking orders and less used to reflecting on and governing by principles in a civilian, non-warlike world.

Looking at Europe, a few things seemed clearly associated with being modern. Secularism was one, nationalism another. Atatürk and his friends completely ignored, it seemed, that the modernization of Europe had taken place organically, to a large extent from the bottom up. European modernization happened in a culture of free exchange of new ideas - and, crucially, criticism of those ideas. In this chapter we will look at the key elements of how the Turkish republic was structured and see how the structures have - ironically - hindered the modernization and democratization that Atatürk - the architect of the structures - was aiming for.

Secularization

In 2017, President Recep Tayyip Erdoğan talked about how much better life had become for the Muslims of Turkey: "Those of us who attended Islamic schools were looked down upon and ridiculed, but now we are the ones ruling the country!"[119] It had been a long and troublesome road getting to a place where the conservative Muslims of Turkey were able to say that they ruled the country. On that road, many a prison sentence had been handed down and many a political party had been banned by the Constitutional Court. In 2001, Erdoğan had been able to establish and then steer a political party that stayed on the right side of the line that could not be crossed: Using religion in politics. The name of the party was *Adalet ve Kalkınma Partisi* (AKP), Justice and Development Party. Erdoğan gradually pushed that line through reforms and legal amendments, and equally gradually, the true, Islamist[120] and nationalist face of AKP became clearer and clearer.

Why had it been so impossible to explicitly base politics on Islam? Mainly because Atatürk and his inner circle thought that religion was an obstacle to modernization and development. It did not matter that a majority of Turkey's citizens were in fact Muslims. Although religion was seen as important for national unity and mobilization, it was also seen as a cause of Turkey's backwardness. Getting rid of - or at least severely limiting - the influence of religion would make way for modernization.[121] "I have no religion, and at times I wish all religions at the bottom of the sea," said Mustafa Kemal.

> My people are going to learn the principles of democracy, the dictates of truth and the teachings of science. Superstition must go. Let them worship as they will; every man can follow his own conscience, provided it does not interfere with sane reason or bid him act against the liberty of his fellow-men."[122]

After he had rid the republic of the caliphate in 1924, an "avalanche of secularizing laws"[123] were passed by parliament, ending with the removal from the constitution of all references to Islam, in 1928.

Secularization did not only mean that the state would not be influenced by religion. For the Kemalists, secularization meant that the state would *control* religion. One important measure was to establish the Directorate of Religious Affairs, which was responsible for the administration of mosques, training of religious leaders and controlling the content of sermons.[124] In 1934 it was forbidden to wear clerical dress outside of places of worship and religious ceremonies. The same year, the hajj, the pilgrimage to Mecca, was prohibited. In 1935, Sunday was made the weekly holiday instead of Friday, the Muslim day of prayer. Courses on religion in primary school were dropped.[125]

With such a large majority of the population being Muslim, it was only a matter of time before the rules that were meant to keep religion in check had to be relaxed. At the end of the 1940s, religious education was reintroduced in schools, Sufi[126] shrines were reopened after having been closed since 1925, and the hajj pilgrimage was allowed again,[127] among other things. After 1950, the Directorate of Religious Affairs grew manifold over the next decades, its bureaucracy becoming increasingly complex. The 1950 election brought the Democratic Party to power, a party which identified itself with the rural population which generally was, and is, more religiously oriented than the urban population. The Cold War had started, and Islam came to be seen as a tool for the state to keep communism at bay.

Letting Islam become more influential in society was a balancing act for the control-minded rulers, not least for the military. Seeing themselves as the guarantors of secularism and democracy - at least their version of secularism and democracy - the generals used the danger of radical religion as an excuse for their coups or interventions in 1960, 1971, 1980 and 1997.[128] Economic hardship during the 1970s pushed people in various extreme and radical directions: to the extreme political left or right, to radical nationalism and radical religion. The generals of the 1980 coup wanted to encourage and expand the moderate section of the population and introduced compulsory religious lessons in schools. They could control the content of these lessons, thus pulling people away from radical Islam. Simultaneously, they hoped, "Islam's green will defeat communist red."[129]

In other words, the rulers of Turkey have behaved as if religion can be controlled and used for whichever purpose serves the state. As if experimenting in a laboratory, the state has sometimes increased the religious ingredient in its "chemistry set," sometimes reduced it, trying to get just the right amount of Islam. This in order to make people happy enough not to become radical, productive enough for economic growth, and so on. But what is radical to a secular general is often not radical to a person of faith. The state's constant attempt to control such a large group of the population inevitably led to a sense of humiliation, the kind that Erdoğan spoke of in his 2017 speech. Humiliation carries substantial political power, as political scientist Francis Fukuyama has explained: "A humiliated group seeking restitution of its dignity carries far more emotional weight than people simply pursuing their economic advantage." [130] A politician that understands this and is able to use it in an effective way will win elections.

Using that insight in an effective way in Turkey has meant staying on the right side of the line mentioned above regarding mixing religion and politics. Before Erdoğan founded his AKP party, several attempts were made at winning elections by appealing to religious voters. Erdoğan's predecessor, Erbakan, almost succeeded with his *Refah Partisi* (RP - Welfare Party) when the party won the general election in 1995. RP received 21 percent of the vote, which made it the biggest party. The ten percent threshold for winning seats in parliament (which we will get back to) meant that the seats that otherwise would have gone to parties receiving less than ten percent, went to those above the threshold. RP was thereby able to form a government, with Erbakan as prime minster. "[A] formerly marginal political element, which lacked legitimacy, found itself accepted into the political establishment."[131] Although this is true, the RP was not sensitive enough regarding the secular boundaries outside of which one could not step. In 1996, a district head of RP was sentenced to four years in prison for a speech where he had said that Muslims would target secular people who "had fallen ill with their own mistakes," forcefully "injecting sharia into their arms."[132] The military would the following year pressure the Erbakan government to resign.[133] The Constitutional Court then declared the RP illegal and banned it.

Learning from this, Erdoğan did not want to become involved with the new party that the former RP leaders founded. He apparently did not have confidence in the ability of the RP leaders to learn from their mistakes. He had himself made the mistake of invoking Islam in a political speech in 1997, resulting in a ten-month prison sentence, of which he served four in 1999. While in prison, he was able to use his network and general popularity as mayor of Istanbul to turn his prison "cell" into an office for preparing the grounds for a new political party. Although it had been a mistake in 1997 to recite the poem that ended him in jail, Erdoğan turned it to his advantage. When he was released in July 1999, he had become a martyr for the cause.

He established the AKP in 2001, holding back his Islamist ambitions. He abbreviated the party name into Ak Party, *ak* meaning 'white,' a metaphor for purity and cleanliness, suggesting that AKP was clean and not corrupt like other parties. The party program made sure not to mention Islam, so there was nothing the Constitutional Court could do to ban the party. The strategy worked, and the AKP could campaign in the general elections of 2002. Partially because of its very good ability to mobilize the grassroots, the AKP received around one third of the vote, but because of the 10% threshold keeping small parties out, it won *two* thirds of the parliament seats.

It is not difficult to understand why the AKP's objection to how the Turkish rulers had interpreted secularism was popular among many Muslims in Turkey. In effect, Atatürk and the Kemalists had introduced measures that limited freedom of religion and had also introduced - arguably silly - practices that they understood to signify secularism. For instance, one of the things Erdoğan did while mayor of Istanbul was to end the serving of alcohol at the city hall. One does not have to be a prude to think that a city hall should not serve alcohol. Seemingly, in the eyes of the Kemalists, secularism and modernity meant that alcohol should flow freely. Even after many years of AKP rule, sale of alcohol is still less restricted in Turkey than in several countries in Europe and North America.

The ban on wearing the hijab in universities and public offices is another example of a silly interpretation of secularism, particularly in a majority Muslim country. The AKP changed this, giving hijab-wearing women similar access to higher education and government jobs as women not wearing hijabs. One female AKP voter explained to a journalist: "The AKP gave me the feeling of having equal value as women who don't wear the hijab. I was suppressed by the old elite because I'm religious."[134]

Thus, it seems imprecise to claim, as has been done by many observers, that AKP has made Turkey much more religious. It seems more correct to say that people are now free to be Muslims in their own way. The increased display of religiosity has, however, brought with it social pressure to "behave more Muslim." But this change does not mainly seem to come from above. It is an organic response to years of suppression followed by the "freedom to be Muslim" that the AKP brought.

Furthermore, Islam is much more visible in cities now than before because of the large scale of urbanization that has taken place. For instance, between 2002 and 2008, 3.5 million farmers and their families went bankrupt and moved to towns and cities.[135] The fact that they did not leave their religion in their hometowns could only be expected.

For secular Turks who are used to the government keeping Islam at an arm's length, the AKP's takeover of Turkish politics has been somewhat of a shocking experience. The 2020 Netflix series Bir Başkadır[136] has portrayed this very well. It shows the everyday encounters between the pious and the liberal lives of Turkey. The perception that Turkey has become something completely different for the secular population than it was before, is described in a conversation between two of the main secular characters. They are both psychiatrists, and one of them is telling the other about how it felt to come back to Istanbul after several years of studying and working in the US. She discovered that Turkey had become a completely different world where "they" (the Muslims) had become the powerful ones. "You and I," she tells her friend, "here in our own country...we are living in an aquarium!" For some of those who have been the most cut off from the Muslim world and lived in a secular bubble, there seems to be a perception that they are now only spectators of society without being a part of it.

A highly regarded Turkish scholar wrote in 2017:

> [Erdoğan] has dismantled Atatürk's secularism in just over a decade and has done so with little mercy for his opponents. He has flooded the country's political and education systems with rigidly conservative Islam and pivoted Turkey away from Europe and the West. (...) Erdoğan is 'anti-Atatürk Atatürk.' (...) Erdoğan desperately wants to change Turkey in his own image in the way that Atatürk did, and herein lies the crisis of modern Turkey: half of the country embraces Erdoğan's brand of politics, but the other half vehemently opposes it.[137]

The Turkish version of secularism caused grievances among religious people in Turkey for a long time. Electing AKP and subsequently keeping Erdoğan in power seems to be a reaction to the decades of suppression that the Kemalist secularism laid upon Muslims in Turkey. Had the Kemalists rather emphasized freedom as a crucial aspect of democracy and modernity, this conflict between

Islam and secularism would probably have been less extreme. Pious Muslims could have been treated on equal terms as non-believers, and everybody could have been free to practice their faith as they wanted. This was not, however, the Kemalist way.

Kemalist secularism certainly did not mean religious freedom, it meant control over religion. Erdoğan has been continuing this control, but in an increasingly discriminatory manner. Sunny Islam is the "correct" religion, and mosques have been built across Turkey with government funding at a fast pace. Other religions are actively discriminated against. In its 2019 report, the United States Commission on International Religious Freedom wrote about the previous year: "the state of religious freedom in Turkey remained deeply troubling," citing a "lack of any meaningful progress on the part of the Turkish government to address longstanding religious freedom issues."[138] The way the state structure is set up regarding religious matters is in itself discriminatory: "The Directorate of Religious Affairs (Diyanet) maintains control over the practice of Islam in Turkey; all other religions are under the auspices of the General Directorate of Foundations (Vakıflar)."[139] The latter makes sure that running a non-Sunni religious institution is no walk in the park.

For instance, the Armenian Apostolic Church was not allowed to elect a new patriarch after the former had died in March 2019. Turkey also required that "Greek Orthodox metropolitans obtain Turkish citizenship in order to participate in the church's Holy Synod."[140] Naturally, these obstacles make the running of an organization very challenging. Furthermore, children from families that are not Sunni Muslim, such as Alevis,[141] frequently have a very hard time being granted exemption from the Sunni Islam "Religious Culture and Moral Knowledge Course," which is now mandatory for primary and secondary school students. There are even cases of schools not granting exemption after a non-Sunni family has won the case in court.[142]

In addition to these practical obstacles to freely exercising one's religion, there are also numerous historical cases of the Turkish government simply having confiscated the property of religious institution. These confiscations happened "most notably in 1936 with the Foundations Law, in 1971 with the Private University Law, and in 1974 when a law recognized only the ownership of religious community properties registered in 1936." [143] Most of these properties have not been returned. One of many examples all over Turkey is the Sanasaryan Han in Istanbul, which was used for educational purposes. The Armenian Patriarchate is still trying to get back the property, seized by the government in 1935.

Even when a decision has been made by a government agency to return property, there is no guarantee that the property will actually be handed back. One example is the case of the properties of the Greek Orthodox Foundation on Bozcaada Island. A government decision was made in 2014 to hand back eleven title deeds to the foundation. In 2019, they still had not been returned.[144]

Does it matter whether Turkey is secular? Why is secularism important? The question has nothing to do with personal preference, or whether you and I are believers. The reason why secularism is important is that the state should not treat one group of people better than another group. If you and I are both citizens, the state is as much yours as it is mine. The state cannot then choose one religion as "special" and give it preferential treatment. The state must be neutral and treat every believer and non-believer - and their institutions - the same.

This is tricky, and no country fully masters it. The United States is one of the most successfully secular countries in the world, with a very high degree of religious freedom, but they still have "In God we trust" printed on their money, used by atheists and believers alike. When Norway revised its 200-year-old constitution in 2014 (not for the first time), they could not resist the desire to mention Christianity in its article 2: "Our values will remain our Christian and humanist heritage." Article 4 takes it further: "The King shall at all times profess the Evangelical-Lutheran religion." Norway has, however, managed to couple this with a very high degree of religious freedom, ranking third in the world in 2019, two spots above the US.[145]

Governing a country is rarely straightforward, and no state will probably ever fully reach the ideal principle of secularism. The control question should be: Does the government treat all believers and non-believers equally? If the answer is not clearly a yes, more energy should be spent to reach the ideal. Turkey has never had this as an ideal and naturally will have quite some distance to cover once it decides to move in that direction.

Nationalism

In the fall of 2019, I took my children to a qualifying football match for the 2020 Euro Cup. The match was played in Konya, and Turkey was up against France, who had won the World Cup the year before. I had never been to a football match in Turkey and quickly realized that the Turks were a different kind of supporters. The noise was out of this world, even before the players had come onto the field. When the French players made their appearance, the whole stadium booed, except for a tiny corner of France supporters. They also booed throughout the French national anthem and whenever France had the ball during the match. They were cheering loudly for Turkey and shouting nationalist four-word slogans that would make the round around the football field, with each of the four sides shouting one word. The noise would quickly switch from general cheering to coordinated shouting of the slogans by all the spectators. One side would start with "*Ne!*" followed by the next side: "*Mutlu!*" and then "*Türküm!*" and "*Diyene!*" (How happy is the one who says: I am a Turk!) Or: "*Vatan! Sana! Canım! Feda!*" (My homeland, I sacrifice myself for you!) The French played as if they were scared, and Turkey won 2-0. After the game, his ears still ringing, my 11-year-old suggested that it might have been better to watch the game on TV.

The first of the slogans, "How happy is the one who says: I am a Turk!" is the last line of a pledge that all school children in Turkey had to recite every morning until 2013. The pledge was written in 1933, was amended a couple of times, and from 1997 went like this:

> Our Pledge
> I am a Turk, honest and hardworking.
> My principle is to protect the younger, to respect the elder, to love my homeland and my nation more than myself.
> My ideal is to rise, to progress.
> O Great Atatürk!
> On the path that you have paved, I swear to walk incessantly toward the aims that you have set.
> My existence shall be dedicated to the Turkish existence.
> How happy is the one who says, I am a Turk![146]

Without exception, Turkish, Kurdish, Armenian, Greek, Laz, Arab and all other school children in Turkey had to recite the pledge daily, proclaiming how wonderful it was to be a "Turk." The fact that

Erdoğan's government decided to stop its daily usage in school after 80 years probably had more to do with Erdoğan's ambivalent relationship with Atatürk, than an acknowledgment of how twisted it is to force children to recite nationalist poetry daily (which, by the way, the US still does with its "Pledge of Allegiance").

From the beginning of the republic, it has been unclear what is meant by being "Turkish." According to some sources it was intended to be a term that encompassed all the citizens of Turkey, not just ethnic Turks or people who spoke Turkish as their mother tongue. The intention was thus to create an inclusive concept for a group of people; the people who lived in Turkey.[147] However, for the groups that did not consider themselves Turks, it was anything but inclusive. When they protested, or simply refused to speak Turkish, it did not lead to an acknowledgment that the term "Turkish" made a lot of citizens feel excluded from Turkey. Instead, it led to coercion, prohibitions, harassment, violence and imprisonment.

At the beginning of the 20th century, because of events described in the previous chapter, the demographics in Turkey went through dramatic changes. Whereas the population in the Ottoman Empire had been around 80% Muslim before World War I, 98% were Muslim in 1923 (remember that the census did not distinguish between ethnicity and religion - the two overlapped[148]). In the cities, the changes between 1900 and 1927 were extreme. In Erzurum, the proportion of non-Muslims (mostly Armenians) went from 32% to 0.1%. In Trabzon, the share went from 43% (large Greek population) to 1%. In Izmir it went from 62% to 14% and, somewhat less extreme, in Istanbul it went from 56% to 35%. Since the Christians had been a more urban population than the Muslims, the forced migration also led to the population becoming more rural. Before the war, 25% of the population lived in cities with more than 10,000 inhabitants. After the war, the share had dropped to 17%.[149]

Regardless of what one today might think about nationalism on a theoretical level, it is an inescapable historical fact that nationalism on a large scale has always been accompanied by suppression of and violence against minorities. This is not to say that nationalism as such, as long as it means nation-building, is bound to be useless. Every society needs a set of shared values and a minimum of common culture. Without this, "we cannot cooperate on shared tasks and will not regard the same institutions as legitimate; indeed, we will not even be able to communicate with one another absent a common language with mutually understood meanings."[150] When the aforementioned Fukuyama writes generally about the need for a shared culture it is as if he is writing specifically about the fall of the Ottoman Empire:

> When a stable, shared moral horizon disappears and is replaced by a cacophony of competing value systems, the vast majority of people do not rejoice at their newfound freedom of choice. Rather, they feel an intense insecurity and alienation because they do not know who their true self is. This crisis of identity leads in the opposite direction from expressive individualism, to the search for a common identity that will rebind the individual to a social group and reestablish a clear moral horizon. This psychological fact lays the groundwork for nationalism.[151]

This is precisely what happened as the nationalists in Ankara were preparing the grounds for a Turkish republic. When the Ottoman Empire disappeared, what was the identity of the people in Anatolia? They had all been Ottoman subjects until then. For the new country to function, something else had to replace the Ottoman identity. The solution was to tell all the citizens that they were now Turks, regardless of how the citizens themselves felt about that.

The Turkish speakers were clearly a majority. Out of a total population of 16.2 million in 1935, 13.9 million were Turkish speakers. Next came Kurdish speakers at 1.5 million. Then followed smaller groups, the largest being the Arabic speakers at 154 000, then came Greek, Circassian, Laz, Armenian, Georgian, Judeo-Spanish, Pomak, variants of Bosnian, Albanian, Bulgarian, Crimean Tatar, Spanish, Abkhaz, Romani, and finally French at 5,400 speakers.[152] A solution could have been to have Turkish as an official language everywhere, and allow for more official languages in areas with a substantial presence of non-Turkish speakers. It would probably have strengthened the feeling among the minorities of belonging and of being accepted as a valuable part of the new country.

But this was the first half of the 20th century. Atatürk chose the absolutist approach. Everybody was a Turk and would speak Turkish. As he explained:

> One of the significant characteristics of the nation is language. One, who regards himself as a member of the Turkish nation, should first of all and in every case, speak Turkish. If, someone, who does not speak Turkish, claims membership to Turkish culture and community, it would not be right to believe in this.[153]

In other words, being a citizen was one thing. Being a *proper* citizen, a Turk, was another.

There was a problem, however. Even the Turkish language was not Turkish enough, and there were too many local variations. First of all, a pure Turkish had to be created. All of the Arabic and Persian words that had become part of the Ottoman language had to be replaced by Turkish ones. It did not matter that some of those Arabic and Persian words had been in use by Turkish speakers for a millennium.[154] In 1932, the Turkish Language Society was formed and given the task of cleaning up the Turkish language and bringing it closer to the language that people in Anatolia actually spoke. This was to be done by gathering words from dictionaries of Turkic languages, and by traveling around Anatolia, recording words that were in use in the provinces. Atatürk, upon hearing that French had more than twice as many words as Turkish, encouraged the guests who attended his infamous daily dinner parties to suggest new words to be added to the Turkish vocabulary.[155]

Secondly, everybody had to believe that Turkish was a glorious language. Enter the Sun Language Theory.

> Atatürk was convinced that Turkish and the Indo-European languages were related and that Turkish was the root of these languages. [The Turkish Language Society] would launch a comparative study of these languages to show that 'the Turkish language was the most influential factor in the development and progress of all the world languages.'[156]

Studying the details of the Sun Language Theory and the "research" that supported it can be a jaw-dropping experience. The conclusions were, not surprisingly, that Atatürk was right: The languages of the world did indeed originate from Turkish, even the native languages of the Americas. For instance, the name of the Amazon river came from Turkish: It consists of the Turkish words *ama* (but) and *uzun* (long), because "the first migrants to South America, who were, of course, Turkish-speaking, exclaimed on seeing the river, 'But (isn't it) long!'"[157] The fact that the name was given by Spanish colonizers only four centuries earlier was conveniently ignored.[158] Some of the loan words were kept, since, after all, they had originally been Turkish before becoming Persian, Arabic or French. When Atatürk visited the city with the non-Turkish name

Diyarbekir in 1937, he declared that from then on, the name of the city would be Diyarbakır, *bakır* meaning copper in Turkish.[159]

Language was one thing, but it was important also to convince the people of Turkey that simply being Turkish was quite magnificent. Therefore, there was a need for a Turkish History Thesis. Similar to the Sun Language Theory, this thesis claimed that most humans descended from Turks, who had "left their original home and moved in all directions to civilize the rest of the world. They went to China in the east; to India in the south; to Egypt, Mesopotamia, Persia, Anatolia, and Greece, and Italy in the west."[160] As a result - and this was an important part of the thesis - all the ethnic groups in Anatolia were in fact Turks. Even the Hittites had been Turks. So, of course, had the Armenians. Atatürk used this when arguing that the areas that had traditionally been Armenian, where in fact Turkish: "The Armenians don't have the least right to this fertile land. The land belongs to you, the Turks. This country is historically Turkish; it is thus going to remain Turkish for eternity. These fertile lands are the profound and fundamental essence of Turkey."[161]

But although they were all Turks deep down, it was important that they also *spoke* Turkish. This was where the thesis became self-contradictory, because it claimed that all inhabitants of Anatolia were Turks, but also that one had to speak Turkish to claim Turkish racial descent. Only those who spoke Turkish would be eligible for membership in the nation.[162] Self-contradictory or not, the important part was that everybody had to speak Turkish.

The "Citizen Speak Turkish" campaign had actually started in 1928 but did not gain proper momentum before the Sun Language Theory and the Turkish History Thesis had gained traction. In Izmir, after the Greeks and Armenians had largely disappeared, the Jews, at more than 10% of the population, had become the biggest minority. They did not speak Turkish, they punched above their weight economically, and when an opposition party emerged in Izmir in 1930 it had the support of the Jews. This made the Jews unpopular among the nationalists. To ameliorate this, some Jewish community leaders encouraged their fellow Jews to speak Turkish, a move that did not go down well among many Jews. In a speech to parliament in 1934, Atatürk's Executive Secretary said that the Jews "will one day learn that they are Turks, and when they join to the Turkish nation, to us, they will understand that they are happy and that they will not be able to find that pride in their previous self."[163]

In 1935, the Speak Turkish Campaign was ramped up. Signs were put up asking everybody to speak Turkish, and those who did not were openly harassed. The campaign lasted well into the 1940s. Even today, speaking Kurdish in public is tantamount to asking for trouble. A Kurd in Istanbul, the city in the world with the largest Kurdish population, told me that people get angry when they hear Kurdish being spoken. "It's funny," he said, "there are so many languages being spoken in this city. But if they hear you speak Kurdish, they will yell at you."

As mentioned above, nation-building has some merit, but was this the right way to do it? It was as if Atatürk and his government refused to learn the lessons from only a few decades earlier. In 1909, the Latin alphabet for the Albanian language had been outlawed by the Young Turks, resulting in armed resistance against the Ottoman government.[164] The government in Ankara knew, based on recent experience, that compulsion and bans with regard to language could have uncontrollable and unintended consequences. Yet they stuck to their absolutist approach to language. And by doing so, they invited the future trouble they thought they had suppressed permanently, namely the Kurdish uprising, which we will look closer at in Chapter 6.

Successive governments have followed up on Atatürk's efforts to suppress anything that smacked of identity preservation outside of the Turkish identity. The measures have been numerous, including resettlement of people to ensure their assimilation, taxing of non-Muslims (usually non-Turkish speakers), and confiscation of property belonging to non-Muslim (and thus usually non-Turkish) religious institutions. By and large, with the exception of the Kurds, Turkey has succeeded in marginalizing other ethnicities than the Turkish.

It is important to remember, however, that the rampant nationalism that led to suppression and assimilation was in no way unique to Turkey. Practically every country in the world forced minorities to assimilate well into the 20th century. France's assimilation of its language minorities and the Scandinavian assimilation of the Samis are just two of many examples.

Although degrading assimilation policies were common in Europe in the early 1900s, the problem in Turkey today is that while other countries have corrected their mistakes - or at least started processes to correct them - the Turkish approach is to defend the assimilation. This may happen in connection with praise for past Turkish military dominance, be it by Ottoman or other warlords. One such warlord is Mehmet I of Karaman, who defeated both Mongols and Seljuks in a battle in 1276. Both in the city of Karaman and in the Museum of Military History in Istanbul he is honored with a statue where he is holding up his famous 1277 decree, stating: "After today, in the palace, dervish lodges, high council, parliament and squares, no other language than Turkish will be used."

Unfortunately, scholars have been surprisingly uncritical of Turkey's nationalism. It is perhaps not so surprising that Clair Price in 1923, when nationalism seemed omnipresent, wrote: "Nationalism in Turkey welds and does not divide. Its cry strikes a sound and healthy note."[165] Consideration of minority issues was not widespread in the 1920s. It is more surprising that Bernard Lewis four decades later would write that Atatürk's "nationalism was healthy and reasonable: there was no arrogant trampling on the rights or aspirations of other nations, no neurotic rejection of responsibility for the past."[166] As if Atatürk's nationalism had nothing to do with the suppression of Turkey's minorities since the foundation of the republic. The Turkish scholar Suna Kili wrote in 1980, "Kemalist nationalism is antiimperialist and recognizes the right to independence of all nations. It views with sympathy the national liberation movements in the oppressed countries of the world. In this the essentially humanitarian trait of Kemalist nationalism can be observed."[167] This is of course only true if one completely disregards how the Turkish, Kemalist state has treated its minorities.

Fukuyama's solution to the populist, ethnicity-centered nationalism that has been blossoming during the past decade is to move the focus away from a national identity based on biology and ethnicity, to one based on the embrace of the pillars of liberal democracy. "Liberal democracy has its own culture, which must be held in higher esteem than cultures rejecting democracy's values."[168] Those values will be looked at closer below. Fukuyama goes on to explain that

> we need to remember that the identities dwelling deep inside us are neither fixed nor necessarily given to us by our accidents of birth. Identity can be used to divide, but it can and has also been used to integrate. That in the end will be the remedy for the populist politics of the present.[169]

Although, thankfully, the Sun Language Theory that Atatürk propagated "was laid to rest quietly when Atatürk died,"[170] the legacy of the bogus identity "theories" of the 1930s undoubtedly shaped the Turkish ethnic identity.[171] It will probably take some time before Turkey starts defining its national identity in the way Fukuyama suggests. In a 2016 speech, President Erdoğan rejected "an understanding of history that takes 1919 as the start of 1,000-year history of our nation and civilisation. (...) Whoever leaves out our last 200 years, even 600 years together with its victories and defeats, and jumps directly from old Turkish history to the Republic, is an enemy of our nation and state."[172] Erdoğan has repeatedly accentuated the Ottoman, i.e. Turkish, greatness, as something God-given and inherent in the current Turkish identity. As opposed to Atatürk, who would rather forget the Ottoman Empire with all its faults, Erdoğan uses the memories of Turkish and Muslim dominance for all it is worth.

Not surprisingly, nationalism is particularly strong in the military. A military officer from a NATO country who had participated in a military sporting event in Istanbul, told me about a parade that had been held as part of the program. "We were 'forced' to watch a dramatized show about Ottoman battles. I felt like I was sitting among extreme rightists. I mean, it was nationalism out of another world! I asked myself: How can this be a NATO country?" During the orienteering event, the Turks had placed several cadets out in the woods, who whispered hints to the Turkish athletes. "The guy who won, who was Turkish, might have won regardless because he was very good. But a lot of the other Turkish runners were helped," the NATO officer told me. It seems that when all that matters is to make one's country look good in the eyes of "one's own," it does not matter how that image is created, or whether the image is based on truth.

The Other Arrows of Kemalism

During demonstrations in 2007 against the AKP government, Kemalist women actively protested what they saw as a threat to women's rights. At the time there was much talk about Kemalism, and the eleven-year-old son of a scholar asked her what Kemalism was. "Exaggerating the task of loving Atatürk," she answered.[173]

Having looked at secularism and nationalism, four "arrows" of Kemalism remain: republicanism, statism, populism and revolutionism. Like secularism and nationalism, these arrows were to guide the governing of Turkey, but it is not immediately clear what they mean. In fact, it is not even clear in academic circles what Kemalism means. "[T]he scholarship on Kemalism is plagued with 'conceptual imprecision.' Indeed, scholars of Turkish politics have described Kemalism in vastly contradictory terms: highly repressive, conservative modernist, right-wing corporatist, self-orientalist, antiimperialist, and modernist."[174]

Contrary to secularism and nationalism, the other four "arrows" arguably have little explanatory power when trying to understand how Turkey got to where it is today. In 1923, there was a need for the regime in Ankara to distance itself from the old ways of the sultanate. The arrows can thus be understood as ways in which the republic was different from the sultanate:

Republicanism was obvious. There would no longer be a monarch, and the role of head-of-state would not be inheritable.

Statism, also called etatism, was less obvious, but was a result of the Great Depression at the end of the 1920s and has to do with economic governance. A market economy had been adopted in the 1920s, but the Great Depression showed that the state could not simply leave the economy alone. Statism gave the government "the right to interfere with, and to control the Turkish economy."[175] Through statism, the state became the owner of the major industries in Turkey (which have since mostly been privatized).

Revolutionism, or *devrimcilik*, signifies the will not to let the modernization that resulted from Atatürk's reforms slide back to the "backward" Ottoman ways, and to keep pushing for "modernization" (whatever meaning with which one fills that word).[176]

Finally, by *populism*, Mustafa Kemal did not mean populism in our current understanding of the word. It simply meant people's rule, democracy, or at least Mustafa Kemal's understanding of democracy. In a speech to the Ankara assembly in 1920, he explained: "I believe the essential reason of our existence now has proven the general tendency of our nation, and it is populism and people's government. It is the taking over of the government by the people."[177] Almost any level of people's rule would be a higher level of democracy than what was in place in the Ottoman Empire, but it seems clear that there has always been some distance between the governing system of Turkey and actual people's rule, that is, rule based on the aggregated will of the entire population, regardless of a person's wealth or ethnicity. We will come back to this below.

Interestingly, Mustafa Kemal's understanding of what was "modern" seems to be at least partially about what he thought was in vogue. He had an obsession about European clothing and loathed the fez, the Ottoman hat that had been introduced in the beginning of the 19th century in order to modernize the Ottoman state. He had himself experienced being ridiculed by European officers for wearing the fez. He was not going to have more of that. At a diplomatic reception he once knocked the fez off the head of the Egyptian ambassador. Furthermore, for a period of time it was forbidden for people to enter the city center of Ankara in non-European clothing.[178]

What could have made Kemalism more useful was Atatürk's regard for science. At least he had a rhetorical regard for science, and had he truly put in place measures to encourage scientific development, Turkey would perhaps have looked differently today. He is known to have proclaimed: "Science, the truest guide in life!" but for some reason science did not become one of the "arrows" of his political party. Education did indeed become much more available to people in Turkey, both basic and university level education. But education must not be confused with science. Education can mean teaching of basically anything, regardless of whether or not it is based on science. And important parts of the education in Turkey have been based on political interest more than science. In coalition governments, there has always been a tug-of-war to control the Ministry of Education in order to shape the minds of future voters, not least with regard to keeping Turkey a secular country, or opposite, allowing more religion,[179] or to keeping the political left at bay. For instance, according to a parliamentarian in the late 1960s: "To give Turkish children a religious and national consciousness, to teach them to be Turkish and Islamic, is the way to ensure that leftism is neutralized."[180] Teaching the children to be Turkish has come at fairly high cost for some. The first years of school in the Kurdish speaking areas have been wasted on teaching millions of children in a language they have not been able to understand.

Science, on the other hand, is the never-ending process of finding out why, based on empirical evidence, the different elements of the universe are and behave in the way they are and do. A basic and absolutely necessary element of science is critical thinking, the free exchange of ideas and critique of research conclusions. In an environment where ideas and theories cannot be freely criticized, the quality of science will naturally be low. It is no coincidence that the US in 2019 had received 385 Nobel prizes, whereas China, with more than four times the population of the US, had only received nine.[181] Turkey has received two Nobel prizes, which still puts it above China if one counts per capita.

Atatürk's party, CHP, the largest party in the opposition, still clings dearly to the six arrows of Kemalism. In spite of its unclear meaning, Kemalism has been central in almost every public debate concerning politics since the founding of the republic in 1923.[182] This is unfortunate - and ironic - because it has been a distraction from the issues that would in fact have ensured basic freedoms for the people of Turkey, thus ensuring democracy and the "modernization" for which Mustafa Kemal, the father of Kemalism, yearned.

Democracy/Turkocracy

A prisoner in Turkey goes to the prison library and asks for a book. "I'm sorry," says the librarian, "we don't have that book. But we do have the author!" The joke is fiction, based on reality. In this section we will look closer at how democracy in Turkey and the values mentioned by Fukuyama are hindered by the government structures themselves, by continuous restrictions on fundamental freedoms and by the lack of rule of law.

"We have to sacrifice some personal rights for the security of the community," wrote the leader of the 1980 *coup d'etat,* General Chief of Staff Kenan Evren, in his memoirs.[183] This could have been the slogan for the Turkish state as such. Instead of striving for a balance in society where all groups are more or less content and nobody perceives the state as fundamentally unjust, the approach of Turkey has been to view dissatisfaction or criticism as treacherous; it should be strangled regardless of whether it is uttered nonviolently or violently. The worship-like approach to Atatürk and "Turkishness" has contributed to this dynamic by criminalizing criticism.

The key problem with Evren's approach - which was similar to that of Atatürk and arguably most of Turkey's heads of state - was that he let his own political opinions shape not only his own politics, but *how politics is done.* Atatürk and his successors assumed that they did what was best for the people, or what the people deep down really wanted, without asking the people. And by holding elections, they would then claim that Turkey was a democracy.

Although elections are important, democracy is so much more. When the great French thinker Jean-Jacques Rousseau in the 1700s wrote about the English system, he wrote: "The people of England regards itself as free; but it is grossly mistaken; it is free only during the election of members of parliament. As soon as they are elected, slavery overtakes it, and it is nothing. The use it makes of the short moments of liberty it enjoys shows indeed that it deserves to lose them."[184] This description in some ways fits Turkey. Elections are being held frequently, but the ability of the people to affect politics is severely restricted because the people lack the basic freedoms that would give them actual political choices. And when election time comes, the people vote for politicians that keep those freedoms away from them.

Freedom is a prerequisite for democracy; if people are not freely able to decide what they want, it is impossible to find out what they actually want. And finding out what people want is a prerequisite for governing the way they want. After all, that is the whole point of democracy: people's rule. In the Republic of Turkey, the freedom of the people to shape their own political opinions has been so restricted - sometimes more so, sometimes less - that it arguably does not make sense to describe Turkey as a democracy at any point in its history. Although there have been short periods of high levels of freedom of speech and of the press, those periods have been in close proximity to periods of politically motivated killings, torture or arrests. During the periods when people have enjoyed political freedoms, people have been acutely aware that the freedoms have not been institutionalized to such an extent that they can trust that they will not be harmed in the future for their political activities. Thus, although they have been "free" on paper, they have not been free from fear of future repercussions.

It is therefore interesting that several Turkish scholars have written about Turkey as a democracy and had their articles published in international, peer reviewed journals. For instance, a scholarly article from 1980 claims: "Turkey has enjoyed a working multiparty democracy since 1946 with the exception of the 'military interventions' of 1960 and 1971."[185] The very same article describes how the Turkish Labor Party that was set up "in the liberal atmosphere of the 1960s" was "closed down by a decision of the constitutional court, following the March 12, 1971 memorandum by the military."[186] Another scholar claimed, in 2001, that Turkey had been democratic for the past fifty years "except for three brief military interventions in the early 1960s, 1970s and 1980s."[187] These scholars seem to disregard that although the "military interventions" took place during the limited time periods mentioned, they had lasting consequences that permanently reduced the political freedoms of Turkey's population. For instance, the closing down of the labor party - a party that had the potential of representing the will of a large part of the population - naturally had major and lasting consequences for the Turkish "multiparty democracy."

Similarly, a Turkish scholar was writing about Turkish politics in 1997, right before the "soft coup" where the government of the Islamist Welfare Party (*Refah Partisi - RP*) was pressured to resign by the military. The scholar was writing about the unprecedented rise of an Islamist party in Turkey, in what he apparently thought was a democracy: "How has this uneasy marriage between democracy and Islam in Turkey been possible?"[188] The question is striking, because it takes as a given that it was democracy on one side and Islam on the other. But it was not "democracy" that ousted the Welfare Party, it was the military. In hindsight, the question the scholar should have asked was how the marriage between Turkey's *military* and Islam was possible. As events would have it a few months later, it was not.

The question is striking for another reason as well, because although the article was written right before the Welfare Party was ousted, the focus of the author was how well the Islamist party got along with the system. It illustrates how extremely difficult it is to predict Turkish politics.

A Structure that Limits the Will of the People

In addition to the lack of freedoms between elections, the government and election structure itself is shaped in a way that limits the will of the people. Until 1950, a free election had not been held in Turkey. The opposition Democratic Party won that election with the slogan "It's enough! It's now up to the people to decide!"[189] But then the military in 1960 decided that the people should not decide that much and staged a coup. They established the Constitutional Court to make sure the political parties were on the right track and in accordance with the secular constitution. Between 1963 and 1998 the court dissolved a total of twenty parties.[190] The political alternatives from which the people could choose were severely restricted by this.

Another restriction on the will of the people is the threshold for winning seats in parliament. Most democracies have some sort of threshold that affects the distribution of seats in parliament, but Turkey has until recently[191] had the highest in the world: ten percent. This means that when small parties have received less than ten percent, votes for those parties have not counted. This has led to the bigger parties being overrepresented in parliament. For instance, when Erdoğan's AKP received one third of the votes in 2002, the party won *two* thirds of the seats in parliament, giving it full control of the legislative assembly.[192]

Locally, too, the government structure restricts the will of the people. After the 2016 coup attempt, a state of emergency was declared giving the government powers it normally would not have. But the powers went far beyond what was necessary to return Turkey to normal after the coup attempt. That is a structural problem. For instance, sixty elected mayors in the Kurdish areas of the east and south-east were put in prison and replaced by government-appointed officials. In addition,

> six elected mayors, including those representing the capital, Ankara, and Istanbul, were left with no option but to resign after being requested to do so by the President. As a result, a third of Turkey's population [in 2017] was not being represented by the people they had elected at the 2016 local elections.[193]

When the government is able to abuse its emergency powers in such a way, without there being any mechanisms for holding it accountable, it is clear that the democratic deficiencies in Turkey are prevalent in nearly all aspects of the governing of the country.

In addition to the problems with the governing system itself, basic freedoms the people need to be able to have a meaningful say in the governing of the country are lacking. Which freedoms are these? As a minimum, for a democracy to function everyone must be free to speak their minds (free speech), they must be free to gather for whatever reason, including to discuss politics (freedom of assembly), the press must be able to write about and criticize the state (freedom of the press), and nobody should be put in jail without being convicted according to the law in a fair trial (rule of law). All of these must be in place and be equally in place for *everyone* regardless of their level of income, ethnicity, religion, or other social category. If not, it will be impossible to find out what the aggregated will of the citizens of a country is.

Free Speech

From the beginning of the Ankara National Assembly onward, finding out what the people want has never been part of the fundamental structure of the Turkish state.[194] "Just as the Ottoman Empire had always put the preservation of the state and the dynasty before all else, including the well-being of its subjects, the burgeoning Turkish nation-state, too, made this primacy of the state its founding principle."[195] As the state evolved it developed a legal system which contained "articles making the freedom of thought in the country a crime."[196] Adnan Menderes, who became prime minister in 1950, made clear that although people should have a certain degree of freedom, that freedom was "not a license to oppose the government.[197]"

One example of criminalizing opinions is the way Turkey's anti-terrorism law is formulated. It defines terrorism in a way that not only includes the violent actions themselves, but the political aims of those actions.[198] In other words, expressing an opinion that is shared by a terrorist organization is a crime. This has rendered it hopeless to discuss the Kurdish question, for instance, because arguing for some level of autonomy for the Kurds will align one with the PKK,[199] and it is a crime to have the same opinions as the PKK. A Turkish intellectual who was interviewed in his prison cell in 1995 said: "In Turkey, the philosophical concept 'I think, therefore I am' is understood as 'I think, therefore I am a terrorist.'"[200]

Amnesty International has made a list of the things one is not allowed by the penal code to say in Turkey. The list includes denigrating the Turkish nation, the government and legal institutions, alienating the public from military service, denigrating people's religious values, devaluing someone's honor, dignity or prestige by swearing, and insulting the president. All of these are problematic from a free speech perspective to begin with, but the articles are enforced in a way that makes everything much worse. Law enforcement authorities do not distinguish between insults and criticism, or between pointing out problems with military conscription and "alienation from military service."[201] People therefore have to accept everything the government does related to these articles, or risk jail if they point out mistakes or express dissatisfaction.

Particularly the ban on "insulting the Turkish Nation"[202] is not clearly defined, so that it has been - and continues to be - used to silence anybody who criticizes the government.[203] Banning insults is highly problematic to begin with, but banning insults to the Turkish Nation is in its own league of problems. President Erdoğan has taken the enforcement of the ban to new heights. In June 2019, a newspaper reported that more than 36,000 people had been investigated for such insults during the past year.[204]

Atatürk did not exactly set an example for the free flow of ideas and opinions. He once participated in a debate in a committee of the national assembly that discussed the future of the sultanate and caliphate. There he said, according to his own records: "If those assembled here (...) see the matter in its natural light, we shall all agree. Otherwise facts will still prevail, but some heads may roll."[205] Not surprisingly, he was frequently described as a dictator, which he hated. When he encouraged the foundation of an opposition party in 1930 - and then changed his mind and made sure the party disappeared three months later - he was the one who named the party.[206] The irony of not wanting to be called a dictator, then deciding the name of the opposition party before disbanding it was probably lost on him.

A few examples from the first decades after World War I illustrate well that speaking up about differing political opinions was dangerous. The first regards the fate of the communist Mustafa Suphi and his comrades. Like the mafia parallels drawn to the Ottomans in the first chapter, the circumstances surrounding this story hints at mafia-like behavior. One source states that Suphi was murdered together with twelve companions,[207] another states that 15 communists were killed.[208] Regardless, Mustafa Suphi was traveling with a group of comrades to Trabzon in January, 1921,[209] after the governor of Erzurum had denied them entry there. Supporters of Suphi were planning a welcoming party in Trabzon, but the guests never arrived. They were instead taken to the harbor where they were met by Yahya, a mobster who controlled the Trabzon harbor. They were put on a boat and taken out at sea, eastwards toward Russia whence they had come not long before. At some point, the communists were thrown into the freezing water and disappeared. It is unclear whether they were shot first.

After this, Yahya himself had to be removed. In July 1922, military authorities ordered him killed to put an end to his strong-arm "harbor government," in Trabzon. With Yahya silenced, it was impossible to confirm that he had received instructions from Ankara to liquidate Mustafa Suphi and his comrades.[210]

The list of political murders is long: Later in 1922, a former Ottoman interior minister, Ali Kemal, who had criticized the Ankara nationalists, was kidnapped in Istanbul and brought to İzmit where he was lynched.[211] In 1923, a member of the opposition in parliament, Ali Şükrü, was strangled by Mustafa Kemal's bodyguard.

In 1926, fifteen opposition politicians were sentenced to death for their alleged participation in a plot to kill Mustafa Kemal. The plot was real enough, but only some of those convicted had been proven to be involved. The court, however, "did not require hard proof; its 'considered opinion' was sufficient, and its opinion rested on guilt by association (...) [The defendants] were all critics of the regime and, sometimes explicitly, of Mustafa Kemal. So they were all guilty."[212] Thirteen of them were swiftly hanged, but two managed to escape. One of them committed suicide upon his capture, the other was hanged. The following year, four more opposition politicians were hanged, out of 46 defendants. The accusations were not clearly connected to the 1926 assassination plot, but more broadly to the "irresponsible behavior" of the defendants during the last decade of the Ottoman Empire.[213] In 1948, the prominent left-wing writer Sabahattin Ali was brutally murdered while trying to escape across the border to Bulgaria. An agent from the Turkish secret service smashed his head in.[214]

Nazim Hikmet has been called Turkey's greatest poet, and his works have been translated into many languages. In Turkey, however, his communist tendencies could not be tolerated. Although becoming quite the international celebrity, he spent much of his adult life in prison or in exile. In 1949, big names like Pablo Picasso and Jean-Paul Sartre campaigned for his release from prison. In 1959 he was stripped of his citizenship. He died in Moscow in 1963. In 2002, to send a very strong signal to a man who had been dead for four decades, Turkey's interior minister asked for Hikmet's birth details to be erased from the state records, "so as to make sure that no traces would be left showing that he had ever existed as a citizen of the country."[215]

The silencing of dissenting voices has continued. In the late 1970s the extreme right youth militia, Grey Wolves, assassinated intellectuals, "journalists, students and trade union leaders with impunity."[216] Labor Day in 1977 became a carnage, with at least 40 demonstrators killed in Taksim Square in Istanbul.[217] In 1978, in the course of one week in December, more than a hundred Alevis, assumed to be leftists, were killed in Kahramanmaraş.[218] After the 1980 coup, there was widespread torture in prisons in Turkey. The torture was frequently not for the purpose of extracting information, but to remove any desire to involve oneself in politics.

Fast forward to the 2000s, and the silencing has not stopped. There are even cases of people being killed for their activism in spite of being outside of Turkey. In 2013, "the assassination of three PKK–connected activists (...) in Paris was widely attributed to the National Intelligence Organization (MIT),"[219] Turkey's military intelligence agency, although MIT denied this. The activists were associated with the PKK,[220] one of them among its founders,[221] but no evidence was provided of their legal responsibility for terrorism. Had such evidence existed, Turkey could have asked for their extradition, or the activists could probably have been tried according to French anti-terrorism law.

An example from 2020 is the deaths of Helin Bolek and İbrahim Gökçek, members of the popular music group Grup Yorum. The group's "defiant left-wing stance"[222] led to the government's banning of its performances in 2016. The government justified the ban by claiming the group had links to a Marxist-Leninist terror organization. Bolek and Gökçek had started their hunger strike while in prison, and continued upon their release, to protest the performance ban and the fact that other members of the band were still in prison. In April 2020, on day number 288 of the hunger strike, Helin Bolek died.[223] A month later, on day 323 of his strike, İbrahim Gökçek died.[224]

Freedom of the Press

Free speech in general is a crucial element of democracy, but there is a group of people for whom free speech is particularly important: journalists. Freedom of the press is absolutely necessary if one is to be able to hold the government accountable for how it wields its power. Without journalists dedicated to informing the public about what the government is doing, to critically interviewing politicians and members of the state apparatus, and to uncovering corruption and power abuse, it is impossible for the people to make rational and fact-based decisions about which politicians or political party to vote for.

It did not start out well for journalism in the Republic of Turkey. Continuing the Ottoman tradition of strictly limiting press freedom, Mustafa Kemal did not like to be criticized. After the Kurdish rebellion in the mid-1920s, two journalists were put on trial for "unfairly and unnecessarily" criticizing the government. Being encouraged to do so, the journalists wisely expressed regret and pleaded for Mustafa Kemal to intercede. That he did, by encouraging the tribunal to show "tolerance." After this, press criticism of the government stopped.[225]

Things have not improved much since then. Today there are (at least) two main ways in which the media in Turkey are held in check by the government. The most conspicuous way is the direct attack and punishment of individual journalists and editors. Turkey has a long tradition of not being willing or able to protect its journalists. Between 1992 and 2016, 25 journalists were killed in Turkey.[226] That amounts to one journalist killed every single year. Importantly, these are only the journalists killed where the motive is known. In addition come the journalists killed with unclear motives or in "accidents" under suspicious circumstances, sometimes after having been threatened by the police or military intelligence.[227] Few other countries described as democracies have such grotesque statistics.

Turkey has an equally long tradition of being the country in the world with the most journalists in jail. In February 2019, there were 157 journalists in jail in Turkey, who had spent a total of 224,423 days behind bars.[228] But the attacks on journalists also come in other forms than violence or jail. It has become "commonplace for top officials, especially Erdoğan, to publicly attack journalists who displease them, and for those journalists to be fired soon after."[229] It is similarly commonplace for top officials to call editors and request specific journalists to be fired.[230]

The second main way in which the government controls the media is economic incentives, either sticks or carrots. The sticks are typically fines that a media company can incur if they publish something the government does not like. For instance, in 2009, the "Doğan Media

Group was hit with a $500 million tax fine, raised in September of the same year to $2.5 billion, four-fifths of the market capitalization of the entire company."[231] Why? Because

> Doğan had enraged PM Erdoğan when its flagship papers, *Hürriyet* and *Milliyet*, gave extensive front-page coverage of a German court case, accusing several prominent Turkish citizens with ties to the top of the AKP of embezzling tens of millions of dollars from a Turkish charity.[232]

The economic carrots, on the other hand, take the form of lucrative government contracts. Turkish media are usually owned by holding companies with a wide variety of economic interests, including in construction and the military industry. A smart move for a holding company is to buy a media outlet and make sure the media outlet says what the government wants it to say. It will then be easier for one of the holding company's subsidiaries to win large government procurement contracts.[233]

Sometimes the line between the government and the media will be blurred. In 2007, a large media group, Sabah-ATV,

> was sold to Çalık Holding. Prime Minister Erdoğan's son-in-law Berat Albayrak was the company's CEO, and Albayrak's brother led the media unit. In an unusual move, two state banks stepped in with financing worth $750 million of the $1.1 billion purchase. Sabah's editorial line rapidly shifted from center-left to ardently pro-government.[234]

Interestingly, and probably because of the strong government influence, the Turkish media has not exactly been united in calling for increased press freedom. One famous editor in chief, İlhan Selçuk, editor of Turkey's oldest newspaper *Cumhuriyet* from 1991 until his death in 2010, was known to speak of democracy as "*cici demokrasi*, sweet democracy, that is; too sweet for the uneducated people."[235] No wonder democracy is kept at an arm's length when even leaders of the press do not want democracy.

Furthermore, the relationship between the military and the media has traditionally been close. For instance, after the "soft coup" of 1997, when the Islamist government was pressured by the military to resign, "large media outlets supported the military with sensationalized and baseless stories about the Islamist threat to democracy."[236] The good relationship between the media and the military lasted until Erdoğan "cleaned up" the military after the 2016 coup attempt.

In other words, the Turkish media have served a variety of financial and other interests and not consistently stood on the side of bringing facts about the state to the people. Those journalists in the country who are actually doing their jobs properly are fighting an uphill battle.

Freedom of Assembly

Turkey does not have a good track record for letting people gather as they want. The authorities usually do not want large gatherings of people when the purpose is to talk politics, especially politics that differ from that of the government. Although it is the duty of the authorities to ensure the security of everybody in the country, it is common for the authorities in Turkey to approach this duty in a selective manner.

A pattern is for the government to warn activists against organizing a political event because it may provoke a violent reaction from one group or another, and then not provide security for the event. If then a violent attack against the event occurs, the authorities will blame the victims for drawing the ire that caused the attack. The worst example of this is the October 2015 terror attack in Ankara, when more than 100 activists were killed in a bomb attack.

Turkey's ability to prevent large gatherings of people was truly put to the test in 2013, when enormous protests erupted across the country. The protests started in Gezi Park in Istanbul and became known as the Gezi protests. As many as 7.5 million people all over the country may have participated in the protests, before the government was able to quell the unrest. The demands of the protesters were multifaceted, and the protests were not organized well enough for a sustained struggle. We will get back to the Gezi protests in the final chapter.

Rule of Law

On November 28, 2015, just before 11 A.M., the human rights lawyer and chairman of the Diyarbakır Bar Association, Tahir Elçi, was fatally shot in the head in Diyarbakır while giving a press conference on the street. He was calling for an end to the fighting between the PKK and state security forces that had erupted four months earlier, after peace talks had collapsed. At the other end of the street, two PKK militants had just shot two police officers and were escaping the scene of the crime, running in the direction of Elçi's press conference. As they approached, several police or security force officers opened fire on them but were not able to stop them. They ran past Elçi and disappeared. The police kept firing, and when it was all over one man was lying dead on the ground: Elçi. The killing of Elçi has never been investigated, although forensic analysis of multiple videos filmed at the incident suggests that he was killed by a bullet from a police gun.[237]

Rule of law is a prerequisite of democracy because without it it is impossible for the state to provide the aforementioned freedoms that are crucial elements of democracy. Rule of law means firstly that no person can be punished without being convicted according to the law after a fair trial. Secondly, every time a crime is committed, no matter who commits it, there is a proper investigation that collects evidence for such a trial. Then, if there is evidence that is likely to lead to a conviction, a trial is always held.

In Turkey, it does matter who commits the crime, especially after the constitution was amended in 2017. The amendment gave the president increased control over "the appointment, promotion, dismissal of and disciplinary sanctions against judges and prosecutors."[238] The consequence of this is that if a prosecutor opens up an investigation into a crime, the president may have him or her fired if the investigation points towards someone the president wants to protect. And since this was written into the constitution, it is unlikely to change any time soon.

Although the amendment happened in 2017, not investigating a crime is a pattern that has repeated itself for decades in Turkey. The question has not so much been who committed the crime, but rather: How will it look for the government, police or military if the truth gets out? Or: Was the person against whom the crime was committed an enemy of a powerful person? If the answer is "bad" or "yes," respectively, it has not been unusual for an investigation to be stopped, restricted, or simply never started.

There can be no fair trial without lawyers. Regardless of how heinous a crime may have been, the defendant must have a lawyer that can make sure that the prosecution is in accordance with the law. The defense lawyer is part of the system's insurance against power abuse by the government. In Turkey, however, a defense lawyer may be seen by the government more as a nuisance than anything else.

To be able to defend his client properly, the lawyer must be able to have private conversations with him or her. But this privileged communication, as it is called, was in practice cancelled under the state of emergency after the 2016 coup attempt. The parliament later passed the cancellation into law. "There is no privileged communication when a meeting between lawyer and client takes place in the presence of a prison guard and the whole meeting is recorded on camera," a lawyer explained to the organization Human Rights Watch. "You can't discuss the case with your client."[239]

To make matters worse, prosecutors have also started going after the defense lawyers with criminal charges. As documented by Human Rights Watch,

> prosecuting authorities have criminalized lawyers for activities undertaken to discharge their professional duties and have associated them without evidence with the alleged crimes of their clients. Some of these prosecutions appear to have come about in reprisal for their efforts to document police abuse and other human rights violations and to protect the rights of their clients.[240]

As a consequence of this, lawyers have become hesitant about taking cases that may jeopardize their own freedom.

Torture is not an unknown phenomenon in Turkish prisons, although the Ottoman reforms in the 1800s explicitly banned it. The ban never quite sunk in. Between 1980 and 1995, "445 people had undergone torture and died in Turkish detention centers."[241] For women, being put in jail means being exposed to a high risk of being raped. Human rights associations in the beginning of the 2000s reported that 80 percent of women in prisons in Turkey had been raped.[242] Turkey has no mechanism in place to prevent torture, no monitoring of prisons with that purpose, and no effective investigation takes place after allegations of torture are put forward.[243]

Turkey cannot be said to be ruled by law. Who you are and who you know is more important than the crimes you have or have not committed. The rule of thumb is that if someone in, or close to, the government is cleared of charges of committing a crime, that cannot be interpreted to mean that no crime was committed. Similarly, if someone who has been critical of the government is convicted of corruption or some other crime, that is no indication that corruption or a crime has in fact taken place. This means that the safest way to stay out of prison is to have power or know people who do. Some periods have been less like that, some have been more. It is difficult not to draw a parallel to the recurring power struggles of the Ottoman Empire, where having power meant being untouchable by the law. Today, this dynamic is being used explicitly for political purposes. President Erdoğan has frequently stepped into the victim role, claiming that his opponents will do to him as they did to President Menderes, who was hanged after the 1960 coup.[244]

The Democracy that Never Was

A famous 1932 biography of Atatürk, "Grey Wolf," concluded that Mustafa Kemal had ruled like a dictator so that Turkey would not be ruled by a dictator again.[245] Mustafa Kemal was convinced that only he would be capable of civilizing Turkey.[246] There is little reason to doubt that a similar line of thinking has been an important motive for heads of state and military leaders in Turkey ever since. But it is completely detached from the reality of human nature: Power corrupts. Absolute power corrupts absolutely.[247] It is a reality that does not seem to sink in among many people in Turkey. When explaining his vote for Erdoğan, one man told a journalist: "We have a long tradition of following strong leaders. Democracy after the European model is not something we strive for."[248] Erdoğan himself has been rather clear that democracy is not what he offers the people. In a famous speech, he said: "We have to discuss democracy. Is democracy an aim or a means? For us, democracy cannot be an aim, only a means."[249] Such an attitude makes sense if one longs for the great Ottoman past, where Muslim Turks had conquered a big portion of the world, and the empire was ruled by a Muslim sultan.

Surprisingly, some of those who oppose Erdoğan do not necessarily want to take Turkey in a direction towards liberal democracy. They, too, want to take Turkey back, not to Ottoman times, but to a time when Atatürk's heritage was the guiding star for the government. One former diplomat explained to me that thanks to Erdoğan, people were rediscovering Atatürk. "Atatürk is way up there. We've realized that our republican past is very precious," he said. He went on to explain that the republic made it possible for people to migrate to cities to pursue economic opportunities, as opposed to Ottoman times when the society was arranged in echelons and people had to keep their place in the hierarchy. Thanks to Atatürk, he said, "children from the street, like Erdoğan, can become president. Süleyman Demirel, too, came from a humble background. He walked four hours by foot each way to school. He graduated with flying colors, studied in the US in the 1940s, became an engineer, then bureaucrat, then prime minister and finally president."

This perspective has some explanatory power. To many influential politicians and intellectuals in Turkey who oppose the Islamist turn that the country has taken, the comparison is not between the current society of Turkey and the society of more democratic countries with better human rights records. The comparison is - still - between the current government and Atatürk's imagined republic. And to argue for the superiority of Atatürk's republic, they do not compare it to current democracies with good human rights records, but to the Ottoman Empire. As long as the expectations for good governance are not raised beyond Atatürk's authoritarian regime, democracy will keep evading the people of Turkey.

4. Security and Unity: Can We Trust Anybody But Ourselves?

Places mentioned in this chapter.

"You know, that trauma! We never completely recovered." Engin[250] told me about Turkey's first military coup in 1960 when I visited him in December 2019. He himself was born after the coup, but the family suffered long after. His family had been heavily involved in politics, and his grandfather was imprisoned by the military junta. "I grew up visiting my grandfather in prison. It was traumatic. My grandfather's friends, who were also in prison, have memories of me growing up visiting him."

Turkey has been through two actual military coups where the military has taken over the government by force, in 1960 and 1980. In addition, there have been two "soft coups," in 1971 and 1997, where the military gave the respective prime ministers offers they could not refuse, so to speak, forcing them to resign. There has also been an attempted "soft coup" in 2007, the so-called "e-coup," which failed. Finally, there was a failed attempt at military takeover in 2016. In other words, the military has intervened every decade since 1960, except for the 17-year break between 1980 and 1997. The two last attempts, in 2007 and 2016, failed.

The Turkish military has seen itself as "the naturally appointed guardians of Atatürk's reforms"[251] and as such the supreme authority on how Kemalism should be interpreted. This has naturally led to the military, on several occasions, putting Turkey back on the "right" track. The generals have tried to keep Turkey away from communism on one side and Islamism on the other, trying to balance the country on some imagined path towards prosperity and modernity. While attempting this, they have failed to properly ask the people what they want by failing to put in place or strengthen institutions that ensure democratic freedoms and practices. While choosing this non-democratic setup of the state, they have also failed to put in place and protect institutions that could have worked effectively against the corruption that inevitably follows authoritarian regimes.

In this chapter we will look closer at how the military meddling in governance happened and how it affected the country. We will see that the military coups had unforeseen consequences several years after they happened, because they gave people power who otherwise would not have it, and they caused lasting grievances among people who otherwise would have been content, or at least more content than they came to be. We will then widen our perspective and look at Turkey's relationship with its immediate neighbors and with Russia, Europe, the US, and NATO.

I have tried to avoid listing events and names of people and political parties, but the reader may still think that there is too much information crammed into the text. The most important points to take away from this chapter are the following: From 1960 onward, the Turkish military started meddling in politics more than before. They have staged two successful coups and some coup-like interventions and have gained substantial and undue influence. This has shaped Turkey to a large extent. It has affected its relations with other countries and reduced the possibilities of developing into a state where the citizens are protected by rule of law and where democracy and human rights have a high standing.

1960 - From Authoritarian to Not Kemalist Enough

After the 1950 election where Atatürk's CHP party lost, the Democratic Party (DP) was the largest party in parliament for a decade, and Adnan Menderes was the prime minister throughout the 1950s. Although the DP had made sure to stay friendly with the military up until winning the election in 1950, after coming to power the general lack of respect for the officers became apparent. The Menderes government also let the salaries in the military lag behind the rapidly increasing costs of living. Furthermore, many an officer was enraged by what looked like corruption among government officials.[252] At this point there had never been a military coup in Turkey. The lesson of keeping the military happy had not yet been learned.

Before the 1950 election, the DP had promised workers in Turkey the right to strike. When Menderes was reminded of this after becoming prime minister, he responded: "Is Turkey to have strikes? Let's have some economic development first and then we'll think about this matter."[253] Towards the end of the 1950s, the CHP became increasingly critical of the Menderes government, accusing it of moving towards becoming a dictatorship. Menderes responded by banning outdoor political activity and limiting freedom of the press and enforced these measures in a way that favored his own party. Menderes also started utilizing the military in a partisan way, for instance by ordering the military to stop a train carrying former prime minister and leader of the opposition, İsmet İnönü, to a political event in Kayseri.[254]

Both political parties were appealing to military officers to win them over to their side. Many officers felt they had to choose between executing the unfair orders of the government or siding with the opposition.

> [It] was these efforts to manipulate the armed forces as a political tool that destroyed the tradition of political neutrality so painstakingly erected over the years. (...) Three middle grade officers, one of whom was the commander whose troops had stopped Inönü, resigned in public protest to the political use of the army by the government. They were promptly arrested for encouraging others to disobey 'military laws' and discipline.[255]

A large enough group of officers in the military had had enough. On May 27, 1960, they staged their coup and removed the government from office.

"The 1960 coup was very vicious and bloody. Merciless." The above-mentioned Engin vividly tells the story as if he lived through it himself. Partially, he did, because when he was born two years later, his family still suffered the consequences. "The coup laid the foundations of later struggles in Turkish politics. The primary goal for us at the center-right became 'revenge' for the coup. It created a divide that even today isn't bridged easily. The military shut down the parliament and hanged three important people, beloved in the party." He goes on to tell me that the families of those who were targeted suffered a lot. Students were unable to continue their education because their parents were jailed; the tuition could no longer be paid. "My mother couldn't graduate because she was flunked by the school, because she was the daughter of the wrong person. Our right to property deeds, everything was frozen."

The military set up a tribunal to prosecute hundreds of people connected to the Menderes regime. 123 people were acquitted, 31 were sentenced to life imprisonment and 418 to lesser terms.[256] In addition, fifteen people were sentenced to death. Of these, twelve had their sentences commuted to life. They were finally pardoned in 1966.[257] Foreign Minister Zorlu and Finance Minister Polatkan of the Menderes government were hanged on September 16, 1961, and Menderes the following day after a failed suicide attempt.[258]

Naturally, the way the military dealt with the ousted regime had long-lasting consequences for those involved. "Certain dates of the year are important to us. To this date, we silently observe our 16-17 September, when the three were hanged. As a young kid I didn't closely associate with it, but when I became older I developed strong emotions about it," explains Engin. He goes on to explain how his generation reacted in mainly two ways. They either left Turkey and wanted nothing to do with Turkish politics, or they "became very vengeful and angry and bitter and never quite came to terms with the loss. Did not find a balance in life, and some joined politics at young ages. Now, time has passed, but still some families keep the grudge," he explains. "Several of us grandchildren are now involved in politics. It's a sort of revenge, it's personal. We grew up with it."

Although the coup caused big personal problems for quite a few families, it also "ushered in the most liberal period the people had known."[259] The military leaders invited academics to come and write a new constitution. "The resulting document enshrined broad freedoms to form associations, publish, organize trade unions, and call strikes -- all limited since the founding of the republic."[260] Unfortunately, the freedoms ultimately allowed for choices of political direction which the military could not tolerate. Only a decade later they intervened again.

Two other important structural changes that affected politics in Turkey after the 1960 coup should be mentioned. Firstly, the Constitutional Court was created, with the power to ban political parties that used religion politically. As previously mentioned, numerous parties were banned during the following decades, only to be reborn under different names. Secondly, the National Security Council (NSC) was established. The council was chaired by the civilian president, but its military members had substantial influence over the assessments made. The council has frequently been criticized for giving the military undue influence over the civilian government. These two structural changes have substantially shaped Turkish politics up until now.

1971 - From Not Kemalist Enough to Mayhem

The DP was dissolved after the 1960 coup, but DP members who were not executed, put in jail or banned from politics formed new parties. In the 1961 election, two parties formed by former DP members won 48.5 percent of the vote between them. The military, however, refused to hand power back to the very people it had taken it from the year before. Instead, İsmet İnönü from CHP, which won 36.7 percent of the vote, was asked to form a government. İnönü had been the prime minister under Atatürk's presidency before becoming president himself until 1950. İnönü had to consider the actual strength of the parties and formed a coalition government with the Justice Party, which was seen as the continuation of the ousted DP. In 1964, Süleyman Demirel became the leader of the Justice Party. He was to become one of the most significant figures in Turkish politics until his last day as president in 2000.

A "self-made man," Demirel was a talented vote hunter who was seen to be "of the people," as opposed to many politicians from wealthy and powerful families. He understood better than the traditional elite what the people wanted to hear and spoke those words well. Particularly he emphasized traditional values and the Islamic character of his Justice Party. This worked well, and his party won more than 52 percent of the vote in the 1965 election. Demirel became prime minister and could rule with majority in parliament.

Although the military had put in place the Constitutional Court which would keep religious politics at bay, the generals did not sanction Demirel's flirting with Islamism. They were more concerned with leftists and communists, who had sprouted up as a result of the freedoms of the 1960 constitution. The right amount of Islam could work as a repellent for communism, they thought. Demirel and the military therefore started limiting the opportunities for leftists and communists to gather and discuss ideas. "People were arrested for publishing communist propaganda, which, in the most famous case, turned out to consist of quotes from an early speech by Atatürk himself."[261] But because of the checks and balances put in place by the 1960 constitution, and because the interests of Demirel and the military did not completely overlap, the limiting of freedoms could only go so far. Demirel could not, like Menderes, evolve into a dictator. The judiciary remained independent, and Demirel had to suffer through criticism from the media.

The limiting of the freedoms was, naturally, not met with a shrug of the shoulders by those affected. Rather, the limitations pushed people towards more radical and extreme political camps. Towards the end of the 1960s, demonstrations and protests by the radical and extreme left increasingly ended in brawls with the police and security forces. The most extreme elements on the left were also responsible for bombings and kidnappings. "But from the end of 1968 onwards, and increasingly during 1969 and 1970, the violence of the left was met and surpassed by violence from the militant right, notably Türkeş's Grey Wolves."[262]

The Türkeş referred to here is Alparslan Türkeş, a military officer who had entered politics after being the spokesperson of the coup-makers in 1960. He and a handful of other officers were dismissed from the military junta in 1960. He tried and failed to found his own political party, but managed to become the leader of a small, conservative party. He ousted the old leadership and turned the party into a hierarchically organized, militant party with an ultra-nationalist programme.[263] The youth organization of Türkeş's party became known as the Grey Wolves after a character in ancient Turkish mythology. Its members received paramilitary training in designated camps. They were to become a destabilizing force for years to come.

Although Türkeş did not receive many votes, he managed to remain an important figure in Turkish politics until he died in 1997.

The violence on university campuses and in the streets around the country increased, and Demirel's government was not able to contain it. On March 12, 1971, the military had had enough of the chaos and the Chief of General Staff demanded that "a strong and credible government be formed that would be able to end the 'anarchy' and carry out reforms 'in a Kemalist spirit'."[264] If this did not happen, the general said, the army would have to take matters into its own hands. If the reader now scratches his/her head, wondering what on earth the Chief of General Staff meant by said reforms, fret not. Nobody knew exactly what he meant. But Prime Minister Demirel knew very well what had happened to Menderes a decade earlier and immediately resigned. The military found - in the right wing of the CHP, the party of Atatürk and İnönü - a person who in the generals' minds was qualified to lead a new government. His name was Nihat Erim, and only led the government for a little more than a year. For his enabling of the plans of the generals, he would later pay a high price.

The leftists in Turkey at first hoped that the military intervention would lead to better conditions for left-leaning politicians and activists. They were disappointed. The military high command remained convinced that it was the leftists and communists who were the main threat to the country. They had to be restrained.[265] Within weeks of the new government taking over, terrorist attacks picked up pace again. Martial law was declared, and the security forces started rounding up terrorist suspects. This in itself might have been justified, but the military used the situation to institute something reminiscent of a witch-hunt against anyone with leftist or just progressive liberal sympathies.[266] Thousands were arrested, including intellectuals and leading members of the Labor Party, and eventually the Labor Party was banned. Conspicuously, the Grey Wolves and other violent actors on the political right were mainly left alone.

Similarly to the 1960 coup, it was time for someone to be hanged. This time it was not members of government, but members of the violent, radical left. Facing strict government restrictions, including arrests, some among the Marxist-Leninists had concluded that the only way to achieve change was through violent means, had acted this conviction out, and been arrested. In July 1971, the trials of 26 members of the Turkish People's Liberation Army began. Several of them, if not all, had received training in Palestinian guerrilla camps in Lebanon, [267] and were responsible for a bank robbery and kidnappings. Of the 26 defendants, Deniz Gezmiş, Hüseyin İnan and Yusuf Aslan were sentenced to death. Several protests and demonstrations were held to overturn the sentences, and there were also violent attempts to free the three. In March 1972, eleven armed men kidnapped three technicians from a military base in order to stop the executions. Ten of the kidnappers were then killed by security forces, and the eleventh was arrested. There was also another kidnapping and even an airplane hijacking before the three convicted were hanged on May 6, 1972.[268]

"My father was part of the second generation of that movement. He met Gezmiş a couple of times," Senem Deniz tells me. She was born a few years after the hanging of Gezmiş, who has achieved a Che Guevara-like status in some circles in Turkey. I meet Senem in her office in Ankara, where she tells me about her family's experiences. She tells me that those who were hanged had done nothing to deserve it, and that "it was seen as a sort of revenge from the hangings in 1960. Süleyman Demirel said: 'They took three from us, we took three from them.'" She goes on to tell me about her father's fight for a revolution in Turkey in the 70s. "Years later, I asked him 'Did you really believe in a revolution?' He said yes. My parents didn't invest in property because they thought there was going to be a communist revolution. Now, he doesn't believe in revolution anymore."[269]

Towards the end of the 1970s, power was shifting hands between two people: The closest thing Turkey has had to a social democrat, Bülent Ecevit from the CHP, and Süleyman Demirel of the Justice Party. Ecevit had been able to rise in the CHP in spite of his leftist sympathies and was even able to win against İnönü for the leadership of the party. Because he tended to lean towards the left, and because they feared he might pull Turkey out of NATO, military officers openly started calling him a traitor while he was prime minister from January 1978 to November 1979.[270] Demirel, knowing he was much closer to the military frame of mind than Bülent Ecevit was, started calling him 'Büllende,' referring to the socialist Chilean president Allende, who was killed in the Pinochet coup in 1973.

The violence and the assassinations were getting more and more out of control. The military tried to control the left wing violence and used the Grey Wolves and other violent extreme rightists in their fight. In 1976, there were 104 political murders; in 1977, the number rose to 230, and by mid-1979, some 20 people were being killed a day. Targets grew more indiscriminate.[271] The following summer, it was even worse, with 25 people killed every day.[272]

Before the violence reached that extreme level, a massacre of leftist Alevis took place in December 1978 in Kahramanmaraş in Turkey's southeast. In a week, more than a hundred Alevis were killed, mainly by the Grey Wolves, actively aided by the military. People sought refuge with the military, but the latter handed them over to the Grey Wolves to be executed.[273] This killing spree had the purpose of instilling fear in the population, undermine Prime Minister Ecevit's position and create a pretext for martial law.[274] Martial law was indeed declared, which gave the generals more power. This made it easier for them to make specific plans for a coup.

1980 - From Mayhem to (Authoritarian) Order

Two related and additional problems to the violence were high inflation and high unemployment. The inflation made the import of raw materials more expensive, which led to decreased production. This, in turn, led to high unemployment, not least among the youth, who became more susceptible to extreme political ideas and violence.

The killing continued well into the year 1980, including that of Nihat Erim, the 1971 puppet prime minister who had overseen the execution of the Marxist-Leninist leader Deniz Gezmiş and his comrades. Two days later, in a twisted form of revenge, the founding head of the Turkish trade union confederation was killed.

> The violence that the military had done nothing to stop provided it with the pretext to stage its coup. On 12 September 1980, the chief of the general staff, General Kenan Evren finally took over as head of state. The killing that had plagued the country since 1975, when the fascist Grey Wolves started assassinating left-wing intellectuals, teachers and students, ceased overnight. (...) All democratic and social rights were abolished. DİSK, the main trade union organization, was banned and its leadership was arrested. Five hundred thousand people, the vast majority of them leftist activists, were incarcerated; 55 people were executed, while several hundred died under torture.[275]

Another source provides the following numbers: 500 were sentenced to death, of which 50 were actually executed. 191 people were killed through torture.[276] A third source is more hesitant about giving specific numbers, stating that "untold numbers were mutilated or killed in the torture chambers."[277]

"It was really hard. It was a military prison. We were treated as enemy soldiers in a concentration camp. The treatment was inhumane," explains Fethiye Çetin, with whom we will get further acquainted in Chapter 7 on the Armenians. She was one of the many who were arrested after the coup. She was held in Mamak Prison in Ankara, known to be the second harshest prison after the one in Diyarbakır, the "Kurdish capital" in the southeast. She tells me about torture and solitary confinement, and the strong bonds that developed between the women in prison. "We were beaten and tortured and denied basic needs, but in our small wards we used to dance, do theater, make fun of the guards, sing songs. We would come back with bruises and tortured bodies, but we cared for each other's wounds and were able to keep each other's spirits up." The solitary confinement would be in a cell that was too small to lie down in, she could only sit. Her longest confinement there was for a whole month. "People could visit me in prison," she explains, "but sometimes they withdrew that right to punish us."

For those who visited, the visit could be quite troublesome. When the above-mentioned Senem Deniz was going with her mother to visit her father in Mamak Prison after the 1980 coup, "we would wait for five hours to see him for ten minutes. We weren't allowed to touch him or hug him. Once a week we had permission to visit. My mom would go every week and sometimes she brought me. I cried a lot when she wouldn't let me come with her." Senem also remembers going with her grandmother to visit her mother in prison. "The prison they used had been a school before, and later it was turned back into a high school, in fact the high school I attended. So I visited my mother in prison, and later attended school in the same building."

It was her mother who was first arrested after the coup. Shortly after her mother was released, her father disappeared. "My mother went to the police station and asked, but they said they didn't have him. Then 45 days later we saw him on TV. He had been held at Mamak Prison in Ankara, where he was severely tortured. In Mamak, the inmates would be beaten by soldiers for eight hours straight." Her father was kept in prison for two and a half years, and her aunts, uncles and mother would every now and then be detained and brought to the police station and kept there overnight. Sometimes they would be thrown in jail for longer or shorter periods of time.

Senem recalls: "I have memories of having stayed - when I was seven years old - at the police station with my mother until the next morning." During one period, both of her parents were in prison so that she had to move to her grandmother's house. "My childhood was about visiting my parents and uncles and aunts in prison."

While inflicting lasting traumas on leftist politicians, activists and their families, the military regime went about changing the system. They wanted to avoid a recurrence of the chaotic circumstances that had evolved - in their eyes - as a result of the 1961 constitution. The period following the 1980 coup is regarded as the most authoritarian period in Turkey after the first free election in 1950.[278] Civil society organizations were by and large outlawed. The three main dangers were, in the eyes of the military junta, communism, Kurdish separatism and Islamic radicalism.[279] Based on their assessments on what needed to change, the generals rewrote the constitution "to limit explicitly freedoms of expression, movement, association, and even scientific research."[280] Twenty years earlier, after the 1960 coup, the military had mainly left the writing of the constitution to civilians. This time they put themselves in the driving seat.[281] In 1982, the new constitution replaced the 1961 constitution.

The purpose of the restrictions of political freedoms in the new constitution was to protect the *security* and the *unity* of the state, two concepts that could be applied to suit the opinions of the military government. Serving both of these purposes was the linguistic intolerance that was incorporated in articles 3 and 42 of the constitution. Article 3 states that the language of the state is Turkish. This in itself may seem reasonable enough; every state needs a language to be used by its administration. In Turkey, however, the article is highly discriminatory because of the large Kurdish population in the southeast. The solution to this would be to amend Article 3 to make it possible for Kurdish to be an official language together with Turkish in regions where the majority speaks Kurdish. Similar arrangements are found across the globe in countries with several languages. Alas, Article 4 prevents any amendment of articles 1, 2 and 3 by stating that those articles "shall not be amended, nor shall their amendment be proposed."[282] Article 4 thus cements the intolerance of Article 3.

Then article 42 comes along and makes it all worse. It states: "No language other than Turkish shall be taught as a mother tongue to Turkish citizens at any institution of education." This means that if

Turkey is to liberalize its linguistic policy and let children be taught in their actual mother tongue, the parliament cannot simply change the law. It has to change the constitution, with is a much more demanding procedure.

One problem with the 1982 constitution is its level of detail. Whereas the US constitution with all its amendments fits in an 18-page document,[283] and that of France fits in a 44-page document,[284] the constitution of Turkey fills 83 pages. When the constitution is that elaborate, it is moving away from being the fundamental law that governs the laws, which a constitution is supposed to be, towards a law that simply governs the details of society, like any other law. The generals of the 1980 coup took away a substantial amount of power from parliament by making it have to change the constitution even for minor legal changes. One could thus argue that the 1982 will of the generals is still superior to the will of the people of Turkey.[285] That is a major democratic problem.

In addition to these systemic consequences of the 1980 coup, it also had long-lasting personal consequences for a large number of people. For instance, after the 1980 coup, many people on the political left were banned from attending university. The ban hit Senem Deniz's father, who could not attend university after being released from prison. The ban was upheld for many years, until 2018. "That meant that my father, after more than 40 years, was allowed to return to university. But now, of course, he's too old for that to be relevant," she explains. For her, personally, one lasting consequence has been that she still does not like the police and soldiers. "They treated my parents badly, and they kept us all under surveillance. It has permanently ruined my relationship with the police and the military."

The coup severely affected Fethiye Çetin's life too. Because of her socialist sympathies, she spent three years in Ankara's Mamak Prison. Although she was released in 1984, she was not absolved of her "crime," and not until the mid-1990s was her case dropped. When she was released she moved to Istanbul, which felt safer. But not until her case was dropped, she tells me, did she feel that she could draw a sigh of relief. She could then, after all those years, start thinking again about the book she had wanted to write since the 1970s. Her grandmother had revealed that she was actually Armenian, and Çetin had wanted to publish her story ever since. The book was finally published in 2004 and became very influential.

I asked her if her prison experience damaged her in any way. "There might be some damages, but I'm not aware of them. I'm more aware of the advantages. It matured us," she explained, almost as if suffering through three years in Mamak Prison had been a spiritual journey. "We truly understand the value of solidarity, especially as women. Us women were treated in a more humiliating way then the men, and we overcame it through solidarity with each other." She went on to explain that she is still in touch with the people she was in prison with. "The friendships from prison are the strongest relationships I now have." Surprising, perhaps, but very similar to what soldiers who have fought wars together say, about how the extreme struggle has created particularly strong bonds.

2016 - The Convenient Coup Attempt

As explained in the previous chapter, the military in 1997 pressured prime minister Erbakan of the religious Welfare Party to resign, because the generals found his party to be too religious. In 2007, the military intervened again, in what has been dubbed the "e-coup." The General Staff of the armed forces published a memorandum on their web page which in practice was a threat against the government. But Prime Minister Erdoğan read the power game well and simply ignored it. Then came the 2016 coup attempt which nobody seems to fully understand, but which led to fundamental changes in how Turkey functions.

"The more closely one looks at what happened that night, the more loose ends one finds,"[286] a foreign journalist investigating the coup attempt wrote. There are too many things that do not make sense, and too many factors pulling in opposite directions, for analysts to be able to draw clear conclusions regarding who were behind the coup and their possible motives. There are three main possibilities regarding the plotters of the coup. The first is that it was yet another effort by secular generals to keep Turkey secular. The second is that the Gülenists were behind it. The third is that Erdoğan knew about the forthcoming coup attempt and knew that he controlled more of the military than the coup plotters did. He therefore let the coup attempt happen, so that he could blame it on the Gülenists and rid himself of all traces of them and others who disagreed with him in the state apparatus.

But who are the Gülenists? To be able to honestly say that we have tried to understand the 2016 coup attempt, we must first look closer at the Gülenists. To do so, we must briefly go back to the first years of the Republic of Turkey, when Sufi brotherhoods (*tarikat*) were banned. They had existed for centuries, and by banning them Atatürk and his comrades forced them underground where they thrived in secret. One of these brotherhoods birthed Fethullah Gülen, who became the leader of an enormous movement, the Hizmet Movement (*hizmet* means 'service').

Born in 1941 in Erzurum, Fethullah Gülen became a preacher like his father, obtaining a preacher's license in 1959. Although he is not himself formally a master within a Sufi brotherhood, his connection to the Nur sect, one of many branches of the Nakşibendi order, is well known. In 1976, he set up the first dormitory for poor students, soon becoming a network of dormitories providing housing for tens of thousands of poor students. In the 1980s, schools were set up in connection with the dormitories, based on the teachings of Gülen. *Fethullahcılar* (followers of Fethullah), also known as Gülenists, would soon be found in every corner of Turkey.

The movement grew further and established schools in Central Asia and Africa, and then in Europe and North America. *Fethullahcıs* who had entered the work force were expected to donate parts of their income to the movement. Some of them established successful businesses which became important sources of revenue for the movement.

Fethullahcıs helped each other into jobs, notably government jobs, which became a useful way of receiving government funding. It was also, crucially, a way of influencing government and politics. Gülen's movement was not the only Turkish Islamic organization to creep into the corridors of power, but it was arguably the most efficient and successful.

The attempts at influencing government were not, of course, an explicit part of the movement's activities. But there is widespread agreement among researchers that it took - and takes - place. In a secret recording of Fethullah Gülen from 1999, which was leaked to the Turkish national broadcaster TRT, he said to his close followers: "You must move within the arteries of the system, without anyone noticing your existence, until you reach all the power centres."[287] Gülen claimed that the recording had been tampered with. Fearing that he would be prosecuted in Turkey, he never returned from a visit to the US, where he eventually, in 2008, obtained permanent residency.

Gülen and Erdoğan wanted the same thing, namely a Turkey where people were more concerned with doing the will of God. This would make Turkey a better country for everybody. It was a win-win cooperation, where they helped each other increase their influence over the Turkish state. This collaboration was explicit and publicly known, although the details of the collaboration were not.

Now we know, or have strong reason to believe, that Gülenists were deeply involved in the infamous "Ergenekon" purge of high-ranking secular police and military officers from 2007 and onward. This purge enabled Erdoğan to replace officers he did not trust with his own officers, increasing his level of control over the police and the armed forces. When Erdoğan had achieved the level of control he sought and won almost half the vote in the 2011 election, he no longer needed the services of Fethullah Gülen. A conflict erupted where Gülenists in 2013 revealed Erdoğan's corrupt practices, upon which Erdoğan fired judges and prosecutors involved in the investigation. Erdoğan came out on top, and Gülen had, seemingly, lost.[288]

Then late in the evening on July 15, 2016, what looked a lot like a genuine military coup started. Soldiers and tanks blocked the bridges crossing the Bosporus strait in Istanbul. Fighter jets were flying above both Istanbul and Ankara. A luxury hotel in Marmaris was attacked by special forces coming for Erdoğan, but he had already left. According to one source, he escaped by minutes,[289] whereas another source claims he had left Marmaris hours earlier.[290] Ankara, which had not been attacked militarily for six centuries,[291] was bombed. The state broadcaster, TRT, was attacked and a few minutes past midnight soldiers forced a news anchor to read on live TV a message from a group calling itself the Council for Peace at Home. According to the message, the government had been deposed in order to reinsert democratic and secular rule by law.

A few minutes later, Erdoğan himself called CNN Türk from his private jet and was broadcast live with video from his cell phone. He called upon all his supporters to defy the curfew and "give their response" to the coup makers.[292] Tens of thousands of people poured into the streets during the night, supporting the police and those in the army who were fighting the coup makers. It turned out that the majority within the army were not partaking in the coup but fighting against it. Shortly thereafter, at 3:20 a.m. on July 16, Erdoğan landed on one of the airports in Istanbul and gave a press conference. He called the coup attempt a "gift from God," saying that now that the enemies had shown their faces, they could be punished. He blamed the coup attempt on Fethullah Gülen, promising to purge his supporters.[293]

In the scrimmages during the coup, mainly in Ankara and Istanbul, both civilians and security personnel were killed, but it is unclear exactly how many. The official number of people killed fighting for the government is 238. According to the government, 34 coup soldiers were also killed, but this number may be significantly higher.[294] The coup was over, and it was time for a reckoning. The coup had given Erdoğan the pretext he needed to rid himself of the long tentacles of the Gülen movement.

The movement was labeled a terrorist organization and given the name Fetullahist Terror Organization with the acronym FETÖ. Soon the media simply referred to FETÖ as if it was real, and as if it had been proven that it was behind the coup attempt. Thousands of personnel from the military were arrested and prosecuted. By July 2019, around 3,600 of them had been convicted while 2,600 had been acquitted.[295] A state of emergency was introduced which removed the normal legal obstacles for arresting people. In July 2019, almost 70,000 people were on trial and more than 150,000 were under investigation on terrorism charges because they were suspected of being connected to the Gülen movement.[296]

The investigation, prosecutions and trials after the coup attempt have been less than impressive from a rule of law perspective. Many of those who confessed to having been involved in the coup later told the court that they had been threatened, pressured or tortured during interrogations. Pictures have emerged of suspects with clear signs of torture on their bodies. One of the pictures "shows hundreds of soldiers sitting closely next to each other, only wearing underwear, their hands cuffed behind their backs. Several of them have visible injuries."[297] The picture was taken in the horse stable of the Ankara police, where the torture allegedly was pervasive. The trials were similarly not by the book. The prosecutors were using anonymous witnesses, and the charges were frequently incoherent and self-contradictory. An incidence could be used as evidence for involvement in the coup in one indictment, whereas in a different indictment it could be used as evidence *against* the coup.[298] In other words, the trials have been held in a way that indicates that nobody will be able to validate the procedures.

In addition to the legal prosecutions, many were punished after simply being accused of somehow being against the government. More than 150,000 public servants were arbitrarily dismissed from their jobs[299] between the 2016 coup attempt and the spring of 2019. They were publicly labelled as having "links to terrorist organizations", in lists attached to executive decrees, without any individualized assessments.[300] Anybody being put on the list would lose his or her job, and there was nothing that could be done to prevent it.

"The worst part about being accused of belonging to a terror organization is that your family and friends don't dare to support you, for fear of being accused themselves," one victim explained[301]. Another victim, a teacher, shared her experience with a journalist: "The headmaster perceived me as bothersome and the leadership knew that I had a political background from a Marxist party that was banned. So when the government asked the school administration to submit names of possible enemies of the state, they put me on the list."[302] Frequently those who have been dismissed do not know what they are being punished for, and there is no possibility of legal recourse. Several of those who have lost their jobs have committed suicide.

The hunt for the so-called "FETÖ" went international. In October 2017, Erdoğan told his party at a congress: "Neither in the East nor in the West is a single member of this organization comfortable as before, nor will they be. If not today, then tomorrow, one day every member of the FETÖ traitors' front will pay for his treason against the country and the nation."[303] Turkey has been able to convince or pressure at least 16 countries to extradite Turkish citizens alleged by Turkey to be Gülenists. They have also been able to pressure at least 20 countries to close down or transfer the ownership of schools in the Gülen network.[304]

But were Fethullah Gülen and his followers really behind the coup attempt? Not surprisingly, Gülen himself was quick to deny any involvement. It is beyond doubt that Gülen had loyal followers in many branches of government, and he seems to have used this influence on a number of occasions. But the actions of Erdoğan and his government before, during and after the coup attempt aroused suspicion that something else was going on. Calling the coup a "gift from God" and having lists ready of people to arrest made the suspicion stronger.[305] The opposition in parliament started referring to the events as a "controlled coup." There are several reasons for this, including the fact that Erdoğan and his inner circle must have known about the coup in advance. He first said that he only learned about the coup when the soldiers started blocking the Bosporus bridges in Istanbul at 10 p.m. A few days later, when the leaders of the military and intelligence service were criticized for not having stopped the attempt, it was revealed that the head of the Turkish intelligence service, MIT, had warned the top three generals in the military at 4 p.m., six hours before the attempt started.[306] It did not seem credible that the top leaders of national security would withhold this information from the president.

Another indication that there was something else, or something more, going on than a failed coup attempt was the discrepancy between the number of generals charged with complicity in the coup and the number of foot soldiers involved. Four days *before* the coup, on July 11, the intelligence service had handed the general staff a list of 600 military officers to be removed from their positions at an August 1 meeting of the military high council. The following day, on July 12, the newspaper Sabah reported on these plans. The message of the news article was that the military council would soon purge the military once and for all of its Gülenists. Then, after the coup, when the arrests started, a very high proportion of generals from military bases all over the country were charged with complicity. Of the total of 400 generals in the military, 163, or one third, were charged. This proportion corresponds badly with the fact that the fraction in the military actively involved in the coup was only at around 1.5%. It led many to believe that the generals were being put in prison for their opinions unrelated to the coup or to Gülen, like their objection to taking a more offensive stance in the Syrian conflict.[307]

The question remains: Was Gülen behind the coup? There are clear indications that several of those involved in the coup were in fact connected to the Gülen network. A few of the officers have admitted to this, but far more have denied it. None of the testimonies in court have explained how Gülen could have been behind the coup.[308] Furthermore, an EU intelligence unit, INTCEN, concluded a few months after the coup that it was unlikely that Gülen had had the means to orchestrate it. There was also no evidence indicating that the secular Kemalists and the religious Gülenists in the military had cooperated to overthrow the government. INTCEN believed the coup was initiated by a mixed group of officers at risk of being purged from the military.[309] In March 2017, the head of the German intelligence agency BND told the news magazine *Der Spiegel* that it did not seem likely that Gülen was behind the coup, but also that the Turkish government had not initiated it. "Before July 15 the government had already started a big purge so parts of the military thought they should do a coup quickly before it hit them too," he explained.[310] This will remain the conclusion of most governments unless contradictory evidence is revealed.

The state of emergency that was introduced after the coup attempt was prolonged, and then several of the measures that the state of emergency allowed were made permanent by law, as described in the previous chapter. The legal changes that came during the state of emergency gave the president powers similar to those he had under the state of emergency. Rule of law and democratic practices were permanently weakened. This will take quite a bit of effort to correct. Erdoğan seems to have been right when he called the coup attempt a "gift from God." It certainly was a gift to him, personally, in the sense of increased power, which in Turkey also means increased wealth. It may not have been from God, but from all the enablers around him who would profit from it themselves.

"Peace at Home, Peace in the World"

Since the foundation of the Republic of Turkey, the keynote in its relationships with other countries has been the fear of being stabbed in the back, attacked, or destroyed by Europe or others, either directly or through its minorities. In itself, the fear of other countries' intentions is of course nothing out of the ordinary; there is a reason why the world spends vast amounts of money on weapons and soldiers. But Turkey has been characterized by this fear to a larger extent than many other countries. This has at least two explanations: the Sèvres complex and the military influence over government.

As we learned in Chapter 2, the dissatisfaction with the 1920 Treaty of Sèvres led to the War of Independence, which in turn led to the Lausanne treaty replacing Sèvres in 1923. Sèvres was truly a divide-and-conquer treaty that reduced Turkey to a fragment of what it is today. The rest of the land was to be divided among World War I victors. Ever since, the suspicion bubbling under - and sometimes above - the surface, has been that the true intentions of the West are to rip Turkey apart. One of the ways in which Turkey resists this imagined, evil plan is to make sure that minorities are supportive of the unity of the state, whether they want to or not. Sèvres, after all, "granted statehood to the Armenians and local autonomy to the Kurds, at the expense of Turkey's integrity."[311] In addition, the treaty restricted Turkey's military capacity and sovereignty in a number of ways. A hundred years after Sèvres, many in Turkey are still convinced that the West is merely waiting for the right moment to implement the Sevres plan.[312]

The second explanation for Turkey's fear of the intentions of other countries is the military's influence over the government. A civilian president without a military background has been the exception, at least during the first seven decades of the republic. Only Celal Bayar, president from 1950 to 1960, had not been a military commander, until Turgut Özal broke the cycle in 1989. In 1950 the military mindset moved towards the background until the 1960 coup, after which the military's influence at the top level of government was formalized through the establishment of the National Security Council. The heavy military participation in decision making has naturally moved the mindset towards security at the expense of international collaboration and dialogue.

Atatürk said that his aim was "Peace at home, peace in the world," (*Yurtta barış, dünyada barış*) a slogan that is still quoted frequently, not least on the many posters, busts, and statues of him around the country in addition to on T-shirts and bumper stickers. (It was this slogan that the 2016 coup makers referred to with their Council for Peace at Home.) One might think that the slogan sounds like a nice ambition, but it hardly moved beyond being a slogan. There does not seem to be a single conflict in the region in which Turkey has not somehow been involved: Iraq, Iran, Armenia, Georgia, Azerbaijan, Bosnia, Kosovo, Cyprus, Greece, Bulgaria, Russia, Tajikistan, Syria, Muslim extremism and war with the PKK.[313]

The "peace" Atatürk achieved at home was, as we have seen, based on the silencing of critical journalists and oppositional politicians - or simply getting rid of them. Furthermore, it was based on the violent eradication of anything that smacked of Kurdish separatism in the southeast. Internationally, Atatürk steered Turkey towards Europe and the US. So far, Turkey has managed to stay clear of outright war with any of its neighbors, which is quite a feat given the constant violent conflicts that have taken place all around it. The military operations in Syria that started in 2016 are, however, clearly a gray zone. In the following, we will look closer at Turkey's relations with its neighbors and with Russia, Europe, the US, and NATO.

Minorities and Water Scarcity Make Bad Neighbors

Foreign policy in this region of the world is usually about much more than what meets the eye. There is frequently a good explanation for a country's behavior that has nothing, seemingly, to do with the matter at hand. Frequently things become clearer when we look at which enemies and friends the countries involved in a dispute have. The enemy of my enemy is, at least when it suits me, my friend.

Turkey shares a land border with eight countries: Georgia, Armenia, Azerbaijan, Iran, Iraq, Syria, Greece, and Bulgaria. Generally, one can say that how the countries in the region relate to each other can be explained, at least partially, by their minorities. For Turkey, it is especially the relations with Armenians, Kurds and Greeks that are or have been the sources of tension.

In 1993, Turkey closed its border with Armenia because of the latter's occupation of the disputed Nagornoh Karabakh region in its war with Azerbaijan. Armenia claims the region because of its large Armenian population. There were attempts at normalizing the relationship between Turkey and Armenia starting in the latter half of the 2000s, but the rapprochement stagnated, and the border is still closed as of March 2024.

Azerbaijan, on its side, has played a role in putting the brakes on the Turkey-Armenia rapprochement, because it wants to keep up the pressure on Armenia. With its ability to withhold oil and gas from going to Turkey, Azerbaijan has some leverage. Then there is Iran, which has a large Azeri minority (more than 10 million), and Iran is not interested in too strong of an Azerbaijan. Shiite Iran has therefore supported Christian Armenia. So has Russia, which has military bases in the country.

The Armenian issue has also affected Turkey's relationship with Israel. In 1992, Turkey marked the 500th anniversary of welcoming the Jews who were expelled from Spain. This became part of an effort to convince the Jewish and Israeli lobby in Washington to work against the lobby efforts of Armenians.[314] The Armenian issue thus affects Turkey's relationship with any country that wants to weaken or strengthen Armenia or Armenia's enemies.

The Kurdish issue is important for Turkey's relationship with the three other countries with a substantial Kurdish population: Iran, Iraq and Syria. None of the four governments want a strong Kurdish population, but neither do they want too strong of a neighboring country. The solution has therefore been to sometimes support the Kurds in the neighboring countries to weaken the government. This is a demanding balancing act. In Iraq, it has led to Kurdish autonomy, inspiring Kurds in the other countries. Why would the Kurds in, for instance, Turkey lay down their arms when they see that the Kurds in Iraq have largely succeeded in their struggle?

For Turkey, it is mainly Iraq and Syria that have been troublesome with regard to the Kurdish question. The Kurdish guerilla group PKK in Turkey, which we will get to know better in Chapter 6, was able to build up training camps in northern Iraq in the 1980s. It is not uncommon for the Turkish military to bomb what it believes to be PKK camps in northern Iraq, and the Iraqi government has usually acquiesced to this.

Syria used to have its Kurds under control, but after the 2011 protests in Syria turned violent, the Kurds have been able to take control over vast areas of land, fighting back both the Islamic State and the Syrian military. It is believed that the PKK has been actively involved in the struggle of the Kurds in Syria. As the Kurds in Syria have gained strength, the government in Ankara has become increasingly worried. Under the guise of securing its border and protecting its people from attacks from Syrian territory, Turkey involved itself military inside Syria. Among its military efforts were Operation Olive Branch in 2018, launched to kick the Kurdish militia out of Afrin, close to the border with Turkey, and Operation Peace Spring in 2019. The 2019 operation was launched to establish a "security belt" free of Kurdish militia inside Syria, along the border with Turkey.

Iran is a neighbor that Turkey has not been at war with since the Ottomans fought the Iranians in 1639. The border demarcated that year is one of the oldest borders in the world.[315] This is not to say that the relationship with Iran has always been friendly. Especially after the 1979 revolution in Iran there has been tension. Tehran denounced Atatürk as an enemy of Islam (something Atatürk himself probably would not have objected to were he to be completely honest). The five million Kurds in Iran have been better off than their siblings in Turkey, being allowed to speak Kurdish and have their own broadcasting. Iran has assisted the PKK with arms and medical assistance and has also allowed PKK combatants to flee into its territory. On a few occasions, Turkey has attacked PKK soldiers from the air inside Iranian territory and been fired at from the ground by the Iranians, without any further escalation between the two countries. Large numbers of Iranians have fled to Turkey from the Iranian regime, some of the most influential of whom have been murdered, either by Iranian intelligence officers directly, or by people trained by them. In 1993, Turkey blamed the murder of celebrated journalist Uğur Mumcu on Iran.[316]

The relationship with Greece has mainly been tense ever since the creation of the Republic of Turkey, after the Turkish nationalists had kicked Greece out of Anatolia. The exchange of people in the aftermath of the war and the subsequent Turkish discriminatory policies and lack of protection of Greeks - not least during the 1955 pogrom of which we will hear more in Chapter 8 - have led to the Greek population in Turkey being reduced to less than 2,000.[317] The war with Greece in Cyprus in the 1960s, where two NATO countries fought each other, and which was never settled by a peace agreement, made the relationship worse. After the 1999 earthquake near Istanbul, however, Greece offered Turkey assistance and the relationship thawed somewhat. During the last decades, historians in both countries have tried to rid schoolbooks of content that demonizes the other country, but there is still some way to go before the relationship can be described as friendly.[318] Furthermore, Cyprus continues to be a recurring source of conflict.

Georgia and Bulgaria are the neighbors that one rarely hears much about in Turkey, and no news is usually good news. Georgia was a Soviet republic and Bulgaria was a Soviet puppet state, and this naturally affected the relationship with NATO member Turkey during the Cold War. Bulgaria has a large Turkish minority, around 10% of the total population, and in the 1980s, Bulgaria tried to assimilate them. In 1989, almost 350,000 Bulgarian Turks fled to Turkey because of Bulgaria's aggressive assimilation policy. Turkey, itself trying to assimilate the Kurds, vehemently objected to the Bulgarian assimilation of the Turks. Most of the Bulgarian Turks soon returned to Bulgaria because they could not find jobs or housing in Turkey.[319] Something similar happened in the early 1950s, when

Bulgaria punished Turkey for its participation in the Korean War by expelling around 250,000 Turks.[320]

After the Cold War, the relationship with both Georgia and Bulgaria has become quite good. The Baku-Ceyhan pipeline going from Azerbaijan through Georgia and Turkey to the Mediterranean was agreed upon in 1999 and is now the main outlet for oil from the Caspian Sea, strengthening the ties between those three countries. Georgia closed its Gülen schools in 2017 upon the request from Turkey do so. Both Bulgaria and Georgia are among the fifteen (at least) countries that have arrested or deported representatives of the Gülen movement after the coup.[321]

Not only the minorities affect the relationships between the neighbors. The rivers Tigris and Euphrates have their sources in Turkey, providing opportunities for hydropower and irrigation. The rivers also give Turkey power over a resource desperately needed in the two countries downstream, Syria and Iraq. The Southeastern Anatolia Project, which is "the largest scale and costliest project in the history of the Republic of Turkey,"[322] is well underway and is not very popular downstream. It involves a plan for building 22 dams, five of which had yet to be completed in 2020. The dams supply the region - on the Turkish side of the border - with electricity and irrigation, and substantially reduce the amount of water carried by the two rivers to Syria and Iraq. In addition to reducing the water flow, the rivers are increasingly polluted due to increased agricultural production made possible by the irrigation. The so-called Master Plan of the project was adopted in 1989, and when the neighbors protested, President Turgut Özal famously said: "We don't tell Arabs what to do with their oil, so we don't accept any suggestion from them about what to do with our water."[323] This attitude is accepted widely in Turkey, including by the media.[324] Fruitless attempts were made in the 1990s to arrive at an agreement between Turkey, Syria and Iraq that would regulate the use of water. Without such an agreement, the issue will remain a source of conflict.

A final factor that should be mentioned when discussing Turkey's relationship with countries in the region is the Muslim Brotherhood. Before Erdoğan, this factor was less prevalent, but after almost two decades of an Islamist party in power in Turkey, the relationship between Turkey and the Arab world has been affected by Erdoğan's support for the Muslim Brotherhood. It may play a role for years to come.

The Muslim Brotherhood has increasingly become a power factor in the Arab world since it was first established in Egypt in the 1920s. Briefly explained, Erdoğan's ideology aligns well with that of the Muslim Brotherhood,[325] and the unification of Sunni Muslims is a goal that goes well with Erdoğan's romantic thoughts about the Ottoman Empire. By supporting Islamists in the Arab world, he seems to try to build a sultan-like image of himself. The governments of most Arab countries, however, see the Muslim Brotherhood as a threat. Qatar is one exception, showing itself as a friend of the Brotherhood, coming to Turkey's aid in times of economic need. Saudi Arabia, on the other hand, is hostile towards the Muslim Brotherhood, contributing to tension with Turkey. This may explain why Turkey, itself having a less than ideal track record on press freedom, made a big deal out of Saudi Arabia's murder of journalist Jamal Khashoggi in its consulate in Istanbul in 2018. Erdoğan is also supportive of Palestinian Hamas, an offshoot of the Muslim Brotherhood. This adds to the current tension in Turkey's relationship with Israel. With the current government in Turkey, it is useful to look at a country's attitude towards the Muslim Brotherhood to understand the broader relationship between Turkey and that country.[326]

Russia

Russia has historically been the nemesis of the Turkish rulers in Anatolia. Between 1586 and 1917, there were over a dozen major wars between the Russian and the Ottoman empires. Russia was always the instigator and usually the winner, forcing the Muslim Circassians and Crimean Tatars ever further into Ottoman territory. After the founding of the Turkish republic, Atatürk "cultivated pragmatic ties with the Soviet Union"[327] and Turkey stayed out of the Second World War. When NATO was established, however, it seemed the safest option to join the alliance; Turkey gained protection against the Soviets, and NATO gained an ally with a very strategic location. After the Cold War, relations between Russia and Turkey were quite good, with booming trade, tourism, Turkish construction in Russia and Russian gas being sold to Turkey. In 2015, the relationship changed when Turkey downed a Russian fighter jet that it claimed had crossed into Turkish air space.[328] After that, both

Turkey and Russia have been actively engaged in the violent conflict in Syria, not fighting towards the same goals. After the Russian invasion of Ukraine in 2022, Turkey carefully played its cards to avoid making an enemy of Russia while staying on decent terms with Ukraine.

One author has described the Russia-Turkey relationship as "a complex affair fraught with contradiction"[329] because of the mix of economic cooperation and regional rivalry. Although the end of the Soviet Union in theory meant independence for the Soviet states, Russia's influence in the Caucasus remained substantial, not least because of its military bases in Georgia, Azerbaijan and Armenia.[330] In the 1990s, Turkey was trying to have an oil pipeline built from Azerbaijan, but Russia "had an almost infinite capacity to cause trouble,"[331] and Turkey had to find ways for the project to please the Russians. The Baku-Tbilisi-Ceyhan pipeline was finally open for business in 2006.

Europe

Although, formally, only the Thrace part of Turkey is a part of the European continent, it is fairly common to encounter sights and attractions in Anatolia claiming to be Europe's second largest or fourth tallest something or other. The aquarium in the Nata Vega shopping mall in Ankara, for instance, claims to have Europe's third longest glass tunnel. The perception in Anatolia of being part of Europe is real.

Europe, however, has not unequivocally welcomed Turkey into the club. In 1963, the Association Agreement between the European Economic Community[332] and Turkey was signed, but the road towards full membership proved to be long. In 1987, Turkey applied to become a member, and in 1995 an agreement was signed with the European Union on a customs union, fully in force since 1996. The customs union lets Turkey and the EU sell each other products without tariffs. Importantly, however, unprocessed agricultural products and coal and steel products are exempt from the agreement. Those three product groups are major parts of Turkey's workforce and economy.[333]

The EU is by far Turkey's largest trading partner, but the accession process for Turkey to become a full EU member has by and large stagnated. In 1997, the European Council stated that "the political and economic conditions allowing accession negotiations to be envisaged are not satisfied."[334] But also stated that it was important to prepare the grounds for accession by bringing Turkey closer to the EU "in every field."[335] In practice, this has meant that the EU will not let Turkey become a member before it reforms its authoritarian structure. Human rights must be upheld, the courts must be independent, elections must be free and fair, to mention a few of the EU's demands. The fact that the National Security Council exists, blurring the line between the civilian government and the military, is another problem. Although the council has been reformed, and other aspects of the civilian authority over the military have improved, a 2019 report from the European Commission pointed out remaining deficiencies: "the military and intelligence services continue to lack sufficient accountability to Parliament and security personnel continue to have wide-ranging legal protection. (...) The legal framework for overseeing military expenditure has not yet been improved."[336]

There is a perception in Turkey that the EU is not treating it fairly compared to the eastern European and Balkan states that were welcomed into the union during the past decade. The Turkish political scientist Soli Ozel has told a joke about how unfair the process is perceived to be:

> After dealing with a number of accession countries for a number of years, the EU becomes sick and tired of the arduous talks, and calls in candidate countries Serbia, Montenegro, and Turkey for a test on European history. The EU tells the three countries that they will be asked one question. If they know the answer, they can join the EU, otherwise they will be rejected. The Serbs are offered the question, 'When did World War I begin?' This is an easy question. 'The answer is 1914.' The doors open, bells ring, and Serbia joins the EU. Then the Montenegrins are asked, 'When did World War I end?' This, too, is an easy question. 'The answer is 1918.' The doors open, bells ring, and Montenegro joins the EU. Finally, the Turks are asked: 'How many people died in World War I, and what are their names?'[337]

Given all that needs to change in the state structure before Turkey can become an EU member, it is somewhat understandable that a Turkish foreign minister in the late 1990s accused the union of behaving like colonial governors.[338]

Will Turkey ever join the EU? Although Recep Tayyip Erdoğan, during his first years as prime minster did set in motion a number of reforms to pave the way towards accession, frustration grew in Ankara as the efforts seemingly bore no fruit. Erdoğan's increasingly authoritarian ways did not outrage a sufficient number of voters to keep Turkey on track towards joining the union. Today, Turkey seems as far away from EU membership as ever.

USA

What is a friend? Someone who knows you, someone you can trust, who knows what you care about and who cares about your wellbeing, perhaps? If these are the criteria for being a friend, it is difficult to characterize the US as a friend of Turkey. Judging by US behavior towards Turkey after World War II, it seems the US has mainly been concerned with keeping Turkey as an ally because of its strategic location, and making sure communism did not spread.

Among the American anti-communist measures was the support of the establishment of militarized underground organizations in mainly NATO countries. These organizations built on the experience of "stay-behind" groups created during World War II, groups that would remain in Nazi-occupied countries for intelligence and sabotage purposes. In the decade after the war, it seemed prudent to establish such groups in case of a Soviet takeover of Europe. The most famous example of this is the Italian Gladio group. In Turkey, the contra-guerilla was established in 1959, but the group did not wait for a Soviet invasion before becoming active. It is probable that the Turkish contra-guerilla played an active part in the violence against leftists around the country up until the 1980 coup.[339]

Until 1979, the US had been able to rely on the shah of Iran since they helped him to power in the 1953 coup. In 1953, the US was at the height of McCarthyism,[340] and the Iran coup was the first of several instances of the US assisting in the overthrow of a democratically elected government, fearing that the government leaned too much to the left. But when Iran was taken over by religious extremists in 1979, it became more important to keep Turkey happy and loyal. At the time, however, Bülent Ecevit, the most left-leaning prime minister Turkey has had, was in power. Ecevit was trying to downplay the cold-war dynamic of being hostile toward the Soviet Union and did not simply obey the US.

When the US lost Iran as a base for their U2 spy flights over the Soviet Union, Turkey would have been a good replacement. But Ecevit declined, fearing that the Soviets might be provoked. In the American communist-vs.-capitalist dichotomy, Ecevit was perceived by the CIA as "neutral or moderately anti-Western."[341] President Jimmy Carter's National Security Advisor, Brzezinski, "more or less openly encouraged the Turkish military to get rid of Ecevit, and to cancel democracy in the name of 'stability'."[342] When the coup finally came in 1980, Carter's staff informed their president that "our boys have done it."[343]

After the 1980 coup, the military junta did not allow Labor Day celebrations. This did not stop people from trying to celebrate, but the military commander in Istanbul arrested those who tried to gather in Taksim Square. When the US general at the NATO headquarters in Brussels heard how the Labor Day celebrations had been stopped, he exclaimed: "Bravo! Now, that's what I call a commander. That's how you install stability."[344] When workers in Turkey have friends like that, what need is there for enemies?

The Americans have not been hesitant about emphasizing the strategic element of the relationship. In 1998, the chair of the US Senate Foreign Relations Committee, Jesse Helms, said: "The United States would be paralyzed in the Middle East without Turkey ... one of the most credible friendly allies of this country."[345] This widely held attitude was followed up by action. During Bill Clinton's administration (1993-2001), Turkey received 800 million dollars' worth of arms every year[346] despite its massacres and forced relocations of the Kurds in the southeast.

In the 2000s, the relationship has fluctuated. After the al-Qaeda terror attacks in the US in 2001, the Americans were looking to cultivate "moderate Islam" to counter the Muslim terror organizations and whatever support they had in the Muslim world. Recep Tayyip Erdoğan seemed promising. American diplomats had been in sporadic contact with Erdoğan since the 1980s, and according to one author, there is little doubt that Erdoğan rose to power with assistance and encouragement from the Americans.[347] But the Turkey-US relationship was strained when the Turkish parliament would not allow the US to use Turkey's territory when preparing for the 2003 invasion of Iraq. The US later allowed the Kurds in Iraq to set up an autonomous region, which went down very badly with Turkey.

In 2016, Turkey had an American pastor, Andrew Brunson, arrested on various charges, including supporting a terror organization and espionage. Brunson had lived in Turkey for two decades. Turkey tried to exchange Brunson for Fethüllah Gülen, the religious leader described in the first section of Chapter 3, whom Erdoğan accused of being behind the failed 2016 military coup. The US did not comply, and instead hit Turkey with economic sanctions to force Turkey to let Brunson go. The Turkish lira was in free fall for a while, but it would be too humiliating to simply let Brunson go. Instead, after spending two years in jail, he was sentenced to time served and released. The lira was not able to recover before the Covid-19 pandemic weakened it even further.

So far, the last major ingredient in the strenuous relationship is Turkey's purchase of the Russian S-400 air defense system. Turkey signed the contract for the purchase in 2017, to loud protests from NATO, particularly from the US. The US was worried that the S-400 system would provide Russia with information on NATO systems, including the new F-35 fighter jet. Turkey went ahead with the S-400 trade, which prompted the US to stop deliveries of the F-35.[348]

The US attitude to authoritarian regimes is usually complex. On one side there is a genuine concern - at least it looks genuine - for human rights. Governments that do not treat their citizens properly may risk various forms of sanctions, including high tariffs on trade and arms embargoes, from the US. On the other side there is the possibility for strategic influence or profit, for instance through arms sales. In the case of Turkey, the emphasis has in sum been more on arms sales and strategic influence than on human rights.

NATO

"It's like a forced marriage where the spouses hate each other. It's the rest of the alliance against Turkey. Nobody likes Turkey. They're stalling every process in Brussels." The NATO officer has agreed to speak frankly with me on the condition of anonymity. Many NATO countries have military attachés at their embassies in Ankara, frequently accompanied by more military personnel. I knew Turkey was different from the other NATO countries but was surprised to hear just how negatively the country is viewed, at least in some circles within the alliance. "It's actually a little sad that someone within the alliance has such a low standing," my officer friend continues.

As the relationship between east and west among the World War II victors became ice-cold shortly after the war, Turkey assessed that an effort should be made to be welcomed into NATO. Communism had never been allowed to fester in Turkey, and the Soviets posed a real threat. The opportunity to show NATO that it was willing to sacrifice for the alliance came in the Korean war, where Turkey sent troops to support the US-led efforts against the communist North. It is now widely believed that it was Turkey's efforts in Korea at the beginning of the 1950s that opened the door to NATO membership in 1952. Its strategic location also helped its candidacy. My NATO source explains: "Turkey's location, from a strategic perspective, is fantastic! They can sail permanently in the Black Sea, which is a very valuable asset. They played an important role during the Cold War because of their location, and they're still exploiting this to the fullest."

In 1957, Turkey had NATO's largest land force with an army of half a million men, armed and trained by the Americans. The US was always convinced that as long as communism existed, Turkey would be one of the most important cards to have on hand.[349] When the Soviet Union collapsed, Turkey had more than a million soldiers.[350] The current size of Turkey's armed forces is estimated at 350,000 active personnel, with roughly the same number of reserve soldiers, making it the second largest military force in NATO after the US. "They're a formidable opponent," my officer friend tells me, referring not only to the sheer size of the army, but also the investments in warships, planes and ground weaponry.

But he explains that their weakness is their rigid way of thinking. "They're not good at thinking outside of the box. The Germans, for instance, are very good at mission-based tasks, leaving the practical decisions to those who will perform the tasks. The Turks tend to micromanage, telling people exactly what to do instead of which goal to achieve." This approach to problem solving makes the Turkish military vulnerable to changes on the ground. While a German task force may be able to quickly adjust to a changed situation because they can make the necessary decisions themselves, a Turkish task force may have to wait for new orders from higher up in the hierarchy.

Will Turkey remain in NATO? So far, egregious breaches of human rights law and the laws of war do not seem to matter much for NATO membership, in spite of the fact that "rule of law" is mentioned as part of the core purpose of the alliance in its founding treaty.[351] And Turkey's strategic location is simply irresistible. If Erdoğan keeps up his behavior, however, flirting with Russia and potentially making NATO systems vulnerable, it is possible that there will be some sort of reaction from NATO. There are, in fact, several people in Turkey, both military and civilian, who believe Turkey would be better off if it pivoted towards Russia and China.[352] If this group gains more political traction, it is not impossible that Turkey will be the first country to leave the alliance, either because they are kicked out because of their disloyal behavior, or because they make the decision to leave.

Göbeklitepe, one of the world's most important archaeological sites, near Şanlıurfa in the southeast. When the site was discovered by a German archaeologist in the 1990s it sent shockwaves through the archaeological world because the site is a kind of temple but made by hunter/gatherer societies. It dates to about 10,000 years ago. Until then, only temples of more recent date, from agricultural societies, had been found.

A bygone era: The ruins of the Hittite capital Hattuşa, three hours' drive east of Ankara.

Early Christianity: In Turkey one finds many of the places mentioned in the New Testament of the Bible. This is the theater in Ephesus, where, according to Acts, followers of the new faith were close to being lynched.

Hagia Sofia in Istanbul, here under restoration in 2018. Called Ayasofya by Turks, the cathedral is an embodiment of Turkey's complex history. The building was completed in 537 and was the largest church in the Byzantine Empire. When the Turks conquered Istanbul in 1453 it was turned into a mosque. From 1935 the building was run as a museum. In 2020, the Erdoğan government decided that it would be turned into a mosque again.

Cappadocia, with its spectacular rock formations, is a popular tourist destination. It is easy to dig caves in the mountains, and people have been doing this for thousands of years. Cappadocia became a refuge for Christians fleeing Roman persecution in the early days of Christianity. They dug themselves safe cave cities in intricate tunnel systems.

Atatürk appears everywhere in Turkey, in all shapes and forms. Paintings, posters, tapestries, mosaics, key rings, car stickers, and so on. In the library where much of this book was written, there was a picture of Atatürk in every room. In the picture of the bust (left), from the Military History Museum in Istanbul, Atatürk is portrayed as the last of the great conquerors from peoples related to the Turks; the bust in the background is Attila the Hun (b. ? - d. 453). Izmir (below) wins the prize for the largest Atatürk figure.

Above: It is common to come across one or more turtles if you take a walk in the Turkish countryside, no matter how far from the sea you may be. These turtles live in a forest in Ankara.

Left: The heroic soldier Seyyid from the Battle of Çanakkale/Gallipoli during the First World War (see Ch. 2). He is said to have carried four 276 kg projectiles up into the cannon and fired them – all by himself – sinking a British ship.

Abandoned by Greeks: Near the coastal town of Fethiye on the Aegean Sea lies the ghost town of Kayaköy. It was called Livissi when it was inhabited by Greeks until the beginning of the 20th century. Several waves of persecution reduced the size of the population, until the population exchange in the 1920s emptied it of the last Greeks.

Left: A common form of public transport is the minibus called *dolmuş*. For very little money one may get a ride. It has a fixed route but no fixed stops and picks up passengers when someone stops it by waving, and it stops when requested by passengers. The drivers sometimes decorate the interior of the bus, and this one is of the nationalist type. On the flag on the ceiling, it says, "Life favors the brave..." and "How happy is he who says, 'I am a Turk...!'"

Stray dogs are found all over the country, to the joy and sorrow of the inhabitants. It is perfectly normal for them to be allowed to stay in the outdoor seating areas of cafes. On the right, the author has an unusually (for him) pleasant moment with a stray dog.

Istanbul is famous for its cats.

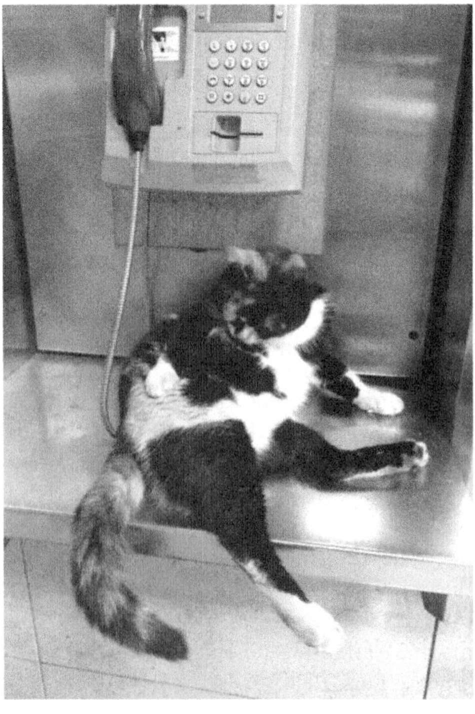

Above: Istanbul. The picture was taken on the European side looking over the Bosphorus Strait to the Anatolian (Asian) side.

Above: The Golden Horn is the name of the estuary that separates the original city of Constantinople (the right side in the picture) from what in later centuries has become the rest of the metropolis Istanbul. To the left, on the north side of the Golden Horn, we see the Galata Tower rising, which 400 years ago is supposed to have been the starting point for the legendary flight (see Ch. 1) across the Bosphorus to the Anatolian side, which we see on the horizon in the picture.

There is no need to be a skilled photographer to take good pictures in Istanbul.

Above: One of the more absurd security measures after the 2016 coup attempt was the fencing off of a human rights statue in Kızılay in downtown Ankara.

Above: "It was not done by experts" (see Ch. 5) can be said about several projects launched by Turkish authorities. Here, the contractor has failed to put up barrier tape around a newly poured pavement.

Left: Outdoor Friday prayer in Trabzon. The fully covered woman on the left is an unusual sight on Turkey's streets. It will typically be Saudi Arabian tourists.

Below: Pamukkale is located midway between Izmir and Antalya and is known for its white travertine terraces which are formed by minerals in the thermal spring water. At the top of Pamukkale lies the ancient city of Hierapolis, where Queen Cleopatra is said to have come to bathe in the hot springs. Pamukkale is Instagram friendly. Below to the left, the pictures are checked before the photographer is instructed to take a few more shots.

Turkey has several lesser-known gems, such as the small town of Amasra on the Black Sea.

It is not difficult to understand what attracts tourists to Turkey. Gems like this can be found scattered all along the Aegean and Mediterranean coasts. This photo was taken near Fethiye.

The town of Kaş is not that far from Antalya, but winding coastal roads make the drive take three hours.

Ulus, the old town of Ankara.

5. Life in Turkey

Places mentioned in this chapter.

"This nation loves its generals, its childhood, and its mothers."[353]

*

I wish I could say that this chapter will give the reader a decent understanding of the Turkish soul, culture, and mindset. It will do no such thing. What it will, is provide the reader with a description of some of the basics - those basics that I have subjectively chosen - that signify living in Turkey. My intention was initially to write about this without involving the way in which the country is run, but unavoidably, many aspects of life are affected or caused by the government. We will not start there, however. We will start with food.

*

Turkish Cuisine

The imam fainted. It is not quite clear why he fainted, but it had something to do with the food that he was served. And the fact that he fainted gave name to a dish, *imam bayıldı*, which simply means "the imam fainted." The dish is said to have its name from the fact that an imam fainted from pleasure upon tasting it. That is the most boring, straightforward version. He is also supposed to have fainted upon hearing how much olive oil that goes into the dish or hearing how expensive it is to make. A more elaborate version goes like this: Upon getting married, the dowry of the imam's bride was twelve jars of the most expensive olive oil. On the first day of their marriage, the imam's wife made an eggplant dish with tomatoes and onions. The imam liked it so much that she made the same dish the next day, and then again on the third day, and so forth. On day number thirteen, there was no eggplant dish. The imam wondered why. His wife then told him that they had run out of olive oil. Upon hearing this, of course, the imam fainted.[354]

It is not unusual for the names of dishes in Turkey to be connected to folklore, although there is usually more than one version of the story behind the name of a dish. The story behind *ezogelin çorbası*, "the soup of Ezo the bride," is slightly depressing. Ezo was a young and beautiful woman from Gaziantep who got married, but the marriage soon ended in divorce because her husband was in love with another woman. She became depressed, but the darker her mind became the more beautiful she became. There was a constant stream of men asking for her hand in marriage, but she turned them all down. In the end her family was able to convince her to get married again, and she married a man who took her with him to Syria. They had nine children, but Ezo was never happy, and she missed her family and homeland. Her mother-in-law was hard to please, and it was for her that Ezo made the soup. She died of tuberculosis, and her final wish was to be buried in the mountains where she could see Turkey.[355]

What is today thought of as Turkish food is, of course, the result of centuries of gathering and mixing of different food traditions in the enormous Ottoman Empire. Some of the names of the dishes are the same as, or very similar to, those in Arabic or Persian, such as the chickpea dish *humus* or the stew *keledoş*. Some have old Turkish names which the Turks probably brought with them from East Asia, like the dumpling *mantı*.

"I spent some time looking at the two dishes in front of me before tasting them. None of them resembled anything I had eaten before, but in a good way; This was some of the freshest and most tasteful food I had ever tasted. When I came to think of it, I actually didn't think I had ever tasted vegetables prepared this well before."[356] For anyone from northern Europe who has eaten the food in Turkey it is easy to relate to this experience of a Norwegian food writer. The two dishes he tasted for the first time was *şakşuka*, an eggplant salad, and *acılı ezme*, a tomato dish resembling salsa. Turkish food has an amazing variation of ingredients from all kinds of vegetables, fruits and spices that simply have not been available in northern Europe until recently. The dairy products one finds in Turkey usually taste differently from those of Europe, partially because they are produced in a different way, and partially because it is more common to use sheep's and goat's milk in Turkey.

The Turkish breakfast tradition is a complete experience, with all kinds of small dishes, vegetables, cheeses, eggs in different shapes and forms, and of course: plenty of tea.[357] If for some reason one wakes up in a bad mood, perhaps after too much *rakı* the night before (see below), going to a place that serves Turkish breakfast will surely change the direction the day seemed to be taking.

For people who appreciate a table full of small dishes, there is another tradition that has even more to offer than the breakfast, namely the meze. Turkey has the meze in common with much of the rest of the Middle East, and it is mainly served as small appetizers, usually with no meat, before the main course which is usually a meat dish. According to the above-mentioned food writer, "it is almost impossible to exaggerate the place of these dishes in the culture, both as dishes of food and as a way to gather family and friends."[358] Although mezes are frequently served as appetizers, a meze table also works perfectly fine as the main course. All the different meze dishes are delicious in their own way, but the purpose of having meze is arguably not to fill your stomach with tasteful food, or to have a few appetizers before the "real" meal. A meze dish is a social lubricant. When a group gathers around a table of meze dishes, they are having a common tasteful experience, and the evening becomes a pleasant memory both because of the conversation and because of the shared joy that the mezes will bring. Eating meze on your own is not a comparable experience.

The origin of the meze can be traced back to ancient Persia, where wine was at the center of the social event. The wine was frequently unfinished, sometimes bitter, so it became common to serve some fruit with the wine. Soon the fruit was accompanied by nuts and small pieces of meat. These small bites were called *maza*, meaning *taste* or *enjoyment*.[359]

In Turkey, the wine has been replaced by something stronger: *rakı*, an anise-flavored grape liquor. Different versions can be found around the Mediterranean: Ouzo (Greece), arak (Arab-speaking countries), sambuca (Italy) and pastis (France). "Rakı is an institution that is not to be joked around with,"[360] according to one observer. When pouring rakı in the glass - which is always a slim, tall, cylinder-shaped glass - it is only supposed to be filled a little less than half-full with rakı. By itself it is a clear liquid. The rest of the glass is then filled with water, and when the water mixes with the rakı, the drink turns white. Some people have very rigid routines for pouring the rakı and water into the glass, with or without ice cubes, to get just the right mix and temperature.

So, if the mezes are insufficient to get the conversation going, the rakı will surely loosen one's tongue. Rakı is supposed to have been the favorite drink of Atatürk, and of course there is a story about Atatürk's wise words about rakı: "In one of the many stories about his parties, he asks one of his guests, 'Tell me what goes best with rakı?' 'Roasted chick-peas (leblebi),' the guest replies, knowing the host's frugal tastes. 'Wrong,' says Mustafa Kemal, 'the best accompaniment to rakı is good conversation.'"[361]

Sometimes a "good conversation" will mean a conversation where one is able to share anything on one's mind, including the sad and dark things. There is actually a verb in the Turkish language that means "to pour out one's grief to each other" - *dertleşmek*. My language teacher explained that what *dertleşmek* actually means is drinking lots of rakı, talking about everything that is going wrong in one's life and crying together. This practice is, of course, not unique to the Turkish context. People going through rough spots in their lives do this all over the planet. Not many languages, however, have a single word to describe it.

The Turkish Language

When a friend of mine heard that I was moving to Turkey he commented on the strange language with all its u-sounds. "Gurumulurul," he said to demonstrate what he thought it sounded like. The reason that it may sound like that is the vowel harmony. In Turkish, suffixes[362] are the key to the language, and which vowel is used in the suffix depends on the last vowel in the word stem. For instance, the verb *görmek*, to see, has the letter ö[363] as the final vowel in its stem, *gör*, and ö turns the vowels in the suffixes to ü. The equivalent of "see you later" then becomes *görüşürüz*. The vowel harmony sounds more extreme when the word itself has many u-sounds before one starts adding suffixes to it, such as the word *kültür* (culture). If one would like to hear about the cuisine of the country of the person one is talking to, one might say "Mutfak kültürünüzü anlatın" ("Tell me about your food culture").

Kültür, of course, is a loan word, and speakers of European languages who try to learn Turkish draw a sigh of relief every time they encounter a loan word from Europe, because they are few and far between. Speaking Persian or Arabic may help, because there are more loan words from those languages, but Turkish is not in the same language family as any of them. The difference is not only the vocabulary but also the sentence structure and all the suffixes.

The Turks brought their language from Asia. It has never been completely established which language family Turkish belongs to. There are some language groups that share enough similarities that some linguists claim that they are part of an Altaic language family. In addition to the Turkic group, where Turkish belongs, one finds Mongolic and Manchu-Tungusic, and even Korean and Japanese are counted as part of the larger Altaic family. The matter has not been settled, however, because skeptical linguists have never been convinced by attempts to show a common source of all these language groups.[364]

Whereas the words in Turkish may be different from anything one has heard before, which makes learning the language quite demanding, reading it is surprisingly easy. We have Atatürk to thank for that. Because of his no-nonsense, swift shift from Arabic to Latin letters, which happened only recently, there is practically no difference between the spelling and pronunciation of Turkish words. As long as one knows how each letter is pronounced by itself, one should be able to read and pronounce all Turkish words correctly.

The same cannot be said of European languages. In English, for instance, all the c's in *Pacific Ocean* are pronounced differently. The spelling of the words *home* and *come* suggests they would be pronounced similarly. In French, with all its silent letters, the word *heureux* (happy) would have been spelt *örö* if it was up to Atatürk.

But language in Turkey is more than Turkish. While most citizens of Turkey today can speak Turkish, many do not have it as their mother tongue (regardless of claims made in the constitution). Senem Deniz, whom we met in the previous chapter, told me that her mother's aunt only speaks Kurdish, and that her grandmothers on both sides started learning Turkish around the age of 16. Kurdish is, like Persian, an Indo-European language. Senem's mother and the other Kurdish children were made fun of by the teachers at school because of their Kurdish accent.

Then there are all the other languages. A young man from Hatay in the south-east told me about the prevalence of Arabic in his home region: "My father says he is Turkish, but he says it in Arabic!" Unfortunately, many of the smaller languages have been successfully killed off by the assimilation policies. Another young man, from İzmit, told me that despite both his parents having grown up in Laz households, his Laz was not very good since they always spoke Turkish at home.

Mother Nature

Turkey is an enormous geographical area by European standards. It is bigger than any of the European countries (not counting Russia), and bigger than Germany and Poland combined. The landscapes to be found in the country vary from the north to the south and from the east to the west. The inland is mountainous, and the tallest mountain is Ararat in the east, where Noah's ark is supposed to have ended up after the rainwater receded. It is 5165 meters tall and according to the Armenians, the mountain is theirs and the border is on the wrong side of it. The area along the Black Sea is quite humid and green, with vast forests. Much of the Anatolian plateau is arid with warm summers and cold winters. Ankara lies at around 1000 meters above sea level (depending on where in the hilly city one is). Then there is the Mediterranean coast, with warm, wet winters and hot, dry summers.

Despite this variation, there are a few things that people in Turkey have in common regarding how nature affects them. One of them is the risk of earthquakes. Anatolia is a seismically active peninsula where several tectonic plates meet. Earthquakes are unavoidable. There are many smaller quakes that bring limited damage and numbers of deaths, but in the 1900s alone there were twelve earthquakes that each killed more than a thousand people. The most lethal one was the Erzincan earthquake in 1939 where more than 30,000 people died. The last large-scale earthquake was in İzmit in 1999, severely affecting Istanbul. More than 17,000 people died.[365]

One would expect the risk of earthquakes to have led to strict regulations on the construction of housing. Unfortunately, being forgiven for having built illegally is quite common in Turkey. More than half of all current buildings in Turkey contravene building regulations, and since 2002, roughly 30 percent of new buildings have not been set up in accordance with regulations.[366]

In 2018, the government introduced an amnesty so that buildings that had been put up illegally could be registered. According to architects and civil engineers who warned against the amnesty, the discussion in parliament focused mainly on how much revenue the amnesty would generate. "We said people will pay for this with their lives, but they did not listen," the head of the Istanbul Chamber of Architects said to a journalist.[367] The chairman of the Chamber of Civil Engineers warned that the amnesty would turn Turkey's cities into graveyards. But the amnesty was approved, bringing in billions to state coffers. The consequences are predictable. In February 2019, a building in Istanbul that had been built illegally and registered through the amnesty, collapsed. 21 people died.[368] There will be more such incidences.

The risk of earthquakes is real, and the next time a city in Turkey is hit by one, it is only to be expected that many people will die. But those deaths will not be evenly distributed among rich and poor alike. The wealthy in Turkey have the resources to make sure that their buildings are safe. The less fortunate usually have other, more pressing priorities, like getting a roof over their heads. That roof may one day fall *on* their heads.

One natural phenomenon in Turkey that does not discriminate is the stray dogs. Dogs do not care if a person is rich or poor. They care if the person has food or seems to be a threat. Their presence on the city streets is a part of normal life. Few people consider this a problem, and the municipality will frequently have some sort of program, more or less efficient, to look after and inoculate the stray dogs.

The Ottomans did not have such programs, and for centuries the street dogs were a public health issue in Istanbul. The Young Turks tried to do something about this and had tens of thousands of dogs rounded up and brought out to Hayırsızada - Good-for-nothing Island - one of the small, arid islands south of the city. There the dogs formed packs that controlled access to rainwater pools and the prey that turned up on the island. If the wind was blowing in the right direction on a quiet day, one could - for years - hear the howling from Hayırsızada in Istanbul.[369]

Unfortunately, or luckily, depending on how one views stray dogs, the Young Turks did not rid the country of the dogs, and they are still to be found in big numbers in the cities. On numerous occasions I have tried to discuss the stray dog issue with people in Turkey, and it is like talking to someone from another planet. From my perspective, which, I realize, is heavily shaped by the fact that I had only lived in places without stray dogs before moving to Turkey, stray dogs should not exist. Dogs have been bred into existence by people, and do not belong anywhere except under the responsibility of people. If the legal responsibility of a dog is not placed with its owner, civilization does not have a place for it. There is no place for it in nature either, because it has been bred, for thousands of years, to be with people. The logical consequence of this is that every dog that does not have an owner must either be kept in a shelter or, if the resources allocated for shelters are insufficient, be put down. This is how most countries in Europe and several other places deal with dogs. Hence, you rarely see a stray dog in those countries.

From the perspective of many people in Turkey, however, my opinions are perceived as cruel, people centric or both. Who have decided that a human is more valuable than a dog? Humans have. A dog would probably not agree.

"We don't have the right to kill other creatures any more than we have the right to kill each other," my Turkish conversation partner would typically say. "The dogs belong here just as much as we do. We have to share the space."

"But the dogs don't leave people alone," I will object. "They sometimes bark at people and scare them, and sometimes they bite, causing risk of incurring rabies or other diseases. Why should people accept that risk in their lives?"

"If a dog bothers a person," they will counter, "it's because the person doesn't understand the mind of a dog. A person has the intellectual capacity to understand a dog and should therefore behave accordingly. Do not threaten a dog by threatening its territory, its puppies or access to food. If people obey the simple rules that govern a dog's world, dogs and people will happily live side by side."

People in Turkey are generally concerned with the well-being of their street animals, and there are organizations raising funds for food and even blankets for dogs. How a dog utilizes a blanket is anybody's guess.

"What about the barking at night, keeping people awake?" I try.

"Well, the traffic is also keeping people awake. Should we ban traffic?" they respond. I look at them and smile with a mix of frustration and fascination at the abyss between us.

Even people who have been attacked by dogs are not necessarily hostile towards them. A friend told me that he had once been attacked by a dog in Ankara. He was walking on the sidewalk by the parliament, and all of a sudden, a street dog that had been lying on the lawn outside parliament ran at him. My friend protected himself with his arm, and the dog bit his underarm. Luckily it was winter, and the dog did not bite through the heavy winter coat. "When a dog bites like that, you shouldn't try to pull your arm away. You should push into its mouth, which will make it want to release its grip," he explains. "While doing this, I looked at the dog, sort of asking 'Hey, what are you doing?!' and it was as if the dog responded 'Oops, wrong guy!' and went back to the lawn and lay down."

I wish I could understand better, and thereby explain to my readers better, why stray dogs are not seen as a problem by most people in Turkey. People do get hospitalized after dog attacks, and in January 2019, a student in Kayseri was even killed by dogs.[370] Sometimes people will take matters into their own hands, poisoning the dogs in their neighborhood, which usually sparks an outcry from the public and from animal rights organizations.[371]

My friend who was attacked in Ankara grew up in the countryside, and he told me that in the village, people know the dogs by name, and the dogs know the people. The existence of street dogs in cities is based on that same "village dog culture," but in the city there are too many dogs and too many people for this sort of relationship to develop - with a few exceptions. Some people actually do develop a relationship with the dogs in their neighborhood, and the dogs will follow them home or to the bus stop when they see them.

Animal rights activists have a big influence on how the authorities in Turkey deal with stray dogs. One might think, then, that environmentalists, too, would be able to affect the authorities in an efficient way. They are not. The key difference between protecting stray dogs and protecting the environment is that the former does not threaten anybody's power or wealth. When the issue is protection of the environment, on the other hand, those involved usually represent a business interest, like a factory or construction work on or near vulnerable ecosystems. In Turkey, the environment usually only wins when those who try to do business have the wrong connections.

Those with the right connections get away with quite a bit of environmental damage. Journalists or others who may feel the need to speak up about it, expose themselves to considerable risk. In September 2019, Bülent Şık, a former deputy director of a research center at a university in Antalya, was convicted to 15 months in prison. His crime was to disclose "classified information" when he published a study he had led, linking pollution in western Turkey to high cancer rates. Ironically, the study had been requested by the Turkish government because of those cancer rates. Upon completion of the study, the authorities were not interested in discussing its findings although Şık urged them to do so. After three years of delays, Şık had had enough and published the results himself. Turkish law allows judges to reduce sentences if those convicted express regret. Şık refused. He actually had connections in high places, but on the wrong side of politics; his brother was an opposition member of parliament.[372]

It is not only industry that damages the environment in Turkey. A lack of proper waste management is a major cause of environmental problems. In the Bosporus, only 26 fish species were left in 2003, down from 160 indigenous species.[373] The main cause of this is the lack of efforts by the city of Istanbul to treat the waste water and sewage before it is dumped in the sea. Because the municipality considers the cost too high, 80% of the sewage does not get properly treated.[374]

To be fair, the problems in the Bosporus have also been caused by the heavy international shipping traffic which Turkey has been restricted from regulating. In the decade between 1983 and 1993, there were 167 large-scale accidents in the strait. They all had very harmful physical and environmental consequences.[375] An international treaty from 1936 did not permit Turkey to regulate the traffic. For instance, they were not allowed to demand that ships hire trained pilots for navigating the difficult currents of the strait. Despite the treaty restrictions on Turkey's powers, Turkey decided in 1994 to introduce measures to reduce the risk of accidents.[376]

"Where Are You From?"

If a person in Istanbul is asked where he is from, he may for instance answer Trabzon. A follow-up question could be for how long he has lived in Istanbul. A typical answer would be: "I was born in Istanbul and have lived here all my life," which may be a little puzzling for a foreigner. Is he joking? Is he lying for the fun of it? Did he forget that he said, ten seconds ago, that he was from Trabzon? No, he is explaining where his parents are from. Usually, that is the answer one will get when asking where a person in Turkey is from.

Engin, the politician we met in Chapter 4, told me in detail where the different parts of his family came from. Not many people in Turkey will be able to give such a detailed portrayal of their family history. This is partially a question of power and wealth, since powerful and wealthy families tend to know their family history well, especially if they have held a certain status for generations. But Atatürk must also take some of the blame because he altered the way the word "Turk" was perceived and used. The Ottomans had not been very concerned with "ethnic purity," and the elite in Constantinople was ethnically quite mixed. When the city was first conquered in 1453, the sultan kept many of the Byzantine aristocrats for governing his newly gained territories. Furthermore, all the sultans of the Ottoman Empire took a Christian-born wife.[377] At the beginning of the 20th century, "'Turk' was used pejoratively and referred to the Muslim peasants in Anatolia; but they did not think of themselves as 'Turks' either."[378]

People's perception of the word and of themselves had to change if Turkey was to become a proper nation. All citizens of Turkey were to think of themselves - proudly - as Turks, so that the country would be a single unit from which no group wanted to secede. This led to the forgetting of much family history. Holding on to the fact that one's family, or a part of it, was actually Kurdish or Armenian could have negative consequences. This is especially true outside of the

Kurdish areas in the southeast. It has led to a situation where a large portion of the population in Turkey do now know for sure what the mother tongue of their grandparents or great grandparents was.

Prime minister Bülent Ecevit, for instance, was over 40 years old when he discovered that one of his grandfathers had been Kurdish. He discovered it when visiting his grandfather's tomb in central Anatolia, where he saw the family name Kürtzade, which means "of Kurdish lineage." More than thirty years later, in 2004, he revealed this to the public.[379] "Back then, such distinctions were not important," he explained.[380] Prime minister Turgut Özal, too, was of Kurdish origin, but this was never openly referred to.[381] Furthermore, many people who thought they were completely Turkish have discovered that their grandmother was Armenian. We will hear more about this in Chapter 7.

The picture is, however, more complex. One cannot simply conclude that most people in Turkey do not know their ethnic background. President Erdoğan has always been open about the fact that his mother's side of the family migrated from Georgia, and that his father's side may be Laz.[382] But this is not about a desire to create harmony between all ethnic groups in Turkey. It is about uniting all *Muslims* in Turkey. For Erdoğan's voters, the fact that his family may be partially Laz, a Muslim group, did not count negatively. For many in Turkey, religion trumps everything, including ethnicity and country borders. That is why, for instance, so many Kurds in the southeast have been voting for Erdoğan's AKP. It is also why so many people in Turkey are voting against their own economic interests. With the exception of the left-leaning former prime minister Bülent Ecevit, most politicians who want to redistribute wealth do not use religious rhetoric. They are usually not religious and sometimes hostile towards religion. Poor and uneducated but devout Muslims have tended to vote for the politicians who best appeal to their "religious feelings." Those politicians tend to do little, structurally, to reduce the poverty in which their voters live.

In cultures where family names have been used for a while, one's family name coupled with where one's parents and grandparents were born will usually reveal quite a bit about one's family history. In Turkey, it is not that simple. It was Atatürk's modernization that brought the Surname Law in 1934, and all of a sudden people who had done perfectly fine without surnames had to acquire one. Humble as he was, Mustafa Kemal chose the name Atatürk, 'father of the Turks.'[383] Many chose names suggesting toughness or masculinity:

"Hard (Sert), Tough (Çetin), Uncowed (Yılmaz), Iron (Demir), Steel (Çelik), Rock (Kaya),"[384] or a combination: Çetinkaya (Tough Rock) or Demirel (Iron Hand).

Some people were concerned with their Turkic heritage and found names of big men from the past. Some names became very popular in some areas, and several families from the same area would take the same last name. In some cases it would be the local bureaucrat simply giving people their names when they did not have a preference, based on where they were from.

Making everybody acquire a last name was one of many steps taken to modernize Turkey. But there could be no modernization without economic development. Wealth and modernity goes hand in hand. How has Turkey fared on this point?

Wealth for Me, Wealth for You?

> Overall, Turkey's economy is a strange combination of enormous successes and huge failures. The country keeps swinging back and forth between prosperity and recession. Success, prosperity, inflation, stagnation and recession – a most peculiar mixture hardly explainable by experts and academics characterize the economy in the past decade.[385]

As we have seen, Turkey has not exactly evolved in a linear fashion since the founding of the republic. It is perhaps not flabbergasting, then, that the economy has had its ups and downs. The country had a rough start, coming out of the First World War followed by the War of Independence. The country's external debt was enormous and had to be renegotiated. Furthermore, the "capitulations" that the Ottomans had been forced to accept gave foreign actors trade advantages in Turkey. By 1929, most of the externally imposed tax and tariff constraints had been removed.[386]

Adding to the economic problems was the fact that Turkey had rid itself of most of its Christian population - the Greeks and Armenians - who had been key parts of the economic machinery. The privileges granted them by the capitulations had contributed to their wealth. They were also generally better educated than their Muslim countrymen, partially because of American missionary efforts during the nineteenth century.[387] In other words, removing the Christians from the economic cycle meant reducing the average level of education, wealth and economic know-how of its population. These deficiencies signified the point of departure for building the country after the wars.

For a few individuals, the vacuum that the removal of Greeks and Armenians left became great economic opportunities. In 1914, more than half of the hazelnut producers in the Ottoman Empire had been Armenian. After the Armenians had been killed off during the First World War, the industry was transferred to Muslims.[388] One of the successful businessmen who were to profit from this redistribution of "abandoned" property was Hacı Ömer. He was only 14 years old when he in 1921, as an orphan, arrived in Çukurova in Adana province. He had walked there on foot from his hometown of Kayseri, 500 kilometers away.

Hacı Ömer was put in touch with decision makers in the bureaucracy in Adana through his family connections. A decade after his arrival, "Hacı Ömer shared the ownership of a cotton gin factory,[389] he had acquired two olive oil factories and the first of four farms, of 1,000 hectares. He admitted that the state had handed him the cotton fields. His business associate had played a leading role in the massacres of the Armenians that took place in Adana in 1909."[390] Ömer went on to build the Sabancı business empire, which is currently "the second largest industrial and commercial conglomerate in Turkey."[391]

In the 1930s, the government put in place large programs for industrialization and the economy grew. Although Turkey stayed out of World War II until the very end, it did not escape the economic troubles the war caused.[392] It did, however, benefit to some extent from the Jewish exodus from Germany. Some of the Jewish scholars who were chased away by the Nazis ended up in Turkey, where they contributed substantially to the building of Turkish research and higher education institutions and to government.[393] Overall the economic growth during the first decades of the republic was respectable, especially considering that there was a depression and a world war during those years: Average annual GNP growth rates have been estimated as 7.4 percent, 1.2 percent, and 7.9 percent for the periods 1923-38, 1938-48, and 1948-53, respectively.[394]

The second half of the 1900s has been described as an economic roller-coaster ride for Turkey. The last severe crisis occurred in 2001, a year before Erdoğan was elected, after which a period of rapid economic growth followed. In 2007 the growth slowed down significantly, and productivity growth stagnated.[395] Then, despite the failed coup attempt in 2016 and the government crackdown, the Turkish economy grew "very fast" in 2017 and 2018.[396] The roller-coaster ride continues.

One thing that has ameliorated the economic downturns is remittances from Turkish workers abroad. Since the 1960s, Turkey has been among the world's top receiving countries of remittances,[397] money sent home by millions of Turkish workers abroad.

One aspect holding back development in Turkey is the fact that whether an investor gets permission to establish a business often depends on how the authorities view him or her as a person. A landowner in the southeast told me that he had applied for permission to set up a solar power plant on one of his properties. According to him, the application was rejected because he was Kurdish and an active local politician for the HDP party. Development is thus held back by politicians who think it is only a certain type of people who should benefit from development.

With a population of 83 million[398] and a GDP of 760 billion USD[399] in 2019, Turkey has the 16th highest GDP in the world and is part of the G20. Turkey is among the world's top food producers, and agriculture is the country's largest employer at around five million workers or fifteen percent of the total labor force in 2019,[400] down from 43% (!) in 2003.[401] Tourism in 2018 accounted for four percent of GDP and eight percent of employment, meaning that 2.2 million people were directly employed in the tourism sector in Turkey that year.[402]

Turkey has become a wealthier country during the last decades. The rich have become richer, and poverty has also been reduced. The gap between the rich and the poor is much larger than in the European countries with the most equality, but only slightly larger than the gap in the US, China and Russia.[403] One specific cause of this wealth gap is the 1980 military coup, which changed the system in a way that made labor unions practically powerless. In 1980, 90 per cent of workers were unionized, while today, 90 per cent are not.[404] During the first years under Erdoğan, the inequality was reduced. Until 2007, the income of the poorest increased more than that of the richest. Then the trend turned around, and income inequality has since risen to new heights.[405]

Where labor unions are weak wages tend to be low,[406] and working conditions tend to be bad, sometimes hazardous. Turkey holds the world record in fatal work-related accidents.[407] In 2019, at least 1477 workers died from accidents at work during the first ten months of the year. The highest number of work-related deaths occurred in the agriculture, construction and transportation sectors, and most victims were seasonal workers in agriculture.[408]

But are people in Turkey happy? Since 2012, a group of researchers have measured happiness around the world, based on a number of indicators including people's own responses to questions related to their happiness. In their 2019 report, the seven happiest countries are the Nordic countries plus the Netherlands and Switzerland. Turkey is ranked as the 79th happiest country in the world, very close to the countries in its neighborhood: Montenegro (73), Croatia (75), Bosnia and Herzegovina (78), Greece (82) and North Macedonia (84).[409] The happiness in Turkey increased slightly from the period 2005-2008 to the period 2016-2018,[410] which may come as a surprise, given that the country became less democratic during those years. But remember that poverty has decreased under Erdoğan while he has implemented very popular, Islam friendly measures. When he came to power, Turkey was a country of mostly poor people. It is now a country of mostly middle-income citizens. Life has improved, and people enjoy better infrastructure and services.[411]

The Organization for Economic Cooperation and Development (OECD) similarly investigates how satisfied people are with their lives. The 2020 "How's Life?" report states that "Turkey has made considerable progress in improving the quality of life of its citizens over the last two decades.[412]" In spite of these improvements, however, it ranks fairly low on most of the measures. In "life satisfaction" it is in the 37th place out of 40 countries, above Portugal, Greece and South Africa.[413] In "work life balance," Turkey ranks as number 38, above Mexico and Colombia. The reason for this is that Turkey has the highest rate of workers in the OECD that work very long hours.

In spite of this, those who have jobs are unable to pull up the average household income for the country as a whole. One reason for this is the high level of unemployment. Turkey ranks as number 39 of the 40 OECD countries on employment because only 52% of people in working age has a paid job. The average in OECD is 68%.[414] An important part of this picture is the enormous gender gap. Turkey has the highest female youth unemployment in the OECD. Whereas 22% of men aged 20-24 are not in employment, education or training, the proportion for women is 44%. The gender gap has increased under Erdoğan's rule,[415] perhaps not so surprising considering his Islamist politics.

Adding to the economic challenges in Turkey is the fact that performance and competence, in many cases, play minor roles in the job market. For the most important jobs it is relationships and politics that matter for whether someone is hired or fired. For instance, a large portion of the population has no actual access to government jobs simply because of their political affiliations or who they are. A natural consequence of this is that people with high skills, frequently the best, are filtered out. This is not something new, although it has varied how much it has affected the job market. As Senem Deniz told me regarding the employment opportunities after the 1980 coup: "Most of my relatives couldn't work for the state because of their political affiliations. They all had to work in the private sector."

Putting "one's own" in the right jobs continues to this day. During the great purge after the 2016 coup attempt, many academics lost their jobs. But for Erdoğan it did not start there. As soon as he came to power in 2003, the government started treating research applications differently. Ilhan Uzgel worked as a political science professor at Ankara University until he was fired after the coup attempt. Uzgel told a journalist about how things had begun to change under Erdoğan's AKP rule. Applications that would usually be approved began to be rejected by AKP-friendly clerks. "Because religious or conservative A.K.P. supporters had felt for decades that they had been shut out of elite academia, now it was their turn to have advantages in academia. They sometimes even said that directly to people, Uzgel heard from other academics. '*It's our turn.*'"[416]

Using employment and unemployment as a carrot and a stick for political affiliation is ostensibly part and parcel of the Turkish system. This systematically keeps the quality of government and academia lower than it could be, because the best qualified people are frequently not hired. In recent years it has caused a brain drain where thousands of scientists have left the country.

"It Was Not Done by Experts."

On November 11, 2019, the Turkish government set a new world record in "Most trees planted in one hour by a team of unlimited size (single location)." A total of 303,150 trees were planted in Çorum.[417] It was part of a nationwide effort in which eleven million trees were planted.

Quite a feat, perhaps, if the saplings had survived. But a couple of months after the event most of the trees were dead, according to the Turkish trade union for agriculture and forestry. The head of the union told a journalist that their inspections had shown that 90% of the saplings had died because of insufficient water. He explained that the timing of the planting had been wrong, there had not been enough rainfall, and the planting had not been done by experts. The Turkish ministry of agriculture and forestry, on its side, claimed that 95% of the trees were alive and growing normally. To this, the union head responded: "Even with normal time and preparation, the success rate is between 65 and 70%. The 95% rate given by the ministry is never true."[418] We can seek comfort in the fact that at least the ministry did not go above 100% in its estimates.

When people are put in charge of large and complex operations because of who they know and what they believe instead of their qualifications, it should come as no surprise that the results will be sub-optimal. It is common for many in Turkey to assume that it is not the best qualified people who perform government tasks. A joke about the Turkish intelligence agency, MIT, is telling in that regard:

The American CIA, the Israeli Mossad and the Turkish MIT were having a contest. A monkey would be let loose in a forest, and whoever found the monkey in the least amount of time would win. The CIA was the first contestant and entered the forest. After five minutes they came out with the monkey. Not bad. Then it was Mossad's turn. After only three minutes they came out of the forest with the monkey. Everybody was very impressed. Then it was the MIT's turn. They entered the forest. Three minutes passed. Five minutes passed. One hour passed. People started to wonder what was going on in the forest. Two hours, three hours, no sign of the MIT. The sun started to set, and the CIA and Mossad agents began packing up their gear. Then the MIT came out of the forest with a giraffe. The CIA and Mossad agents scratched their heads. As the MIT agents approached with the giraffe, one could see clear marks of torture on the giraffe's body. Then the giraffe said: "I am the monkey."

The joke sums up both the lack of faith in government agencies and the awareness of the use of torture by security forces. In addition to the fact that people know that competence is not the most important thing when recruiting for the public sector, there are also other things that contribute to people's lack of faith in government institutions. One of those things is the Ergenekon case that started in 2007, briefly mentioned in the previous chapter. There was a mass arrest of high-ranking military leaders, judges and journalists who were accused of belonging to an organization called Ergenekon. The organization was said to be responsible for most political murders in Turkey since the 1970s. The purpose of the Ergenekon organization was said to be to keep Turkey secular.

While the court cases against roughly 500 "Ergenekon members" were still ongoing in 2010, information about a plot to oust Erdoğan emerged. The plot was said to have been called "Operation Sledgehammer" and involved leading military officers. It led to the conviction of around 300 officers in 2012, who were sent off to jail. In addition, 275 defendants were convicted in the Ergenekon case.[419]

Throughout the investigation and court cases related to Ergenekon and Operation Sledgehammer, journalists revealed that the investigators had planted and fabricated evidence. Those journalists risked being accused themselves of being Ergenekon members. Several were arrested.

It turned out that both Ergenekon and Operation Sledgehammer had been dreamed up by investigators and judges, most likely belonging to the Gülen network. In other words, Gülen supposedly helped Erdoğan get rid of high-ranking secular officers in the military. On this point, the interests of both Gülen and Erdoğan overlapped: They both wanted to reduce the influence of the secular officers in the military.

Then came the backstabbing. When the collaboration had led to the desired results for Erdoğan, he turned against the Gülenists in order to reduce Gülen's influence. Starting in 2014, he let new rounds in the courts reveal the truth about the Ergenekon and Operation Sledgehammer investigations. The courts found that both Ergenekon and Operation Sledgehammer had been made up by the prosecutors and that the evidence had been fabricated. Over the course of two years the convictions were overturned and those in prison were released. But their military careers were over.

Erdoğan's achievement was to kill two birds with one stone: Both rid himself of secularists in the military, and then make the Gülenist network weaker by revealing its existence in a formal and public way.[420] Another "achievement" was that the public was given yet another reason not to trust their government agencies.

Conspiracy Theories

In November 1996, something happened that to many in Turkey confirmed what they had been suspecting for a long time: That there is a "deep state" in Turkey protecting certain interests relating to nationalism and security. On November 3, after dark, a car was driving at high speed through Susurluk, a small town between Izmir and Istanbul. The car crashed into a truck and three of the four passengers were killed. As the ambulance personnel arrived, they were surprised to discover who the passengers were: A senior police chief, an ultra-nationalist gang leader and drug smuggler, a Kurdish member of parliament of one of ruling parties, and a beauty queen. What were they doing in the same car?

It all looked very suspicious and three separate government investigations were started. It was revealed that some of the members of government were somehow connected to the people in the Susurluk car crash, but the investigators had too limited powers and were given too little time to find enough evidence for proper prosecutions.[421] "Predictably, the parliamentary investigation of the Susurluk incident ran into insurmountable walls of silence. It reported nothing significant."[422]

In spite of this, some of the investigations, including those done by courageous journalists, showed a clear link between drug smuggling, far-right and violent gangs, and the government and/or security forces. The conditions were ripe for people to fill in the missing facts and draw historical lines. Among Islamists the lines were drawn back to the Young Turk Black Hand Society that came into existence during the Ottoman Empire. The claim was that the Black Hand Society had become the "Deep State" of the Republic of Turkey in order to keep Islamists at bay. People on the political left had their own ideas about the deep state. Neither the Islamists nor the leftist-liberals who claimed the Deep State existed, however, clearly articulated precisely who was part of this clandestine organization.[423]

Badly performed investigations after events like the Susurluk car crash make people prone to create their own conspiracy theories about what is *really* going on. Two other aspects of Turkey contribute to the flourishing of conspiracy theories. One is the heavy restrictions on press freedom, often preventing the truth from being reported accurately. The other is the way ideological convictions - instead of science - steer education. This leads the education system to leave gaps of theory and knowledge for people to fill themselves. For instance, Darwinism was taken out of the curriculum for Turkish school children in 2017.[424] The Turkish public is left with a government and media they cannot trust to provide facts, and with a reduced capacity to assess information themselves.

Politicians use this to their advantage and spice up their political arguments with conspiracy theories. Erdoğan, for instance, blamed the 2013 Gezi protests, in which millions of people participated, on foreign powers aiming to destabilize Turkey. His supporters accepted this explanation. Years later, one professor told a journalist that his students frequently asked him why the EU and western media organized the Gezi protests.[425]

One popular conspiracy theory is that the 1923 Lausanne Treaty which laid the foundation for the republic has a secret, 100-year expiration clause. This means that in 2023, British troops will reoccupy forts along the Bosporus strait and Greece will reestablish a version of the Byzantine Empire inside Istanbul's old city walls. On the bright side, Turkey will finally be able to exploit its vast, secret oil reserves.[426] Of course, there is no secret Lausanne Treaty clause or secret oil reserves, but that does not keep people from believing that they exist.

In fact, a Reuters Institute study from 2018 found that Turkey was the country most exposed to misinformation among the 37 countries surveyed.[427] When the Covid-19 pandemic spread around the world, the theory that the virus had been planted in China by the US military was widely believed in Turkey.[428] The media did not exactly help to clarify matters. When it took a while before the first case of virus infection was found in Turkey, it was seriously discussed in the media whether perhaps Turkish genes were somehow superior to the virus.

It seems that it does not matter where on the political spectrum people are; Both Islamists and secularists propagate conspiracy theories. It is not unusual for the theories to have anti-Semitic elements. For instance, is Erdoğan secretly a Jew trying to weaken Turkey vis-a-vis Israel? Or: Is it a coincidence that the important 1923 treaty was signed in Lausanne, Switzerland being the center of world Zionism? Should we just wait for a Christian-Zionist or Euro-American invasion?[429]

There are also plenty of conspiracy theories that do not involve Jews, like the claim that the conflict between PKK and the Turkish government is kept alive by the Dutch dairy industry. In this way, production in Southeast Turkey is reduced and Turkey stays reliant on dairy imports. Other conspiracy theories are more banal, like claims that Abdullah Öcalan, the PKK leader, is living a life of luxury on his prison island, with young, beautiful women being transported out to him by the government.

Conspiracy theories seem to thrive among people who do not trust the sources of information that they should be able to trust, such as the government and the media. And when politicians refer to conspiracy theories to undergird their argument, they exacerbate the matter.

Corruption, Nepotism, and Power Abuse

Misinformation is an excellent way of blurring the facts about use and abuse of power. In Turkey, this seems to mean that if one has power, misinformation is a friend. If one can control both what the government says and what the media says, there is little to fear, politically, in terms of consequences of power abuse.

Politics in Turkey has a lot to do with patronage, perhaps as much as ideology. That means that it is important to get "one's own people" in positions of power, in a quid pro quo dynamic. This naturally leads to certain people prospering under certain prime ministers or - currently - presidents. "Turks tend to think of those who prospered in the 1980s under the prime ministry of Turgut Özal as being the 'Özal rich' as opposed to the 'Demirel rich' of the 1990s. If the 'Erdoğan rich' of the following decade seem more powerful, this is in part because the economy is so much bigger."[430]

One reason why Erdoğan's AKP became so popular at the beginning of the 2000s may have been all the corruption scandals that took place in the 1990s. AKP seemed clean compared to the parties that had recently been in power. When the Islamist Welfare Party won the 1995 election, two other parties teamed up to form a coalition government without the Welfare Party. One of those two government parties then worked with the Welfare Party to press corruption charges against Tansu Çiller, the leader of the other government party. Tansu Çiller left the government coalition and made a deal with the Welfare Party: If they helped her avoid corruption charges, she would help the Welfare Party form a new government. This she did. "Through its shameless willingness to conceal corruption, the Welfare Party attained government power and shielded Çiller against corruption allegations and parliament inquiries -- some of which they had put forward."[431] Then, a number of bribery scandals were uncovered during the reign of the Welfare Party[432] (which was outlawed in 1998 for its mixing of religion and politics, as mentioned in Chapter 3).

All the corruption at the top level of politics, together with other corruption scandals in the 1990s, made it difficult to have faith in the political system. So, when Recep Tayyip Erdoğan's AKP entered the scene of national politics, many believed that things would now be done differently. Erdoğan had said for years that the system was broken. During the first years of governing Turkey, he did indeed seem to play by the rules. But after a while in power, it was revealed that Erdoğan was not as clean as people had hoped.

In 2007, several prominent people with ties to Erdoğan's AKP were involved in a court case in Germany, accused of embezzling millions of dollars from a Turkish charity. As we learned in Chapter 3, the Doğan media group had to pay a high price, literally, for publishing information about the court case. It was fined 2.5 billion dollars.[433]

Two years later, in 2009, the newspaper Aydinlik obtained a recording of a conversation between Erdoğan and a wealthy businessman. In it, Erdoğan requests the transfer of a sum of money to his daughter in the US. Not surprisingly, Erdoğan claimed the recording had been fabricated. Two weeks after the revelation, several of the employees at the newspaper were arrested.[434]

When the conflict between Erdoğan and Gülen peaked in 2013, police arrested 52 people allegedly participating in grand corruption. They were all connected to the AKP, and three of them were sons of government ministers. Internationally the case mainly became known as a gold smuggling case linked to Iran, with the gold trader Reza Zarrab in the midst of events. In Turkey, the case mainly revolved around all the enablers connected to the AKP. In the homes of those who were arrested police found a total of 17.5 million dollars in cash.[435] Although Erdoğan himself was not directly and publicly accused of taking part in the smuggling scheme, embarrassing tapes of what appeared to be conversations between him and his son about managing millions of dollars of cash were leaked to the public.[436]

In the mid-1990s, Erdoğan said in a speech: "Our people can see that the current system in Turkey has gone bankrupt."[437] He should have added "and if I get the chance, I will make it worse." He is neatly fitting into a predictable pattern of human behavior; Populist politicians who criticize the corrupt elite, only to become even more corrupt once in power.[438] In 2012, Erdoğan oversaw the pulling of teeth from the Court of Accounts which is responsible for monitoring government spending. A new law took away its ability to audit public institutions.[439] This made it easier for the leaders of those institutions to enrich themselves and their family and friends with public funds.

Erdoğan's personal wealth has been estimated to be in the tens of millions of dollars. It has grown together with his power. When he was mayor of Istanbul, he entered into a business deal with the chocolate producer Ülker, through a company he had established with his brother and brother-in-law. Ülker has become an international conglomerate having bought up the Belgian Godiva and the British United Biscuits. Erdoğan's company gained monopoly rights to sell Ülker products in large parts of Istanbul. As Erdoğan's political power expanded to the national level, lucrative business deals were entered into by companies he established. After he sold his stocks in the companies with Ülker contracts in 2005, it has become increasingly difficult to trace his income.[440]

His children are "swimming in money"[441] after having done a series of very good business deals where they have been able to buy property or company stocks far below market value. When the father can make the arrangements that he can, it makes sense to offer his children generous deals. And it seems the father can make those arrangements ever more lucrative. In 2018, he appointed himself chairman of Turkey's wealth fund. His son-in-law was made deputy chairman. At 200 billion dollars, the fund's assets include shares in Turkish Airlines, telecom companies and banks.[442]

Unfortunately, the corruption does not limit itself to enriching oneself financially. It also prevents non-financial crimes from being properly investigated. In 1998, Erdoğan's eldest son Ahmet Burak hit singer Sevim Tanürek with his car in Istanbul an killed her. According to some sources, she had a green pedestrian light for crossing the street. Ahmet Burak is said not have had a driver's license and to have fled the scene of the accident. The prosecutor concluded that he was guilty of killing her and requested a prison sentence. Erdoğan was then the mayor of Istanbul, and in the final court hearing his son was absolved of all the allegations. The court process left people unconvinced about Ahmet Burak's innocence.[443]

The corruption in Turkey is not unique, and Turkey is not shockingly corrupt compared to the rest of the world. The world is a corrupt place, and according to Transparency International, Turkey ranks in the middle at number 91 out of 180 countries. But for foreigners from countries with less corruption who try to understand life in Turkey, it is necessary to be aware of the effect that corruption has on the decisions that are made.

6. "The Kurdish Problem"

Places mentioned in this chapter. A substantial proportion of the population in the darker area on the map are Kurdish.[444]

"Our only friends are the mountains."
Kurdish saying.

"Hello, this is Tor," I say in English.

"Hello, am I speaking with Tor?" the other end replies in Swedish.

Swedish? I hesitate for a split second before I answer in Norwegian.[445]

"Yes...who is this?"

"This is Mehmet.[446] I'm on my way to the airport."

I am told to look for a Toyota pick-up that will arrive at the terminal within ten minutes. I first find a seat indoors because it's too hot outside and few opportunities for finding shade. After a few minutes I go out, the pick-up arrives and out of the car steps a smiling Mehmet. We greet each other and my suitcase is thrown in the back of the car.

It turns out that my man in Diyarbakır in South-East Turkey has lived for many years in Sweden, where he arrived as a refugee in 1980. In 1986, Turkish authorities offered an amnesty to everyone who had gone underground or left the country, as long as they had not participated in violence. It seemed safe enough to come back, and Mehmet travelled home to Diyarbakır for a visit while his family remained in Sweden. For a few years Mehmet traveled back and forth between Sweden and Turkey. His daughter found herself a Kurdish husband in Sweden, and after a while Mehmet moved home to Diyarbakır with his wife, his daughter, her husband and their three children. For Mehmet's grandchildren, however, Diyarbakır was not "home," as the eldest was eight when they left Sweden and he had never lived anywhere but in Stockholm.

Mehmet's father was born around 1915 in the town Mardin. In 1931 he was put in jail, according to Mehmet because "he was considered a threat against the system. The government armed people to pressurize others. Dad resisted this, and so they came up with something and put him in jail. They let him out in 1941."

His father married, and Mehmet was born in 1945. When Mehmet was six months old his father died unexpectedly, and his mother married her deceased husband's brother, which was the custom for a widow at that time. With her new husband Mehmet's mother had six more children. Mehmet, as the eldest, married early. His parents agreed on his engagement with another family among their relatives when he was 15, and he married at 17. "I was only a child, I didn't know what an engagement was!" he explains and shakes his head.

Their Own People

Around the same time that Mehmet left for Sweden, another Kurd around the same age, Abdullah Öcalan, left Turkey. Öcalan had in 1978 established the organization PKK with likeminded Kurds. PKK was to fight for the independence of the Kurdish areas in Turkey, and the establishment of a Kurdish state. Öcalan was by no means the first person to think of Kurdish separation. It had been tried before, multiple times, but the attempts had been brutally repressed by the Turkish government. So brutally, in fact, that the Kurds did not seriously attempt something similar for many years. A British diplomat who travelled in the Kurdish areas in Turkey in 1956 noted that he could not find a hint of Kurdish nationalism. This was in stark contrast to the Kurdish areas of Iraq, where he found nationalism to be prevalent.

The first time the Kurds revolted in the new Turkey was in 1925. The Turkish Republic had recently been declared, and it was a time for uniting the country and become a proper nation like the nations in Europe. The French were French and lived in France. The Germans were German and lived in Germany. Turkey was to be the Turkish country, where the Turks lived. Turkey was a nation just like the nations of Europe, thought Atatürk and his powerful likeminded friends. The Kurds did not completely agree with this description of reality. They had their own language, their own culture, their own identity. The Kurds in Turkey had more in common with the Kurds in Iran, Iraq and Syria, than with the Turks of Anatolia. Why should the Kurds pretend to be someone they were not?

Few people groups, including the European ones, can claim as much "ethnic purity" as the Kurds. They have lived in the same environment for about 4400 years and led the same nomadic lifestyle until recently. The nomadic life has resulted in a certain spread of Kurds around their core area, and there are even a few in Afghanistan. The only thing that has changed significantly is the language. Around the twelfth century B.C.E. the language was heavily influenced by Persian and Median. The current Kurdish language is actually not one, but five closely related Indo-European languages belonging to the Iranian/Persian branch. Of the five, Kurds in Turkey speak mainly Kurmanji and Zaza. Some of the five are mutually understandable, but the two main languages, Kurmanji and Sorani (the latter is spoken in Iraq and Iran) are, according to some linguists, grammatically as different from each other as English and German.

"It is the Kurds who belong here," explains Mehmet. "We are the ones who have always lived here. Other countries and authorities have come and occupied and tried to turn it into their land, but in the end, it is the Kurds who have remained."

Ostensibly the Kurds have had to continually tolerate being formally subjected to the rule of foreign kings and emperors. Usually, they have managed to maintain some sort of autonomy. They have particularly opposed two signs of submission: Taxation to and military service for the external ruler. This resistance has led to a sort of chronic condition of revolt in the Kurdish areas. When Turkey decided that the whole country would be Turkish, it was quite predictable that the Kurds, yet again, would resist this type of external influence and control.

The problem was that the Kurds had not been able to unite sufficiently to make their demands known to the European powers when the borders of the Middle East were being redrawn after the First World War. The academic Andrew Finkel has said that while the Turks were the last ethnic group in the Ottoman Empire to get their own country, the Kurds came too late to the party.[447] Although the Kurds were promised the possibility of their own state in the Sèvres Treaty (signed by the Ottoman Empire in 1920), it was the Lausanne Treaty (1923) that determined the future of the land after the Turks, led by Atatürk, won the War of Independence. The Lausanne Treaty says nothing about the Kurds. In it there are only commitments towards the non-Muslim minorities, but the Kurds are not considered part of this group since they are by and large Muslim. In many ways it was the system of the Ottoman Empire that was continued; The different groups (millet) in the empire had a degree of autonomy and enforced their own jurisdiction within the empire. A Christian should not have to comply with the laws of Islam, and vice versa. But the Kurds were considered part of the "Muslim nation" (umma). Potential ethnic, linguistic, or cultural differences were not to matter in the new Turkey.

Kurdish Diversity

There are two factors that have particularly contributed to the lack of Kurdish unity. One factor is the fact that the Kurdish culture is tribal. Only in the tenth century C.E. did (a portion of) the Kurds live in one kingdom, but the kingdom did not survive longer than the king who gathered it. In the 1920s, 90% of the Kurds in Turkey were divided into tribes controlled by powerful landowners. The tribal cleavages and the hostility between the tribes were aggravated by the competition for limited resources. The last hundred years have changed a lot of the tribal culture, and the urbanization and general migration, among other things, have contributed to the weakening of the tribal ties.

The other factor contributing to a lack of unity is religion. Since the Lausanne Treaty, the Kurds have been defined as Muslims, but this is partially wrong and partially a coarse and not very useful simplification. As with any other religious people, the Kurds are religious in their own way. No proper survey which could have provided accurate numbers has been done, but according to estimates between 60 % and 80 % of Kurds are Sunni Muslims. "Compared to a nonbeliever, a Kurd is a Muslim," is a description of Kurds that says something about how the Kurds are perceived by other Muslims.

Although they have Sunni Islam in common with very many Turks, most Kurds follow the Shafi'i school of Sunni Islam, while most Turks (and Arabs) follow the Hanafi school. The differences concern among other things the time for the morning prayer, how the hands are to be used while praying, what leads to ritual impurity. These things may seem insignificant, but they do bring forth a sentiment of "our group" and "the others." This has been actively used from time to time for nationalistic purposes. Another aspect of the Kurdish version of Sunni Islam is the role of mysticism. Traditionally there have been numerous mystical orders or brotherhoods (tarikat) among the Kurds. The mysticism may concern practices including meditative repetition of the name of God, breathing techniques, or different ways in which to show humility. A brotherhood is led by a sheik, and the sheiks gained an important role from the mid-1800s when the Sultan abandoned the semi-autonomous emirates. The emirs had tried to keep the conflicts between the tribes in check, but when the emirs disappeared the feuding increased. The only leaders with authority across the tribes were now the sheiks.

Another substantial religious group among the Kurds is the Alevis. A researcher estimated in 1991 that there might be more than a million Kurdish Alevis in Turkey. Like so many other minorities also the Alevis have been persecuted throughout the centuries, which led them to withdraw towards more inaccessible mountain areas. One of these were Dersim (the name of which was later Turkified into Tunceli), which was to become a central arena in the Turkish-Kurdish conflict.

In addition to Sunni Muslims and Alevis there are also Yezidis, Christians and Ahl-i-Haqq ("Those who are devoted to truth") among the Kurds, but these are minor groups today because of continuous persecution. The Jewish minority that could be found in many Kurdish towns have by and large disappeared. Most of them migrated to Israel, where they are known as Kurdistani Jews. An estimated 200.000 Jews with a background from the Kurdish areas live in Israel.

Kurdish religiosity is multifaceted, and this has had an impact on how united the Kurds have stood against Turkish authorities. The relationship between Kurdish nationalism and religion has been strained and ambivalent. The nationalists have tried to point to religion as a divisive factor but have experienced that criticism or ignoring of religion has made recruitment difficult. To reach a broader audience they have had to adjust their rhetoric to make their message more palatable to religious Kurds.

Revolt

When the first Kurdish riot in the newly established country Turkey took place in 1925, the relationship between the Turkish authorities and the Kurds had for some time deteriorated substantially. The abolition of the caliphate had big consequences for the Kurdish perception of fellowship with the Turks. Islam had united Turks and Kurds after the First World War against the infidel victors and the local Christians (Armenians and Greeks). Consequently, the new government started a nationalization process that prevented the Kurds from living out their identity. Teaching Kurdish and using Kurdish language in public was banned, and influential landowners and tribal leaders were moved by force to western Turkey. This happened even though Atatürk during the War of Independence had promised the Kurds local autonomy and free use of the Kurdish language. Naturally the disappointment and feeling of betrayal was strong among the Kurds.

A sheik by the name of Sa'id was the leader of the 1925 rebellion. Islam was used actively to mobilize people to rebel, but this met with resistance from the Alevis who objected to Sa'id's initiative.[448] The divide between the Kurds contributed to the ease with which the Turkish military could end the riot. Sheik Sa'id and 46 of his supporters were hanged at a square in Diyarbakır.

"One of the brothers of my father told me about this riot," says Mehmet. "My grandfather lived in Mardin. They were a rich family, leaders of the clan. But always against the system and the authorities.

The brother of my grandfather was hanged together with Sheik Sa'id. My grandfather was not as active during the riot and saved his life by keeping quiet."

In 1926 a new, more local riot broke out as a continuation of the riot the year before. This rebellion lasted for four years, and when the government finally was able to control the situation numerous Kurdish leaders were executed and more than 20,000 Kurds were moved by force to western Turkey. This marked the beginning of an active denial of Kurdish existence. In order to avoid trouble, some Kurds agreed to call themselves Turks. "They said they were Turks, but they said it in Kurdish! They didn't know Turkish," Mehmet laughs.

Smaller riots continued in the mountains in the southeast, until a big riot erupted in 1937. This took place in large parts of Dersim (Tunceli) and it was an Alevi riot. Hence, it was not supported by the Sunni Kurds. This riot was also brutally struck down and thousands of Kurds were forcefully moved to the west. In addition, many Kurds were forced to move from the mountains and summer pastures they had used for thousands of years, down to the flatlands to farm. The area was later perceived to be a source of trouble from the Alevis, nationalists and radical leftists. After the military coup in 1980, Tunceli became the subject of military operations to establish peace and quiet, and the area has since been a priority for Turkish security forces.

The Mountain Turks

The Kurds were – and are – the largest language minority in the country. Although official censuses do not register ethnicity, Turkish authorities have put the proportion at 7 per cent, while a Kurdish estimate is 24 per cent. Mehmet's number is 30 million (which would be more than a third of Turkey's population). CIA World Fact Book estimates the proportion to be 19 per cent (15 million), while a conservative estimate based on surveys of the use of Kurdish language puts the proportion at around 13 per cent. If the latter estimate is true, around eleven million Kurds live in Turkey (but probably a few million more do so). For the sake of comparison: More than two thirds of the EU member countries have less than eleven million inhabitants.

With such a substantial population the Kurdish movement was seen to be the greatest threat towards the new Turkish republic. The Turks had just won their independence and had had bad experiences with the Armenian separatist inclinations during the First World War. The near history suggested that it would be best if the country was as unified as possible, if all inhabitants pulled in the same direction. Part of the solution was to ban things. The authorities banned all religious brotherhoods (tarikat). All organizations or publications that could be perceived to disturb law and order were banned, dissolved, and shut down. Regarding the Kurds, the solution was to ban anything that could be perceived as encouragement of separatism. Strict restrictions on the use of Kurdish language and music were introduced, many newspapers were closed down, and publications were closely monitored. Since Turkey was to be the land of the Turks – and only Turks – the Kurds were, after the final rebellion in 1938, officially referred to as "Mountain Turks."

The Turkish response to unique Kurdish traits has been a mix of denial, disregard, coercion and violence. Since the early years of the republic, Turkey has tried to assimilate the Kurds through bans and coercion of the population, in combination with rewards to the willing elite. In school the children were taught in Turkish. What one's mother tongue was did not matter; if the school was in Turkey, the teaching was in Turkish.

"When I started school, I only knew Kurdish," says Mehmet. "I had to learn Turkish in school, I didn't know a word of Turkish! It was the same for all the children, nobody knew Turkish. The teachers had pictures of different words – horse, book, human being – which they used to teach us the language. The teachers came from Istanbul or Ankara and of course they didn't know Kurdish. The children weren't allowed to speak Kurdish in school. After a few years we learnt the language."

It is still the case that Kurdish children are taught only in Turkish in school. Naturally this reduces the quality of their education, as their first years in school are lost in following teaching in a language they only partially understand. The economic costs from such ineffective education must be assumed to be substantial.

With this "Turkification" of the children followed, naturally, a perception of what was right and wrong, what one should be proud of and not. In addition to the language and the authorities' version of the subject of history, the children also had to repeat the oath that all Turkish school children started their day with.[449]

"We stood to attention and shouted it, every day. As we got older, we woke up and realized that it was pure bullshit!" Mehmet uses the primeval Swedish word "skitsnack!"[450] He continues: "Mom and dad didn't know a word of Turkish – they hadn't gone to school. They didn't know a word of Turkish. I was embarrassed when mom came in her Kurdish clothes. 'Mom, dress more modern, more Turkish!' I would say. But as time passed, we learnt that we were indeed Kurds, not Turks. We got to hear our own history, but in secret."

The official response to Kurdish resistance has been incarceration, violence and forced relocation. Since, in the eyes of Turkish authorities, there has not existed Kurds, only Mountain Turks, the government has focused on a sort of education in how the system, the country and the society works. It appears as if the authorities have been thinking that if only the Mountain Turks could learn how to be and act, all the problems would be solved; that if they stopped resisting, they would be offered the same services that the rest of the Turks receive; that they can thank themselves for the bad conditions where they live. The authorities have categorically refused to talk about a "Kurdish problem," there has only been talk of a "situation," a "terrorism problem" or "socio-economic problems." When government representatives make statements in the media it is common that questions about identity are dismissed, and emphasis is put on economic needs. Highlighting anything but the economical, material situation is branded as "political." For instance, a claim that cultural identity is at the core of the conflict can be brushed aside by labeling it as a political claim. Thus, it is not the problem of those in power and the responsibility is pushed onto other politicians, those who agree that identity is at the heart of the conflict. In this way, those in power disclaim their responsibility of the situation.

It is worth noting that not all Kurds are over-enthusiastic about the term "the Kurdish problem," since it implies that the Kurds are the problem. For the Kurds, of course, it's the other way around; Turkey, Syria, Iraq, and Iran are the problem. Although many Kurds are not concerned with this, several Kurds consciously avoid talking about a "Kurdish problem" and opt for more neutral terminology, such as "the Kurdish issue" or "the Kurdish question." "The Kurdish problem" is a legacy from the European powers, who always knew that the Kurds were there and that they might be considered a separate country, but this did not go well with European interests.

Thus, for the Europeans the object, Kurd, became a problem. When I use "the Kurdish problem" in this book, it is with a sense of irony. Calling the Kurds a problem is itself a problem because it is a biased perspective.

Ironically, the fact that the authorities consider the main problem as socio-economic does not render many practical consequences. Poverty and unemployment in southeastern Turkey are much worse than in the rest of the country. This, of course, is related to the consequences of long-standing war, but it is also a contributing factor in keeping the conflict going. Millions of Kurds were driven from their farms to the cities in the southeast or elsewhere in Turkey. This has contributed to persistent unemployment in the cities. In the large city of Diyarbakır in the southeast, unemployment was estimated at between 30% and 70% in 2000-2002. In 2014, unemployment was measured at 17% in the Kurdish southeastern region, and 24% in the Kurdish eastern region, against the national average of 10%. It should not surprise anyone that frustrated young people who have the opportunity to "do something" about their hopeless situation by fighting for the PKK choose this.

PKK

When Abdullah "Apo" (uncle) Öcalan - the PKK founder and undisputed leader - came to Ankara and Istanbul in the late 1960s and early 1970s, the awareness of the Kurds about their distinctive identity had begun to resurface. The first generation born after the rebellions in the 1920s and 1930s had grown up, and the memories of the authorities' brutality were not as vivid for them as for their parents. As a political science student in Ankara in the early 1970s, Öcalan came in contact with left-wing student groups. He attended a protest in 1972 (not long after the 1971 military coup) and was arrested with the other protesters. During his imprisonment he was educated by the other political prisoners, and when he was released after seven months, he was a changed man. In addition to his own experience of being imprisoned for months for participating in a nonviolent demonstration, the experiences of his fellow prisoners had convinced him that armed revolution was the only way to bring about a change.

After a couple of years of encounters with likeminded Kurds in Ankara, a group that called themselves the Kurdistan Revolutionaries eventually came into being. In 1977, Öcalan began touring the Kurdish areas of the southeast to hold secret meetings with supporters of the revolution. One evening in November 1978 a secret meeting was held in a village some distance from Diyarbakir. Most of the twenty participants in the meeting had previously been involved in the work of starting an illegal political party. At the meeting the party program was adopted, and the party was named PKK (*Partiya Karkeren Kurdistan* - Kurdistan's Labor Party). The party was not to participate in the official Turkish political system or run in parliamentary elections; it was to lead the armed struggle for an independent Kurdistan.

When the PKK was founded, there were already nine - perhaps more - illegal organizations that, at least in theory, had Kurdish independence as their purpose. They were all on the political left and, as seems to be the fate of parties on the outer left, the number grew as disagreements about ideology led to separation and founding of new parties. The PKK stood out by pointing to violence as the only sensible means of change. Öcalan was not gentle in his criticism of the other groups, and debates could develop into violence. Even before the PKK was founded, the Kurdistan Revolutionaries had participated in skirmishes against other groups for domination of territories. For Öcalan and his followers, it was about clearing away the internal Kurdish quarreling so that the revolution could start, so that the shooting could be directed at the right target, namely the Turkish state.

Some of the powerful landowning Kurdish tribal leaders were very unpopular further down in the social hierarchy. They collaborated with Turkish authorities and were seen as blood suckers who stole from the poor. After years of oppression, the Kurdistan Revolutionaries - and later the PKK – were perceived as people who could finally do something about the problem. Öcalan's group was of course considered a threat by the powerful landowners and in May 1978, one of Öcalan's men was shot and killed in the town of Hilvan, probably as a result of the Kurdistan Revolutionaries attempting to gain influence in the city. Öcalan was aware that a revenge attack could trigger a blood feud but had to demonstrate that he and his group were serious. After a couple of months, the Kurdistan Revolutionaries returned and killed the tribal leader. In the fighting that followed, Öcalan demonstrated that his group - unlike the other groups - believed what they were saying about fighting the oppression that the landowners, collaborating with the government, were responsible for. A later attempted assault on another powerful tribal leader reinforced this image of the PKK.

The late 1970s were a very turbulent time in Turkey, with many murders and arrests. So also in the southeast. In addition to armed struggles between Kurdish groups, where the PKK by the other groups were perceived as overly aggressive, there were rumors of an impending military coup. The military reinforced its presence in several places in the southeast, and in the spring of 1979 the PKK Central Committee member Şahin Dönmez was arrested. He knew the addresses of the PKK's hiding places in Diyarbakır, and Öcalan decided to escape the city. He sought refuge with sympathizers, but it became too risky for people to house PKK members. In July 1979, Öcalan fled to Syria. He was not to return to Turkey until 20 years later, in Turkish detention.

The military coup came on September 12, 1980. Order was re-established and tens of thousands in political opposition from all persuasions were arrested over the next three years. Torture in prison was widespread. The PKK in particular was hit hard by the arrests, and Öcalan decided it was too risky to maintain the organization's presence in Turkey. From Damascus he traveled to Beirut in Lebanon, where he got in touch with local Kurds who were mostly migrants from Kurdish areas in Turkey. He eventually got in touch with a Palestinian group who agreed to teach a handful of PKK members in guerrilla warfare. Not long after, more PKK members came to receive military training, and they were distributed among several Palestinian camps in Lebanon. Öcalan kept working strategically to ensure the survival of the PKK outside Turkey. He entered into an agreement with the powerful Kurdish leader Barzani in Iraq to establish PKK camps in the mountains of northern Iraq, close to the border with Turkey. Öcalan was thereby able to turn the flight of the PKK from a weakening to a strengthening; PKK soldiers were trained in Lebanon and learned to survive under harsh conditions in the mountains of northern Iraq.

The Ankara military regime handed over power to a civilian[451] government in December 1983. The mood in Turkey became less tense, and Öcalan decided in the first half of 1984 that the PKK was ready to launch the war. In the evening of August 15, two small PKK groups attacked military camps in two small towns in the southeast. The government soldiers were completely unprepared for such an attack and remained in the barracks under threat of being shot if they came out. The rebels were able to read their message in the town square in peace, and curious residents came and listened. In one city, the rebels filled up a truck with weapons from a storage building in the military camp and drove off. The attack was over, and the guerrilla soldiers went to hide in the mountains, as planned. The military initiated a searching operation for the perpetrators, but with no result. It is difficult to find a Mountain Turk who does not want to be found.

The war was underway, but how was information about this to be spread to the Kurdish villages? The PKK could not leave to the unreliable media to inform about what had happened. The rebels began to move from village to village, talking to the residents. The message that the fight was necessary and that there was no other sensible way to fight than with weapons, aroused interest, but people weren't immediately convinced. Wasn't this risky? How would the government respond? In October, while President Evren was traveling in the area, the PKK struck again and killed three soldiers. The army was shocked, and the (Kurdish) people were impressed. The army with several thousand soldiers in the area was unable to fight back against the guerrilla attacks of the PKK. Young men were convinced that the struggle made sense and they reported for duty to the PKK. Some joined the guerrilla groups in Turkey, others were sent to Iraq for training, yet others were asked to stay at home and be ready to be called upon.

In parallel with the war preparations of the PKK in the early 1980s, there was a bloody internal process that made it clear that the PKK had one leader. Period. Any attempt to question the decisions of Abdullah Öcalan was harshly dealt with. Stalin's purges in the 1930s were seen by several senior PKK members as the way to go. One of the victims was Çetin Güngör, who worked to gather support for the PKK among Kurds in Europe and was a senior member of the European PKK Committee. He was critical of the authoritarian way in which the PKK was ruled and believed people should discuss and make independent decisions based on their own experience and judgment. He wanted to discuss this at the PKK's second congress in August 1982. Öcalan protested and wondered if he had let himself shape too much by the Europeans. Others at the congress considered Güngör's concern as a diversion. Here they were, preparing for war. Why would they spend time and energy talking about totally unrelated things? Disappointed, Güngör returned to Europe but said that he would continue to address this issue. Öcalan responded by sending senior PKK members to Europe to talk about Güngör with others in the European Committee. Was Güngör really competent enough? Was he well grounded? Did he really have the PKK's and the Kurds' best interests in mind? The smearing campaign worked, and the pressure on Güngör increased. He finally announced, in October 1983, that he would leave the PKK but that he would continue to fight against the organization's "dangerous ideology." This led to the internal PKK newspaper calling Güngör a traitor at the beginning of 1984. Things had become really dangerous for Güngör. Already in 1977, two activists in the Kurdistan Revolutionaries had been killed when they said they would start their own group. The standard for how the PKK dealt with "traitors" had been set then.

After a bit of underground writing, Güngör decided to stop hiding. In November 1985 he attended a meeting for Kurdish activists in Stockholm. In a break, a young Kurd came up behind him and shot him dead. The killer insisted that the murder was about a personal conflict, but no one doubted that the PKK wanted the murder. In an information letter, the organization stated that the provocateur Güngör had been rightfully punished by "our people."

In addition to Güngör, at least ten other high-ranking PKK members (some of them former members) were killed from 1983 to 1985. Öcalan did not always explicitly order someone to be killed, but in classical mafia style it was made clear who was marked for death. For example, if you were branded as a "traitor" there was no doubt what had to be done. But also, people who had had ties to the traitor, or questioned the murder, could be killed. If you were perceived as a quarrelsome person who wanted to discuss all kinds of things, you were also at high risk.

But it was not only internally in the PKK that these purges took place. People in the Kurdish areas who were considered to be state collaborators were also killed, often with the whole family.[452] Particularly vulnerable were villages and families who had "village guards" among them. The guards were villagers who had been enlisted by the Turkish army to protect their village from the PKK. They received weapons and wages from the army, and it could be difficult to decline the much-needed extra income. The PKK did not like this and were not content with attacking only the village guards. In the first two months of 1987, at least 35 villagers were killed by the PKK, of which at least seven were children. In June of that year, 16 children and six women were killed in an attack on a village. The PKK newspaper warned that collaborators (i.e. people who cooperated with the state) would be annihilated. External criticism of the PKK's murder of civilians was met with a shrug; a PKK spokesperson explained that it was a war, and that people die in wars.

However, PKK's brutality did not arise in a vacuum. The government army has not been particularly eager to distinguish between civilians and combatants either. In addition, people were chased away from their villages, which were then burnt down to prevent PKK soldiers from having access to food and shelter. Since the war began in 1984 until today, it is estimated that as many as four million Kurds have been displaced from their villages and forced to settle in cities in the southeast or west. In 1994, the chief of the Turkish military called this strategy the "go hungry and surrender" strategy. A similar approach to one's own citizens is probably difficult to find among military strategists in other NATO countries. The PKK justify their methods by pointing to those of the Turkish military. Öcalan said at one point: "The whole of Kurdistan has been cleared [of its Kurdish population] by the Turks; is it so bad if the PKK clears a few fascist villages?"[453]

In addition, the PKK has killed many people in occupations that have symbolized the state's influence in the area. Teachers have been particularly vulnerable. In 1992, ten teachers were killed, the following year 34 teachers were killed. Many teachers who were sent to work in southeastern Turkey chose to quit instead of risking their lives for their jobs. Several schools were burned down, and hundreds of schools were closed due to a lack of teachers. To instill fear and loyalty, public employees and former PKK members were also murdered. In 1992 and 1993, the PKK killed about 500 "collaborators."

The government, in turn, killed people considered to help legitimize the struggle of the PKK, such as nationalist intellectuals and journalists, albeit in a less obvious way. Between 1992 and 1994, about 1,200 people were killed by "unknown perpetrators." In 1995, a parliamentary investigation commission concluded in this way: "`illegal formations' within the state bear some responsibility for mystery killings."[454] Who in the end were ultimately responsible for the killings will probably never be known. The authorities dismissed the murders as unimportant and claimed that the victims had not been real journalists. Prime Minister Demirel even claimed in 1992 that the journalists who had been killed so far were actually guerrillas. This competition between the government and the PKK to be the most ruthless party in an attempt to win has become a vicious circle that has hit the civilian population hard.

A relevant question is whether the PKK can rightly claim to represent the Kurdish population. The truth is that so far this has not been possible to find out. The government's limitations on freedom of expression mean that it has not been possible to discuss in an open and transparent manner what the Kurds really want. To the extent that nationalist movements have birthed leaders who have been able to formulate Kurdish requests, these leaders have been sentenced to imprisonment for years for separatism or supporting terrorist activity or both. The most well-known example in recent times is the head of HDP (*Halkların Demokratik Partisi* - People's Democratic Party), Selahattin Demirtaş, who was imprisoned in 2016 and sat for two years without judgment before being sentenced in September 2018 to four years and eight months for "spreading terrorist propaganda." Amnesty International and other human rights organizations condemned the verdict and court process, and the EU Human Rights Court ruled in November that year that the imprisonment and the verdict were against both international human rights and Turkey's own legal system.

But also the PKK in general and Abdullah Öcalan in particular have done their part to prevent the Kurds' wishes from being freely discussed. Two points in particular show this. One point is Öcalan's efforts to stop any discussion within the PKK. The way he shaped the PKK is in many ways reminiscent of a cult. A former PKK member explained it like this: "The thinking inside the PKK was that we were doing something that was holy, sacred. In that atmosphere, how could someone go and criticize you? (...) Ocalan laid out the path, and the rest of us followed."[455]

Academics have described Öcalan as a classical charismatic leadership type, defined by Max Weber as "deriving its legitimacy not from rules . . . but from a devotion to the specific and exceptional sanctity, heroism, or exemplary character of an individual person."[456] Although the PKK had statutes from 1978 and various regulations, "none of these functioned independently of Ocalan, who applied, manipulated, ignored, and changed everything at will."[457] He was also totally immune to hints that his strategy or tactics could go – or worse, had gone – wrong. If the PKK failed to achieve a goal, it was those in charge of implementing the mission who had made mistakes; a plan never had faults if it came from Öcalan. At the PKK congresses, all analyses had to be in line with Öcalan's vision, and "he freely rewrote reports to incorporate his interpretation of what had happened and who was to blame."[458]

Öcalan, on several occasions, forced the PKK leaders to undergo humiliating and comprehensive self-criticism exercises, similar to those conducted during the Chinese Cultural Revolution. Öcalan's own brother escaped his own execution by writing a number of self-critical texts, one of them 106 pages long. The fact that the leaders carried out such self-criticism without protest (something that would be life threatening) helped strengthen the perception that Öcalan was infallible. The PKK was Öcalan and Öcalan was the PKK. When the PKK's most acclaimed military commander, Şemdin Sakık, protested to Öcalan's unrealistic military objectives, Öcalan gave him an impossible mission in Hatay. The PKK had no particular presence there as the population was (and is) quite ethnically mixed with both Turks, Arabs, Armenians and Kurds. In addition, the terrain was flat - there were no mountains in which to hide. The mission would be meaningless and probably deadly. Sakık deserted and was eventually arrested by Turkish security forces. Öcalan "put protecting his leadership first, to the point that he would destroy his chief military commander."[459]

The second point showing that the PKK and Öcalan have prevented free discussion among Kurds is linked to one specific event, namely the 1993 "national assembly." The stated intention was to establish a kind of legislative assembly, which would also represent the Kurds internationally. The PKK invited participants broadly, also from the Kurdish diaspora in Europe, but having learnt from earlier PKK treatment of nonconformists most people without PKK connections stayed away. However, several were elected as delegates to the assembly, which was held in a PKK camp in northern Iraq in the spring of 1993. A total of 130 delegates made sub-committees, elected ministers among themselves for different issue areas, and wrote hundreds of pages of law. In August of the same year, Öcalan changed his mind and wanted to dissolve the assembly, but the assembly leader refused. All delegates were asked to write a report where they agreed to dissolve the assembly, but the leader, a former politician, wrote that he did not accept a dissolution, that no individual could dissolve the assembly, and that the assembly reflected the will of the people. A vote was held and more than 100 of the 130 delegates voted against dissolution. However, Öcalan's decision was taken, and the congregation was simply terminated by the PKK soldiers.

The congregation had made provision for concrete and real Kurdish self-determination, and it was under Kurdish control in northern Iraq, beyond the reach of Turkish authorities. Although many Kurds had failed to attend because it was organized by the PKK, the congregation had potential as a first step towards legitimate Kurdish policymaking. The form of the meeting facilitated a genuine, free and relatively representative exchange of views. But when Öcalan's romantic thoughts of Kurdish self-determination began to take shape, it became clear that the power of the congregation would be at the expense of PKK's and Öcalan's power. This was too much. The PKK was unable to prove its legitimacy in the face of reality.

More War, Less War

While the assembly was gathered in northern Iraq, the PKK declared a unilateral ceasefire. President Özal had since becoming president hinted that it might be possible to come up with a solution for the Kurdish problem. In 1991, he acknowledged that Kurdish did exist and that there were about 12 million people who spoke Kurdish. The same year, he lifted the ban on the use of Kurdish language in public which was introduced by the military regime in 1983. With the assistance of Kurdish leaders in northern Iraq, he had established a form of communication line with Öcalan, despite the protests from the government and military leaders. Was he really going to negotiate with terrorists? The PKK suspected there could be opportunities for real progress for the Kurds and did not have much to lose by declaring a ceasefire. President Özal, however, had to be very careful not to be perceived as giving in to terrorists. On April 16, 1993, Öcalan declared that he extended the ceasefire. He also called on Ankara to guarantee Kurdish cultural rights, put an end to ill-treatment, provide a general amnesty, and lift all restrictions on Kurdish broadcasting and education. The day after, Özal died suddenly of a heart attack, 65 years old.

"Özal was a good president," says Mehmet as he drives me back to the airport. "He had these roads built. He said he would fix the Kurdish problem before he died. He was himself Kurdish, you know. But two weeks later they killed him." Who killed him, I wonder.

"MIT," replies Mehmet, and by that he retells one of many conspiracy theories that abound in Turkey in general and perhaps particularly among the Kurds. Truth is, as the saying goes, the first victim of war. When news is manipulated and the truth is obscured by the men with weapons, it provides good breeding ground for speculations about what is actually going on. MIT, the Turkish intelligence service, is supposed to have killed Özal and made it look like a heart attack. The rumors of this have evidently been resilient, because in 2012 an autopsy was performed, but no evidence of poisoning was found. Regardless, the perception that he was killed lives on.

Öcalan repeated his promise of a ceasefire, but to no avail. Without Özal in the presidential chair, no one was pushing to investigate why the Kurds were so dissatisfied. The military, in turn, had little regards for the PKK's ceasefire, and several PKK positions were attacked, and several guerrilla soldiers killed. At the end of May 1993, Öcalan announced to his soldiers that they could strike back if attacked. This was interpreted differently by different commanders. A PKK commander set up roadblocks in his area, and the guerrilla soldiers stopped a bus full of unarmed government soldiers and four teachers. They were ordered out of the bus and shot - all the teachers and 33 of the 35 soldiers were killed. This marked the end of the ceasefire and the battles resumed with full force.

The war was at its most bloody in the mid-1990s and included Turkish attacks on PKK camps in northern Iraq.[460] The civilian population was forced to flee to the cities, and many were killed. In addition, the army changed its strategy. Instead of staying in the military camps and carrying out brief raids on areas where they believed the guerrilla soldiers were, they began to remain in the mountains for weeks at a time. The guerrillas could not move as freely anymore and partially lost contact with their supply lines. Several surrendered. Requests to Öcalan for a change of tactics fell on deaf ears.

Öcalan realized that something had to be done but thought the right thing to do was to start a mass mobilization and establish battalions that could stand against the government army. The commanders did not believe what they heard. The rural areas that the PKK had been so dependent on had been emptied out of friendly Kurds, and many guerrillas had been killed. The recruitment had also decreased. Not surprisingly, Öcalan stood his ground, and little changed on the battlefield. The guerrillas were more defensive, but to some extent managed to maintain their fighting power. In addition, the PKK began to use more desperate measures, such as suicide bombing, mainly by female guerrilla soldiers. The war continued with the PKK on the defensive but still able to carry out attacks and to retreat to the impenetrable mountains of northern Iraq. Turkey managed to reduce the PKK threat but not to remove it and chose not to do anything about the deeper Kurdish grievances.

In October 1998, Turkey had had enough of Syria's hosting of Öcalan and threatened with war if the country did not extradite him. The threat was taken seriously, and Öcalan realized he was no longer welcome. He disappeared from Syria, but neither central PKK figures nor Turkish intelligence knew where he traveled. He flew from Damascus to Athens because he believed that Greece, due to its poor relationship with Turkey, would give him asylum. But he was wrong and went on to Russia, then to Italy where he was detained by the authorities. This became a big news story. While Italy contemplated their next move, Öcalan was held in a form of house arrest on the outskirts of Rome. Weeks went by. In January 1999, Öcalan decided that Russia was perhaps the best option after all and returned there but was not well received and eventually ended up in Athens again. Like a piece of hot coal, Greece sent him in the direction of the Netherlands via Belarus, but there never came a plane to transport him to the Netherlands, and he was returned to Athens, passed on to Corfu, and finally to Kenya where he would stay with the Greek ambassador until he received a residence permit from an African country. It is unclear which other country's intelligence services were involved, but somehow Turkish intelligence lured Öcalan inside a car and transported him to the airport. From there, the journey went directly to Turkey.

Probably in an attempt to avoid the death penalty, Öcalan agreed to a number of confessions and provided details about PKK's activities and supporters. He was also full of praise for Turkish history and Atatürk. He acknowledged the suffering of many Turks but said nothing about the Kurdish suffering. "He is a coward," Kemal Burkay concluded, an important voice in the Kurdish diaspora in Europe.[461] Burkay had criticized the PKK and the organization's violence from the beginning. He explained to a journalist that the Kurds and the PKK were shocked by Öcalan's exaggerated willingness to co-operate.[462] Unfortunately for Öcalan, his repentance did not affect his sentencing. On June 29, 1999, on the same date that Sheik Sa'id and his co-conspirators were hanged in 1925, Öcalan was sentenced to death. Two months later he gave public orders that the PKK should withdraw from Turkey and end the armed struggle.

The Kurds were astray. What should they make of Öcalan now? Had they lost their family members in war to no avail? For many, it was easiest to continue believing in Öcalan and the PKK, and to interpret Öcalan's change as a sensible strategic change. After so many years of war and death, trying out other ways to achieve basic rights for the Kurds did not seem entirely wrong.

The Kurdish areas entered a less violent period. In 2002, the Turkish parliament adopted reforms to comply with EU membership requirements and abolished the death penalty. Öcalan's punishment was turned into lifetime in prison. That same year, Recep Tayyip Erdoğan's AKP came to power, and parliament slightly relaxed the restrictions on Kurdish language and culture. Time went by and not much occurred. Turkey had seemingly won over the PKK; why make a lot of concessions then? For the Kurds, however, the road towards equal citizenship between Turks and Kurds was still long, and in 2004 Öcalan lost patience and canceled the ceasefire. The fighting and violence resumed. The years that followed were marked by fights between the PKK and Turkish security forces. Terrorist attacks were also carried out, among other things by the group Kurdistan's Freedom Falcon (TAK), with unclear (but very probable) connections to the PKK. While the PKK has mainly sent its bombs to the military and police - though with significant civilian casualties - TAK has to a larger extent targeted civilians, including tourists, in cities including Istanbul, Ankara and Izmir. TAK carried out a limited number of terrorist attacks until 2016, when the group suddenly assumed responsibility for nine bomb attacks in the course of one year (February 2016 - January 2017). The last one took place in Izmir on January 11, 2017. Two people were killed and nine were injured. The rest of 2017 and all of 2018 progressed without terrorist attacks.

In parallel with the increased violence from 2004, there were also processes that pulled in the direction of peace. The PKK alternated between declaring ceasefires and carrying out attacks. Prime Minister Erdoğan was good at saying the right words and claiming the problems in the east were completely possible to resolve through democratic means. This gave him and AKP votes in the election in 2007, including from the Kurds. In 2009, Erdoğan officially launched "The Democratic Opening," which was a series of reforms that would facilitate constructive, solution-oriented processes. A few years earlier, he had replaced the military group that communicated with

Öcalan in prison, with a civilian intelligence group closer to himself. This led to a number of secret negotiation meetings, including in Oslo (hence the name "the Oslo Process"), which seemed to be important steps in the right direction. In October 2009, Turkey was going to allow 34 Kurds to "come down from the mountains" in northern Iraq and offered amnesty as a trust-building measure. Eight of the Kurds were PKK soldiers, the rest were people who had fled to a PKK-led refugee camp south of the border. Large groups of Kurds traveled to the border station to celebrate their return. The celebrations, which were perceived as triumphant cheering, were hard to swallow by the Turkish authorities. According to them, the agreement was that the Kurds would come in a nice and quiet way without much publicity. The media in the west reported in capital letters on the celebrations, and the authorities felt betrayed by the PKK's inability to be discrete. The amnesty arrangement did not go so well and in June 2010, the court filed criminal cases against all eight guerrilla soldiers.

The so-called Oslo Process ended with a violent incident in the town of Silvan near Diyarbakır in July 2011, one month after Erdoğan's AKP had received 50% of the votes in the parliamentary elections. The army lost 13 soldiers and the PKK lost seven. Both sides blamed each other. Just two months earlier, the army had killed 19 guerrillas in two different attacks, and the PKK had responded by attacking Erdoğan's electoral bus, killing a policeman in the attack. Violence escalated again. In particular, the Turkish air raid in December 2011, killing 34 villagers that were smuggling oil products from Iraq to Turkey, aroused the anger of the Kurds. It became the most violent period in the conflict since the 1990s, and about 1000 people were killed until the spring of 2013. New peace talks started in late 2012, in parallel with sporadic violent incidents. The talks ended in July 2015 with a suicide bombing allegedly committed by the Islamic State (IS) in the border city of Suruç. Thirty-two people connected to the political party HDP were killed, and violence erupted in several Kurdish cities. This led the PKK and the Turkish military to take up the fight again. The year 2016 was very bloody with over 2200 killed including civilians and soldiers on both sides. After this, the violence has decreased somewhat; in 2018 a little more than 500 people were killed.

Obstacles to Peace

It does not seem that any of the agenda-setting leaders who have made sure to keep the violence going have had any sort of eureka moment. After almost 40 years of killing, forced relocation, imprisonment and torture, there is ostensibly no acknowledgment that the method does not work if the goal is to end the violence, or to have it one's way. Unfortunately, the politicians have not ensured a free press which could have helped them look at the problem from different angles. For fear of the consequences, journalists have basically said whatever is safe to say. The popular newspaper writer Oktay Ekşi wrote in 1988: "[I]n Turkey there does not exist a 'Kurdish minority.' (...) What does exist are some Turks who accept or think that they came from an ethnic group known as Kurds.[463]"

But there are also journalists who have chosen the risk that comes with challenging the official narrative. Ahmet Altan tried to get his readers to join him in a thought experiment in an article in 1995:

> What if Mustafa Kemal had been an Ottoman pasha born not in Salonika, but in [the Kurdish region of] Mosul ... and the republic formed was called the Republic of Kurdey? What if it were said that in Kurdey there were no Turks and everyone in fact was a Kurd and those who thought themselves Turks were, in fact, sea Kurds. Would we Turks have agreed to this ... Or would we have insisted that our Turkish identity, our language, our culture be accepted, that we be accepted as equal citizens in this country? ... Democracy is accepting that what we Turks would have wanted if we had lived in the Kurdey Republic, are the same desires that Kurds today are raising.[464]

Because of the article, Altan was fired from the newspaper Milliyet and was given a suspended sentence for encouraging ethnic hatred. Another journalist, Cengiz Çandar, wrote the following when PKK leader Öcalan was arrested in 1999: "This is the time to act in a cool-headed manner, however difficult that may be. I think that the 'Kurdish problem' created the PKK and Apo [Öcalan], rather than vice versa. The solution lies ... in making democratic arrangements which would enable [Kurds] to fully express themselves politically and culturally."[465] In other words, let the Kurds live out their identity and you will see that the violence disappears. It does not require great cognitive abilities to acknowledge that Çandar was probably right. After all, the Kurdish desire to be Kurdish has been an explicit part of both nonviolent and violent attempts at change since Turkey was created. However, there are several obstacles that contribute towards Turkey not choosing this path. These obstacles can be called war factors because they contribute – each in their own way – to increasing the likelihood of the war continuing.

The lack of a free press is certainly a war factor, and it is closely connected to another important war factor, namely the law and the way it is enforced by the judicial system. It is a crime to encourage "separatism" and to "support terrorism," something that may sound plausible. But the police can keep people imprisoned for years before their cases are tried in a court, so that they may be in prison for a very long time before they get the opportunity to prove their innocence. In addition, the courts have adopted a very broad interpretation of "separatism" and "supporting terrorism." The aforementioned Demirtaş[466] case is the latest and most well-known, but there are countless others who are in jail because something they have said is linked in a creative way to "separatism" and "terrorism."

If you run a high personal risk by suggesting that the Kurdish problem should be dealt with differently, it is safest to continue as before: Consider the problem as only separatism and terrorism and hand it over to the military to be dealt with. On the Kurdish side the law and the judicial system contribute to the Kurds' choosing violence and the PKK rather than nonviolence and civil society. The punishment for fighting for Kurdish rights is so high no matter what method one chooses, that for many Kurds it seems more sensible to enlist as a guerrilla soldier than to pursue nonviolent activism and politics.

A third war factor is the lies that Turkish authorities and media have spread about what has happened during the war. The term "lie" is, however, a simplification, as it has been a mixture of lack of information, selective information, and direct lies. Authorities have effectively prevented journalists and non-governmental organizations from establishing the facts about skirmishes and killings. In addition, law enforcement has looked away. For example, when the government army forced villagers away from their villages in the 1990s, the authorities claimed that the evacuation took place voluntarily and as a result of pressure and harassment from the PKK. In addition, the government's demonization of the PKK contributed to an undermining of all forms of Kurdish activism, including demands for universally acknowledged rights. Disinformation has thus affected Turkish public opinion, but it has also affected the

Kurdish in an unintentional way. When the PKK has committed abuses, and the media or the authorities have conveyed information about this, many Kurds have not taken it seriously. When it has not been possible to rely on information provided by the authorities, why should the Kurds suddenly believe in (true) stories of PKK abuse? Thus, a situation has arisen where many Turks dismiss everything that comes from the Kurdish side as separatism and support for terrorism, while many Kurds do not believe that the PKK has committed abuses, and they consider the PKK to be a legitimate representative for the Kurds. Why should the Turks make concessions when there are no legitimate demands from the Kurds? And why should other Kurds than the PKK convey demands when the Kurds already have a legitimate spokesperson?

A fourth war factor is the loss suffered by thousands of Turkish families when their sons and daughters have been killed in war. The sacrifice and grief of the families are used politically as arguments for not giving anything to the Kurds; what has a Turkish family's son died for if the authorities are going to give the PKK what they are asking for? Ironically, it is the PKK's violence that keeps this factor alive. The intention is to forcefully demand rights for the Kurds, while the consequence is that their violence causes politicians to go against reform and ask for "tougher" (that is, more violent) measures against the guerilla fighters.

An obvious fifth war factor mirrors the fourth; all the losses that Kurdish families have suffered, both because of the military's warfare, but also the government's persistent discrimination and ill-treatment of Kurds. Also, the killings by "unknown perpetrators" and the evacuation of millions of Kurds from their villages have caused their share of the Kurdish frustration and sense of injustice. The behavior of the government has thereby driven many a frustrated young Kurd to the PKK. This too is ironically the opposite of the intention behind the state's actions, which has been to stop recruitment to the PKK.

A sixth war factor is the inability of the Kurds to formulate exactly and specifically what they want. This leads to Turkish fears that what the Kurds really want is separation and establishment of their own state. A relevant example is the vague concept of "democratic autonomy" which PKK leader Öcalan launched in 2004. It is constantly being used in different contexts, and it is usually unclear what the person using it means. "Democratic autonomy – ordinary people don't understand what this means. I don't think BDP understand what they mean [when they say it]. It's just a phrase coming from Öcalan," Nebahat Akkoç, an activist for Kurdish women's rights, said to the International Crisis Group in 2011.[467] Another Kurdish leader, Ahmet Türk, tried to explain: "We just want a kind of autonomy. This could mean local parliaments, control of health and education. We just want a share. We see it in Spain, in Scotland, in Ireland; Italy has 27 regions ... we don't say federalism,[468] we say autonomy."[469]

The lacking ability to formulate specific desires is of course linked to both the authorities' and PKK's limitations on freedom of expression, mentioned earlier. Combined with the authorities' discrimination against the Kurds,[470] this leads to frustration that causes the Kurds to demand their rights in an angry but vague way. This, in turn, causes "mainstream Turks [to become] more suspicious and deepens mutual misunderstanding."[471] Thus, it may seem safer to reject the demands rather than examine what they are actually about.

A seventh war factor is NATO's support to Turkey, ostensibly regardless of the acts of violence Turkey is committing against its own population. The allies have in their treaty committed themselves to "safeguard the freedom (...) of their peoples, founded on the principles of democracy, individual liberty and the rule of law." Turkey blatantly and openly went against this in the mid-1990s (and still does, although on a smaller scale). Nevertheless, especially the United States, but also Germany, the United Kingdom and France have poured weapons into Turkey's military escapades.[472] The beautiful words about democratic principles, individual liberty and the rule of law do not seem to have any practical consequences within the alliance. Turkey is not in a situation where the country should alienate itself from its most important guarantor against being invaded. If NATO let it have consequences when member states broke with the treaty, Turkey's relationship with its Kurds could look quite different.

The conflict between the Kurds and the Turkish state has two main layers; one is the basic, deep conflict that is about identity, and the other is the way in which the conflict has played out between the PKK and the government. The latter has received the most attention. About 40,000 people have been killed and four million have been displaced from their villages. Naturally, this has enormous social and economic consequences for both the region and the country.

When Turkey became a country, Diyarbakır was ranked number three in the government's socio-economic development index. Since then, it has steadily declined, to 63rd place out of 81 cities in the ranking in 2003.[473] By that same year, Turkey had spent well over USD 300 billion on fighting the PKK,[474] equivalent to nearly two times the 2017 government budget.[475] However, the government has not been close to fulfilling its international obligations to meet the needs of victims of warfare, which would have cost many more billions. The real costs of the war (if we only look at those costs that can be measured in money) are in other words much higher.

The two layers of the conflict have influenced each other, and the losses, wounds and traumas caused by the violent conflict have reduced the political willingness to do something about the underlying causes of the conflict. In order to break the cycle, a large enough group of both decision makers and people at the grass roots, on both sides, must choose to break it.

7. The Lost Armenian Fatherland

Places mentioned in this chapter. At the beginning of the 1900s, the largest single concentration of Armenians lived in Istanbul, but the majority of Armenians lived spread across the east. They did not constitute a majority of the population in any province but constituted a majority in an area around Lake Van and northeast of Adana.[476]

"What I have seen and heard passes all imagination. I thought I was passing through a part of hell. They arrive by the thousands. (...) As far as the eye can reach are to be seen mounds where 200 to 300 corpses are buried in the ground pell mell."[477] This is how an eyewitness described the scene in a telegram that was published by the American Committee for Armenian and Syrian Relief during the First World War. The author of the telegram had visited the concentration camps in Deir ez-Zor in the Syrian desert. The Ottomans had set up the camps in Syria and Iraq to manage the hundreds of thousands of Armenians who had been forced to walk from different parts of Anatolia since the spring of 1915. Another eyewitness had visited a camp, or rather an area (which in his eyes could not qualify as a camp) close to Aleppo in Syria where thousands of Armenians were held. The Armenians were

> living in the open air, herded together like cattle, without any protection against heat or cold, almost without clothes, and given very irregular and entirely inadequate food. ... Under a tent measuring about five or six square metres I saw roughly four hundred orphan children [sic]. They were starving. These wretched children are meant to receive 150 grams of bread per day. It often happens that they receive nothing for two or three days. The death rate is naturally extremely high.[478]

They were mainly women, children and elderly who had survived the torturous march from their respective hometowns in Anatolia to Syria. The march ended in concentration camps in current Syria and Iraq where the Armenians died by the tens of thousands from disease and starvation. Most of the Armenian men of fighting age suffered a different fate: They were usually rounded up separately and killed. It had been the decision of members of the Young Turk government of the Ottoman Empire, panicking from how badly things were going during the First World War. Too many Armenians behaved treacherously, they thought, and therefore none of them could be trusted. They had to disappear from Anatolia.

Hayrenik - The Fatherland

At the beginning of 1915 there were probably between 1.5 and 2 million Armenians in the Ottoman Empire.[479] The largest single concentration of Armenians was in Istanbul, but the majority resided in the eastern provinces of Anatolia, although they did not constitute a majority in any one province.[480] Armenians considered this area their fatherland - an area where their forefathers had lived since time immemorial. We do not know exactly how the Armenians ended up in what is now known as the Armenian Highlands, east of the Anatolian Plateau, but most historians and archaeologists agree that it is related to the migration of the Hittites into Anatolia around 2,000 B.C., that is, around 3,000 years before the arrival of the first Turkish tribes into Anatolia. The Armenian language is - like the Hittite language - Indo-European. Historical and archaeological studies suggest that several people groups moved into the Armenian Highlands and formed a federation of people known as the Armens.[481]

Armenia prides itself with being the first Christian country in the world. The Armenian King Tiridates III became a Christian in the year 280, and in 301 declared his realm as Christian. As early as around 390 A.D. the Bible was translated into Armenian (more than a thousand years before Martin Luther translated it into German). In 2001 Armenia celebrated 1,700 years as a Christian country. This is not to say that the Armenia over which Tiridates III ruled has been a stable, singular country since then. Armenia has at times been independent, at times occupied, at times more than one kingdom, at times one or more vassal states. When the Seljuk chief Alp Arslan won the battle of Mantzikert in 1071 (see chapter 1), this marked the start of a grand period not only for the Seljuks but for the Armenians too, who were able to take strategic fortresses and become a dominant force in Cilicia. The period coincided, however, with various invasions from Turkic speaking tribes.[482] At the beginning of the 16th century, the Ottomans conquered Armenia, but the Persians to the east did not simply accept this. The Persians and Ottomans took turns governing Armenia. Towards the end of the 19th century, Russia moved in from the north and took control of the eastern parts of Armenia, while the Ottomans controlled the western part.

Around the middle of the 19th century, Armenians were the largest ethnic group in the six eastern Ottoman provinces Van, Bitlis, Erzurum, Diyarbakır, Kharput and Sivas. Five of those province names are still in use in Turkey - only Kharput is no longer in use (but all the provinces are smaller. In the latter half of the 19th century, the area that is now approximately Turkey consisted of 16 provinces. Turkey today has 81 provinces.) There was also a concentration of Armenians along the coast of Cilicia (Turkey's southeast).[483]

Although the relationship between the Armenians, Kurds and Turks was not characterized, generally, by conflict and violence, it is probably an exaggeration to claim that the Christians and Muslims were living peacefully side by side. How one understands the word "peacefully" determines the accuracy of the claim. If we are talking about so-called "negative peace," meaning that injustice and tension between groups are prevalent, but there is little overt violence, then it makes sense to use the word "peaceful." As explained in chapter 1, the Ottoman system was set up in a way that led to Christians dominating the business sector, and the capitulations gave many Christians competitive advantages. This pulled in the direction of making the Armenians wealthier than their Muslim neighbors, causing inequality. Pulling in the other direction was the discriminatory taxation of non-Muslims vs. Muslims. This had local variations. An Ottoman document from 1847 conveys the complaint from an Armenian community in Sivas Province:

> Muslim and Armenian residents in the village of Zara used to pay equal annual taxes as required. Recently, however, Muslims forcefully reduced their own tax and added [the reduced amount] to the non-Muslims' tax. They imposed a tax on non-Muslims that was one and a half times the amount of their [own] tax.[484]

There are many Ottoman documents like this, recording the way in which Armenians felt unjustly treated by the authorities.

The injustice that people experienced was not always the result of intentional discrimination by the authorities. Sometimes it was the lack of government control that contributed to resentment between groups. When, in the 1840s, the Ottoman government attempted to implement reforms in the eastern provinces, the local rulers resisted, realizing that this meant they themselves would lose power. When the central government responded by removing the local rulers, a power vacuum arose that the government was unable to fill. Several small tribal groups, mainly Kurdish, started harassing the sedentary population, both Muslim and Christian.[485]

Adding to the damage was the fact that Armenians, being Christians, were not allowed to keep arms. This meant that in a context with limited state capacity to enforce order, non-Muslims could not protect themselves and were more vulnerable to bandits and other types of aggressors. Especially in the east there was a problem of Kurdish groups attacking, plundering and sometimes taking the land of non-Muslims.[486] The Armenian-Kurdish relationship was the cradle of the larger conflict yet to come between the government and Armenians.[487]

Naturally, the discriminatory nature of the Ottoman system led to increased nationalism among the minority groups. It started off as demands for reform or demands for the rights that had already in principle been given to them through reforms without being implemented everywhere. The Armenians requested guarantees of life and property and fair taxation. When this did not seem to happen, some Armenians lost their patience and founded organizations that would promote demands they believed to be representative of the Armenians. The two best known groups were the Hanchak (founded 1887), which used violence, including terrorism and assassinations, even against more moderate Armenians; and the Dashnak (founded 1890), a group that advocated for reform within the empire. One missionary based in southeast Anatolia wrote in his memoirs about the efforts of the Hanchak to raise a rebellion in 1895:

> During the summer three revolutionary emissaries had passed through Aintab [now: Gaziantep], preaching an immediate uprising, and attempting to levy funds for the same. They had been given a hearing, but little more, only one timid man contributing to their exchequer. They passed on to Marash [now: Kahramanmaraş] and Zeitoon [now: Süleymanlı], and we heard alarming rumors of their success in that region. One of the leading pastors of the Protestant Armenian community, at considerable risk to himself, went with me to Marash in the attempt to dissuade the foolish people from any idea of an armed uprising. We assembled some twenty leading men from the different Armenian communities, and tried to reason with them; but they were carried away with their revolutionary schemes and would listen to no one. When the storm they raised blew over there were but two of that score of men alive.[488]

Between 1894 and 1896, the sultan, Abdülhamid, had had enough of the noise coming from Armenian groups and "encouraged massacres of Armenians in order to unify his populace and scare people from flirting with (the wrong type of) nationalist ideas, and as many as 200,000 may have been killed."[489] The wrong type of nationalist idea was any idea that diverged from seeing the Ottoman Empire as the best solution for its inhabitants.

Although nothing, of course, can justify these killings, the sultan had reason to be worried about Armenian nationalism. A decade and a half earlier, in 1878, when the Treaty of Berlin was signed after the war with Russia, an Armenian delegation had been present during the negotiations. They had been able to get the participating states to insert an article into the treaty requiring the sultan to implement "reforms demanded by local requirements" in the provinces where Armenians lived.[490] An Armenian bishop later described this as the unveiling of the name of the Armenians, which "for the first time is acquiring a political appearance" rather than "a mere religious appearance." It was through this international treaty that the Armenian problem was "turning into an international problem."[491]

The Armenian delegation as such, however, was not content with the treaty article, which could mean whatever the sultan wanted it to mean. They formally protested against a result which did not include an independent Armenian state: "The Armenian delegation will return to the east carrying with it the lesson that without struggle and without insurrection nothing can be obtained. Nevertheless, the delegation will never cease addressing petitions until Europe has satisfied its just claims."[492] Not only was it clear that the Armenians would keep fighting for more autonomy, they were also explicit about working internationally to put pressure on the Ottoman government.

The "struggle" and "insurrection" led to a heightened consciousness among Armenians that an alternative to their current situation was possible, but it came at a high price. Interestingly, before the Armenians started to work for reforms during the last decades of the 19th century, "they were famously considered the 'most loyal community' among Ottoman Christian citizens."[493] After the killings in 1894-96, there were no major massacres of Armenians until 1909.

In 1908, the coup of the Young Turks had resulted in the reintroduction of the constitution that Sultan Abdülhamid had abolished in 1878. This brought with it a number of concessions to the minorities; Armenians could run for parliament, serve in the army, Armenian newspapers were allowed to be published, and the Armenian national assembly was unbanned. Raids on Armenian villages by Kurdish nomads decreased. Leading Young Turk figures, such as Enver Pasha and Talat Pasha, who a few years later became key architects of the genocide, went around the country and preached unity and fraternity. They

> went to Armenian churches, schools, and graveyards, where they paid respects to fallen Armenians who had died in the antisultan struggle, and made powerful speeches pointing to cooperation between Turks and Armenians. Enver told 'children that the old days of Moslem-Christian strife had passed forever and that the two peoples were now to live together as brothers and sisters.'[494]

At this point the Young Turks did not see the Armenians as a threat to the Ottoman regime. The emphasis was on the Ottoman identity, and as long as the additional, ethnic or religious identity was not being used in a separatist manner, it was viewed a normal aspect of being Ottoman.[495]

The seemingly bright Armenian future within this new, constitutional Ottoman Empire would soon look dark. On April 13, 1909, there was a countercoup where those who had lost power and privilege the year before were able to reinstall the sultan for a period of ten days. The Young Turks who had taken power in 1908 were forced to resign, and Sultan Abdülhamid promised greater attention to Islamic law.[496] As recounted in Chapter 2, the Young Turks quickly sent for reinforcements and were able to retake power and replace Abdülhamid with his brother Mehmet V.

During these turbulent days in April in 1909, the drama mainly took place in Istanbul, but far, far to the southeast, in Adana, massacres took place that have not yet been fully understood or explained by historians.[497] In a matter of a couple of weeks, more than 20,000 Armenians were killed, within the city and in the surrounding areas.[498] Some sources claim that it was Sultan Abdülhamid who gave the order for the massacres. The killing was done by soldiers with a "massive participation of the Turkish population,"[499] illustrating the resentment many Muslims (of different ethnicities, not necessarily Turks) felt towards the Armenians. The Armenians owned a lot of property, controlled much of the trade, and had introduced tractors and other machines that potentially threatened the jobs of many of their workers. There were internal pockets of resistance to the madness taking place in Adana, however. The local Muslim religious leaders are known to have objected to the killings and stood in solidarity with the Armenian Church.[500] Given the extremely violent context, these Muslim leaders protested at great personal risk.

Naturally, the Adana massacres affected the loyalty of the Armenians. In addition, the Ottoman territorial losses following the Balkan wars in 1912 contributed to the perception among the Young Turks running the government that centralization and a streamlining of society was necessary to prevent the empire from disintegrating. They changed from being liberal and egalitarian to becoming "extreme chauvinists, bent on creating a new order."[501] One of the key Young Turk intellectuals wrote that a nation "must be a society consisting of people who speak the same language, have had the same education and are united in their religious and aesthetic ideals--in short those who have a common culture and religion."[502]

Furthermore, the fact that hundreds of thousands of Muslims had been chased from their homes in the Balkans, and the Albanian secession from the Ottoman Empire, increased suspicion and hostility towards the Christian minorities still within the Empire.

In this context of disintegration, Russia made matters worse by starting to collaborate with Ottoman Armenians to put in place reforms that would improve the Armenian situation. Russia had earlier been very skeptical towards accommodating Armenian demands but changed its assessment when realizing that a major Armenian uprising in the Ottoman Empire, with demands of a separate, Armenian state, might encourage Russian Armenians to do the same. Reform was better than uprising. After negotiations the Ottomans agreed to put in place a reform plan, which entailed the creation of two Armenian zones, one consisting of the aforementioned six provinces in the east, and one being the Trebizond province (now: Trabzon). These zones were to be administered from Istanbul by two neutral European inspectors. The tasks of these Europeans included overseeing liberalization reforms in the zones, and they were given the authority to "appoint and dismiss all officials and provisional judges" and given "the command of the gendarmerie and the disposal of the military forces for the maintenance of order." [503] (Talk about willingly handing over sovereignty!) Britain, France and Germany were present at the negotiations, but the final document was only signed, in February 1914, by the Ottomans and Russians.[504] The Ottomans were furious at this external meddling in internal affairs, but signed the plan nonetheless, probably hoping that they would now be left alone.

The fury of the Ottomans was not only directed at the Europeans, but also at their own Armenians who were blamed for this international humiliation. At a time of territorial crisis after the Balkan losses, the Armenians had not helped ameliorate the situation, but instead expanded and escalated it. The Young Turk government felt increasingly pressurized from all kinds of angles.

And then came a war more deadly and destructive than any war the world had seen.

Darkness

The assassination of the Austrian Archduke Franz Ferdinand on June 28, 1914, precipitated World War I. The Ottoman Empire had entered into an alliance with Germany, becoming the enemy of Britain, France and Russia. The Ottomans were not ready for another war, but Germany pressured them into attacking Russia's naval fleet in the Black Sea, causing both Russia, France and Britain to declare war on the Ottomans in the beginning of November 1914. The Ottomans would soon face a three-front war, against Russia in the east, the British and French in the west (Çanakkale/the Dardanelles), and the British in the south (Iraq). The Russians were aided by tens of thousands of Armenian voluntary soldiers, winning the Battle of Sarıkamış (near Kars). The Ottomans on February 25, 1915, ordered the disarming of their Armenian soldiers. As they retreated, the Ottoman forces massacred Armenian villages[505].

The Young Turk leadership panicked. They were losing in the east and the British and French were determined to get to Istanbul through the Dardanelles in the west, causing massive Ottoman casualties. With the extreme pressure that their enemies put on the Ottomans, threatening the very existence of the empire, how should the numerous treacherous Armenians be dealt with? In reality, far from all Armenians were fighting for Armenian independence, but dealing humanely and precisely with a politically complex, multiethnic reality proved to be too demanding under the given circumstances. The militarily minded Young Turk leadership decided that their main priority was to secure the survival of the empire, at any cost. With that mindset, and under that pressure, it seemed better to exaggerate to make absolutely sure that the "Armenian threat" disappeared, than to spend time and energy on assessing what a sufficient and humane measure would be.

Many of the official Ottoman records "disappeared" after the war, and access to relevant archives is still restricted by the Turkish government. Because of the lack of access to key official documents, researchers do not have a complete picture of who made the decision to exterminate the Armenians, but there is consensus that Enver Pasha, the minister of war, Talat Pasha, the minister of interior, and Cemal Pasha, the military commander of Istanbul, were key figures. The research community is clear that although the lack of public documents "makes it hard, if not impossible, to prove the exact extent of the involvement of the different persons and institutions, (...) it can no longer be denied that the CUP [Young Turks] instigated a centrally controlled policy of extermination."[506]

Despite the insufficient amount of Ottoman documents, there is a wealth of other sources to draw on to determine what went on in the minds of the Young Turk leadership. They gave public speeches, they sent telegrams and they had meetings with foreign diplomats. Enver Pasha told the American ambassador Morgenthau the following in the spring of 1915, after having explained to him how the Armenians had recently revolted in Van:

> [W]e cannot permit people in our own country to attack us in the back. We have got to prevent this no matter what means we have to resort to. It is absolutely true that I am not opposed to the Armenians as a people. I have the greatest admiration for their intelligence and industry, and I should like nothing better than to see them become a real part of our nation. But if they ally themselves with our enemies, as they did in the Van district, they will have to be destroyed. (...) During peace times we can use Platonic means to quiet Armenians and Greeks, but in time of war we cannot investigate and negotiate. We must act promptly and with determination.[507]

Talat Pasha similarly explained to the ambassador that the Armenians

> have openly encouraged our enemies. They have assisted the Russians in the Caucasus and our failure there is largely explained by their actions. We have therefore come to the irrevocable decision that we shall make them powerless before this war is ended.[508]

Enver further told Morgenthau that if the Armenians attacked Ottoman forces or helped the Russians in doing so, the Ottomans would "be compelled to use extreme measures against them."[509] The German ambassador Wolff-Metternich had a conversation with Talat Pasha towards the end of 1915, where Talat told him that they had discovered a "Russian-engineered large scale conspiracy" among Armenians near Aleppo and the border areas towards Russia. "It had been impossible to single out any individual culprit from the masses of these people. Only the deportation of the whole could ensure security."[510]

The "extreme measures" began as seemingly proportionate responses to specific Armenian threats. When thousands of Armenians who had fled to Van - where there already was a substantial Armenian population - started attacking police stations, killing large numbers of Muslims and burning down their houses, the government on April 24 undertook mass arrests of Armenians, which they had also done in Trebizond a few days earlier. The fighting in Van lasted one month and included the arrival of a Russian Armenian army that came to the assistance of the Ottoman Armenians. They massacred part of the Muslim population and set up an "Armenian state."

On May 27, 1915, the "Deportation Law" was passed, authorizing the deportation of Armenians in the Van province. Armenians elsewhere, notably in Zeytun and Maraş, were also rounded up and deported to southeast Anatolia and what is today the north of Syria. Then came the order to transport the Armenians further south, to the Syrian desert. Soon the orders for deportation of Armenians were cast ever wider and ended up including almost all Armenians in Anatolia.[511]

The word "deportation" may not sound all that inhuman, but actual deportation was only a minor part of what transpired. Firstly, adult males of fighting age were mainly not deported, but rounded up and executed, usually by shooting, throat-cutting or drowning in rivers and lakes or at sea. Secondly, women, children and elderly were ordered to walk to their destination (although there are exceptions. Some were allowed to go with carts and donkeys).[512] They were not given enough food and water, and when their shoes wore out, they had to continue barefoot. Along the way, many were raped in the villages and town they passed by the local population who were encouraged to do so by the soldiers transporting them. Many were killed afterwards, others died of starvation or thirst. Some pregnant women had their bellies cut open. Those who were able to hang on to life and made it all the way to the Syrian desert, ended up in concentration camps where they died in large numbers because of disease, thirst, starvation, and executions. The pattern of the "deportation" was "remarkably similar from one area to the next, indicating a well-orchestrated plan."[513]

> At the beginning of the war numerous bands were sent from Istanbul to Anatolia. They consisted of murderers and thieves freed from prison. They were trained for a week in the War Ministry square and then sent to the front with the help of the Special Organisation. It is these bands which committed the worst crimes in the Armenian atrocities.[514]

The Special Organization was a clandestine group of officers that at first had been under the direct control of Enver Pasha, and during the war played an important role in suppressing separatist behavior, especially in Arab parts of the empire, and became involved in terrorist attacks against Greek businesses in the west.[515] The Special Organization also became instrumental in the "deportation" of Armenians, under the direction of the Young Turk central committee member and medical doctor, Bahaettin Şakir.[516]

Most people do not spend time studying genocide, so it may be difficult to comprehend what exactly is meant by "atrocities" or "extreme measures." It is difficult to find the right words to characterize the nature of genocide. One could use words like darkness, insanity, or evil, but people fill these words with different things. In order to comprehend the gravity of the genocide, both the individual actions and the sum of them all, the scale; in order to comprehend what a human is capable of doing towards other humans, we have to look at some of the individual stories.

One well-known and well-told story is that by Fethiye Çetin. Çetin did not come to know that she was quarter Armenian until her grandmother Heranuş, a few years before she died, revealed that she was in fact Armenian. On the "death march" to the Syrian desert, Heranuş's mother saved young Heranuş's life by letting a Turkish officer adopt her. Heranuş was given a Turkish name and raised as a Turk and a Muslim.

The story of Heranuş begins in a village near the town Palu, north of Diyarbakır, where she had a happy childhood until she reached 4th grade. Her father had left for America in 1910 and he was still there in 1915. One day during the spring of 1915, gendarmes came and gathered everybody in the village. They killed the village headman, gathered all the men, young and old, beat them up and took them away. Nobody ever saw them again.

The women and children were taken to Palu, where people from other villages had also been gathered, including some men.

> They shut the women into the church courtyard. The men remained outside. Before long the women and children could hear blood-curdling screams from over the walls. Because the courtyard walls were very high, they could see nothing of what was happening on the other side. They stood there staring at each other; mothers, grandmothers, children were holding each other and shaking. The entire courtyard was trembling. Heranuş and her brothers clung to their mother's skirts, but though she was terrified, she was desperate to know what was going on. Seeing that another girl had climbed onto someone's shoulders to see over the wall, she went to her side. The girl was still looking over

> the wall; when, after a very long while, she came down again, she said what she had seen. All her life, Heranuş would never forget what came from this girl's lips: 'They're cutting the men's throats, and throwing them into the river.'[517]

The women and children were then allowed to return to their villages, only to find that their homes had been looted. The gendarmes soon returned and once again rounded up everybody in the village. This time they were ordered to start walking. The death march began. They soon ran out of food and water and had no means of acquiring more. The sick and tired started falling behind. Many years later Heranuş told her granddaughter Fethiye:

> At the back of the line we could hear people crying, screaming, pleading. Every time this happened, my mother would walk a little faster, to keep us from looking over our shoulders. On the evening of the first day of the march, two of my aunts came running from the back to catch up with us, and they were crying hysterically. (...) My aunt – my uncle's wife – was ill, and she couldn't walk, so the gendarmes killed her with a bayonet. They threw her body to the side of the road. (...) The elderly, the infirm, the ones who couldn't walk – throughout the march they'd kill them with their bayonets and leave them lying there, just where they fell. They left them lying there, unprotected, on the mountaintops.[518]

Desperate parents and grandparents did not know how they would save the lives of children who were too exhausted to walk and too big to carry. Heranuş was one of the lucky ones, being adopted by a Turkish officer along the way. Others were not so lucky.

> After crossing the bridge at Maden – at Havler – my grand-mother threw two of her grandchildren into the water. These were my uncle's daughters. They'd lost both their mother and their father, and they couldn't walk. One of the children sank right away but the other child's head bobbed up in the water. My grandmother – my father's mother – pushed her head back underwater. The child's head popped out of the water again, and this was the last he [sic] saw of the world, for my grandmother pushed him back under again... Then she threw herself into the madly rushing water and disappeared from sight.[519]

Heranuş came from a large Armenian family, with grandparents and many uncles and aunts. In the end, only two of the adults survived the death march; Heranuş's mother and aunt. Most of the children died, except for a few who were taken in by Turkish, Kurdish or Arab families. One survivor described the death march experience like this:

> We had become like animals, without much feeling. We had reconciled to crying, being hungry, walking. We knew this was our fate. After a while I was no longer afraid because no feelings remained in me. We were concerned only about where we were walking and where we could get food and water.[520]

The ethnic cleansing of Armenians soon spread westward and in July 1915 reached Ankara. Before the war, almost 30,000 Armenians lived in Ankara (which at that time was a fairly small town. Twelve years later, after Ankara had been the capital of Turkey for four years, a census counted only 74,500 inhabitants).[521] The government replaced the Ankara governor with someone they knew would comply with the orders of removing the Armenians from the town. His name was Atıf Bey, and he soon became known for his ruthlessness. According to an officer stationed in Ankara at the time, "[t]he atrocities of this governor are unforgettable. Atıf Bey, acting governor of the Ankara vilayet [province], is an example of unparalleled cold-bloodedness."[522]

Armenians were arrested and "interrogated," and starting on August 14 (1915), Armenian detainees were tied together in pairs and escorted out of town. In the course of 5-6 days, around 1,200 men were killed. The recruits of the Special Organization returned to town showing off their booty, such as shoes and trousers, taken from the Armenians. Upon realizing what was going on, the commander of the gendarmerie in Ankara resigned.[523] In the beginning of September, thousands of Armenians were detained and held for more than three weeks at the train station. "This was a period long enough for their property to be extorted, and persuade the most attractive young girls to convert and marry a Muslim."[524] The Armenians were then sent to Eskişehir, then Konya, and then finally awaited the death march to the desert of Syria.

A few thousand Armenians were allowed to remain in Ankara, for different reasons. They may have been useful craftsmen for the army, or they may have been allowed to stay in order to reduce the protests from foreign diplomats. After the war, the Armenian Patriarchate counted 14,300 Armenians in the Ankara province. This number increased somewhat when deported survivors returned in the beginning of 1919. It proved challenging, however, to reestablish their lives in Ankara. Their houses could be occupied by others, or they could have been burnt to the ground. Adding to the difficulties, a few years later the government of Mustafa Kemal imposed heavy taxes on Greek and Armenian families in Ankara. As a consequence, a substantial number of Ankara's Armenians decided to resettle in Istanbul.[525]

All the killing from the "deportation" resulted in vast amounts of dead bodies. This was a logistical problem that the Ottoman authorities tried to take seriously. Orders for digging deep enough graves were often not followed, however, to the great frustration of the authorities. Telegrams used as evidence during the trials that were held in 1919 and onward revealed that a governor-general of one of the provinces in the east was less than impressed by how the local administrators had (not) dealt with the problem of the amassing corpses. In one telegram sent in August 1915, he complained about the "many corpses littering the roads" with the "numerous inconveniences that engenders," that corpses that had been buried had not been properly so (making it easy for dogs to get to them), and ordered officials who had been negligent in this regards to be duly punished.[526] In another telegram from September 1915, he repeated his complaints about corpses that had not been buried. "It is not appropriate, from the point of view of government and for reasons of hygiene, that one finds [corpses] in the open air, in a state of decomposition."[527]

It was mainly the corpses away from rivers or lakes that became a problem for the government. A frequently used method of killing Armenians without having to consider what to do with the bodies was to drown them in rivers. Especially the Tigris and the Euphrates became the graves of many Armenians. They would typically be tied together, back-to-back, and thrown in the river. Upon drowning the river made the bodies disappear. That was the intention, at least. Since the number of bodies floating down the river was so great, the bodies at some points along the river dammed up the water, making it necessary to clear away the decomposing bodies with explosives. Dead bodies polluted the rivers for thousands of kilometers, some drifting as far as the Persian Gulf.[528] The contaminated rivers in several instances caused disease among people living downstream.

Those who survived the death march, around 870,000 people according to one scholar,[529] ended up in concentration camps in current Syria and Iraq, where the mortality was high because of starvation and diseases like typhus, cholera and dysentery caused by unsanitary conditions. During the winter people froze to death. A German missionary, Béatrice Röhmer, who visited one of the camps reported the following on November 26, 1915:

> The Islahiye camp [close to Aleppo] is the saddest thing I have ever seen. Right at the entrance a heap of dead bodies lay unburied (...) in the immediate neighbourhood of the tents of those who were down with virulent dysentery. The filth in and around these tents was something indescribable. On one single day, the burial committee buried as many as 580 people.[530]

Some of the camps were enormous, and in 1916 the Ottoman government started replacing local administrators with Young Turk officials who had been given the task of exterminating the Armenians in some of the camps. One such operation took place in the Ras ul-Ayn camp, where Kerim Refif Bey was put in place as the new sub-governor. In the middle of March 2016, he started the process of systematically executing the 40,000 internees in the camp. In April, a German consul reported: "Every day or almost every day for a month 300 to 500 victims were taken from the camp and slain in a place about 10 kilometres from Ras ul-Ayn. The corpses were thrown into the river."[531]

As the Armenians kept arriving from Anatolia, they were being sent from camp to camp, finally arriving at Deir ez-Zor by the Euphrates in the east of Syria. When the camp at Deir ez-Zor was out of room, internees were sent onward to Mosul or other locations, which meant days more of walking. The Armenians in many of these convoys were simply killed once they reached desolate locations.[532] "The indictment of the Young Turk leaders, read out at the first session of their trial on 27 April 1919, states that 195,750 people were murdered in Zor in 1916."[533] A scholar who in 1974 visited the sites where the camps in Syria had been, saw large areas where human bones were still scattered.[534]

Many aspects of the mass slaughter of Armenians are disputed, including the actual number of people that were killed. One scholar explains that

> about 250,000 managed to escape to Russia, either over land or (...) by sea. Of the remaining 1,600,000 about 1,000,000 were killed, half of

> whom were women and children. Of the surviving 600,000 about 200,000 were forcibly Islamised; and the wretched remnant of 400,000 was found, starving and in rags, by the Allies (...) at the end of the war. A further figure of between 50,000 and 100,000 were killed off during the Turkish invasion of the Caucasus in May-September 1918; and probably another 250,000 or so during the years 1919- 22, when surviving deported Armenians returned home to face further organised killings.[535]

Many Armenians would say that one million killed is too low of an estimate, but academics seem to hesitate regarding the actual number of people killed, and in the literature one finds any number between 600,000 and 1.5 million.[536] A more recent source than the one quoted above claims that around 300,000 Armenians survived the deportation and killings in the desert, of which most migrated abroad. Currently around 60-70,000 Armenians live in Turkey, mainly in the Istanbul area.[537]

The Ottoman Justification

Could the extermination of the Armenians be justified in any way? Turkish authorities have argued that there is no point in trying to point fingers, because it was a war situation. Armenians killed many Muslims, and many Armenians were killed in return. Unfortunate, of course, but war is hell. Chaotic hell.

This line of thinking does not, at first glance, seem invalid. Tens of thousands of Armenians, in no subtle manner, and in a very violent way, turned against their own government. In the east, there were massacres of a substantial number of non-Armenians at the hands of Armenians. Of course, a government should do what it can to protect its citizens from violence, to maintain the integrity of its territory, and to deal with any threat to this integrity in an efficient manner. The problem is the way in which the Ottoman government dealt with the Armenian threat, the lack of proportionality in its response, the fact that it did not distinguish between actual threats and potential threats, and its complete disregard for the principle of not targeting civilians with violence.

So why did the Ottoman government choose this course of action? One theory, mainly promoted by Armenian researchers, has been that the extermination of the Armenians was premeditated. The

Ottoman government was waiting for an opportune moment, and when the First World War came the war did not cause the extermination of the Armenians, it became a pretense for it. This theory has by and large been rebutted, partially because other theories are more convincing, and partially because some of the source material that back up the theory has been shown to be forgeries. Furthermore, some of the source material bears the traits of being Allied wartime propaganda instead of objective, historical documents.

The increasingly accepted explanation for the Ottoman government's behavior is related to the fact that the government was under extreme pressure. The decision to remove the Armenians from Anatolia by any means was taken at a point during the war when battles were taking place several places at the same time. Ottoman losses were high. A group of key people within the Young Turk government in Istanbul were convinced, "though mistaken (...) that there was a deliberate and coordinated Armenian uprising in the East, with Empire-wide ramifications."[538] It was these key government members who decided that the integrity of the empire must be prioritized above all else, including the survival of an entire ethnic group. It was not a willed policy by the government as such.[539] The key members of the government, notably Talat Pasha, Enver Pasha and Cemal Pasha, referred to as the triumvirate, were able to execute their decision to "deport" the Armenians, despite on several occasions meeting resistance and protests from local administrators and officers. Those who resisted, however, were replaced by people willing to obey orders, regardless of the inhumanity of their content.

Were the genocidal decision makers in Istanbul a specific breed of evil men? One of the most respected historians on the issue, Gwynne Dyer, has suggested that they were not as much evil as they were

> desperate, frightened, unsophisticated men struggling to keep their nation afloat in a crisis far graver than they had anticipated when they first entered the war (...), reacting to events rather than creating them, and not fully realizing the extent of the horrors they had set in motion in 'Turkish Armenia' until they were too deeply committed to withdraw.[540]

Although this is probably an accurate description of what went on in the heads of these men, it cannot be disputed that had they had more compassion for Armenians in general, they would have chosen a less lethal way of managing the Armenian threat. They did not.

Trials, Assassinations, and Denials

When the war came to a close, several of the men who had been responsible for the mass slaughter of Armenians realized that they would be prosecuted and maybe executed by the victors if they remained in the Ottoman Empire. Talat, Enver and Cemal, together with four other key individuals, left Istanbul in the night of 1/2 November, 1918, on board a German destroyer, traveling first to Crimea and from there to Berlin.[541] Those who had been involved in the genocide and did not flee were arrested and prosecuted in what has been called the first war crimes tribunal in history.

Sultan Mehmet V died in July 1918, and it was his brother, Sultan Mehmet VI, who set in motion the establishing of a military tribunal. This was done mainly in an attempt to soften the terms of the Allies during the peace negotiations. The first investigations began in January 1919, and the trials of 120 wartime government officials began in late April. Official documents and testimonies from Ottoman Muslims were used as evidence. The court concluded that the mass slaughter had been orchestrated by the Young Turk central committee. In May the court decided to transfer 67 of those on trial to Malta, for fear that the prison in Istanbul would be stormed. A number of others were released. The seven who had fled were tried in absentia, found guilty and sentenced to death. Trials were then held for people who had been involved in various massacres, but the momentum gradually came to a halt as the Independence War picked up speed and the real power was shifted towards the nationalists in Ankara. By the fall of 1920 the proceedings had stopped.[542] This was perhaps not so surprising, given that several of those who became part of the new regime in Ankara, had also held important positions in Istanbul.[543]

The seven who fled justice on board the German warship in November 1918 were not to live long and happy lives in exile. They would all, except for Enver, be systematically hunted down and killed by Armenian assassins over a few years. Enver was killed fighting Soviet forces in Central Asia. Perhaps the most controversial of the seven, Talat, seen as the mastermind behind the extermination of the Armenians, found refuge in Berlin. There, on the street, he was shot and killed one morning in March 1921, by the Armenian survivor

Soghomon Tehlirian.[544] Tehlirian made no attempt to get away with the murder, and when he was tackled by the German bystanders, he shouted "It's nothing to do with you!" pointing out that both he and his victim were foreigners.[545]

Tehlirian was arrested and put on trial and, remarkably, acquitted. He had killed a man in public, in broad daylight, and was acquitted by a German court. Among the evidence that was put forth during his trial, the court had heard witness descriptions of the horrors that had transpired in Anatolia and Mesopotamia during the First World War. Both Johannes Lepsius, quoted at the beginning of this chapter, and German officials who had been in a position to closely watch the Ottoman killing machinery, gave their testimonies to the court.[546]

How could a German court acquit a murderer like this? Today it is completely unthinkable that someone in Germany would get away with it, but this is a century ago. The rule of law has made major advances in western European and many other countries since then. A similar case from the 1920s in western Europe is that of Sholom Schwartzbard. He was a Jew who killed the former chief of the Ukrainian National Army in Paris in 1926, and like Tehlirian, Schwartzbard was acquitted. The Ukrainian army chief had been responsible for the mass slaughter of Jews in Ukraine in 1919 and 1920. More than 100,000 Jews were killed, and hundreds of thousands more were raped and pillaged. When the police in Paris arrested Schwartzbard, who had made no attempt to escape, he announced: "I have killed a great murderer!"[547] Both Tehlirian and Sholom were acquitted, with a few years apart, in western Europe. The fact that they killed their victim in public and then gave themselves up for arrest, show that they wanted "a show trial, one that showed the world the truth and the horrors of the pogroms against Jews and Armenians."[548] They managed to do both this and get away scot-free. Tehlirian later moved to San Fransisco, where he died in 1960. A plaque on the monument raised at his grave in Fresno, California, proclaims:

> This monument has been erected by the Armenian people in memory of Soghomon Tehlerian,[549] the national hero who, on March 15, 1921, brought justice upon Talaat Pasha, a principal Turkish perpetrator of the Armenian genocide of 1915 which claimed the lives of 1,500,000 Armenian martyrs.

The killings of the top decision makers responsible for the Armenian genocide could possibly have been the end of the matter. What more was there to do, after those responsible had been punished with death? Well, there were around 300,000 survivors and only a handful of those who actually partook in the killing were punished. It should not come as a complete surprise that this was not over. In addition, the government of the new Turkish republic started denying the gravity of the "deportations." Although Mustafa Kemal Atatürk had been highly critical of the actions of the Young Turk central committee, he did little to formally distance his government from the extermination of the Armenians. He supposedly said the following about Talat Pasha: "Talat was one of the causes of the Great Turkish disaster, but we have to be grateful to him, as the unhappy results on his political shortsightedness stimulated our national rebirth."[550]

It would get worse. After having executed hundreds of people in the opposition during the first years of the republic, Atatürk had created an atmosphere where there was little room to differ on politics. There was therefore little room to challenge the government approach of keeping Turkey as ethnically "clean" as possible, and of discriminating against the minorities. When Atatürk died in 1938 and İnönü took over, it became important for the latter to try to put a dent in the ostensibly invulnerable image of Atatürk, and to try to step out of his shadow. One opportune moment came in 1943, when Nazi Germany, in need of friends, offered to send the remains of Talat to neutral Turkey. İnönü accepted, and a great funeral was held in Istanbul in February 1943. A first secretary at the British embassy wrote at the time:

> It seems that he who praises those whom Ataturk did not like is sure to please Ineunu (sic). For three days the Istanbul Press has been devoting entire columns to Talat Pacha calling him the "symbol of Turkish patriotism," without Ataturk being mentioned once. The purpose is obvious: Ataturk must be forgotten.[551]

In other words, according to this diplomat, the celebration of Talat in 1943 was not so much an embrace of the extermination of the Armenians, as it was an attempt from İnönü to claim his spot in the sun by going against Atatürk. That is not to say that Talat is not remembered with honor in Turkey today. There are still places, streets and public buildings bearing his name, such as Talatpaşa Boulevard in Ankara, or Talatpaşa Primary School in Şişli in Istanbul.

Then came a period when the Armenian issue seemed to fade away. Three decades passed after the moving of Talat's remains to Turkey when in January 1973, near Santa Barbara in California, a 78-year-old Armenian genocide survivor shot and killed two Turkish consular officials[552]. In the coming decade and a half, several more Turkish officials would be killed around the globe, including in Austria, France, Lebanon, Italy, Spain, the Netherlands, Greece, Australia, Switzerland, Canada, and the United States. The two secret Armenian organizations Justice Commandos against the Armenian Genocide (JCOAG) and the Armenian Secret Army for the Liberation of Armenia (ASALA) had decided that it was time, several decades after the Ottoman government had in practice exterminated the Armenians from Anatolia, that Turkey, or rather Turkish officials, pay the price.

ASALA built close links with the Palestinian Liberation Organization (PLO) from whom they received training, and the ASALA headquarters in Lebanon were next to the offices of the PLO. The location in Lebanon was no coincidence. The civil war there had fueled the anti-Muslim sentiments among the Christians, and Lebanon had a substantial Armenian Christian population. Another factor that contributed to the Armenian terror attacks in the 1970s and 1980s was how well the Armenian communities had integrated into their host countries, particularly in France and the United States. For the young generation of Armenians growing up in these countries, the main thing that marked their identity was the memory, told by their parents and grandparents, of the genocide.[553]

By 1983, Armenian terrorists had organized over 100 attacks on Turkish targets in over fifteen countries, involving in all nearly fifty murders including twentynine Turkish diplomats or their dependents.[554] ASALA also targeted countries that arrested its members. Swiss targets were attacked to force the release of Armenian terror suspects. In the end Swiss authorities gave in to the demands. When Swedish authorities arrested an Armenian terror suspect, ASALA threatened to kidnap Swedish tennis stars in Paris. When the French arrested 51 suspects after a bombing in Orly, Armenians bombed the Air France office and French embassy in Tehran.[555]

ASALA demanded that eastern Turkey be handed over to Armenia. In a TV news story from an attack on Turkey's embassy in

Ottawa in 1985, where the attackers killed a guard and took hostages in the embassy, one can hear a reporter talk on the phone with one of the hostage takers:

> Reporter: What demands are you making?
> Hostage taker (in broken English): To..to Turkish government...demand..to... We want our land back. And we want the Turkish government to recognize the Armenian genocide in 1915.[556]

The attackers then surrendered after four hours of negotiating with Canadian police. To ASALA, the demands seemed reasonable considering the events after the Holocaust: West Germany had paid reparations to Jews, and the Jews got their own country (albeit not in Europe). To Turkey, of course, the demands were completely out of the question, and Turkey became adamant in fending off "the 3 R's: genocide recognition, leading to demands for financial recompense, and eventually territorial restitution."[557]

Turkey did not sit idly by while its diplomats were killed. After the 1980 military coup, a covert paramilitary organization was set up, with the mandate to track down and kill Armenian assassins who either had not been arrested, or who had served their prison sentence and been released. The authorities also put pressure on the Armenian community in Turkey, asking prominent Armenians to tell the Armenian terrorists to stop the attacks. "The Armenian patriarch (...) had to issue press releases condemning the attacks and to hold mass in honor of the assassinated Turks."[558] Turkish authorities also allied with Israel and their lobbyists in Washington, D.C., to counter the work of Armenian lobbyists trying to get the US to recognize the genocide.

Does It Matter What We Call It?

In 1944, the law student Raphael Lemkin, a Jew born in Poland, used the killing of Talat on the street of Berlin as an illustration of a legal conundrum. Lemkin was puzzled at the fact that Talat Pasha could live freely in Germany, whereas his killer was put on trial: "It is a crime for Tehlirian to kill a man, but it is not a crime for his oppressor to kill more than a million men?"[559] Clearly, this did not make sense, and his reflections set off a process that led him to coin the word "genocide," and his lobby work at the UN became important for the adoption in 1948 of the Convention on the Prevention and Punishment of the Crime of Genocide.[560] In other words, the term "genocide" was created to describe what had happened in recent history, including the "deportation" of Armenians from Anatolia.

The Genocide Convention came three decades after the events in Anatolia and the word "genocide" did not exist in 1915. This does not mean that the definition of genocide cannot be used to describe occurrences that took place before 1948. In fact, the convention itself clearly states that "at all periods of history genocide has inflicted great losses on humanity." Most historians now agree that it makes sense to call the "deportations" genocide, and in 2003 the International Center for Transitional Justice, a non-governmental organization based in New York, issued a legal opinion stating that the "deportations" were genocide according to the legal definition[561], which reads as such in the convention:

> genocide means any of the following acts committed with intent to destroy, in whole or in part, a national, ethnical, racial or religious group, as such:
> (a) Killing members of the group;
> (b) Causing serious bodily or mental harm to members of the group;
> (c) Deliberately inflicting on the group conditions of life calculated to bring about its physical destruction in whole or in part;
> (d) Imposing measures intended to prevent births within the group;
> (e) Forcibly transferring children of the group to another group.[562]

Considering what happened to the Armenians, and what the Young Turks leaders shared with diplomats about their intentions, the reader may or may not agree that there was "intent to destroy, in whole or in part" the Armenians, and that at least one of the acts listed was committed.

Why is it so impossible for Turkey to acknowledge that what the Ottoman regime did was genocide? Even Atatürk himself admitted and condemned the killings of Armenians several times in the years following the war, and his nationalist movement even agreed that accountability was necessary. But after the founding of the republic, denial set in.[563] As earlier mentioned, several important people from the Ottoman regime joined Mustafa Kemal in Ankara, including in the government. In addition, the lesson about how external powers had used the Ottoman minorities against the Ottoman government had been learnt well. The Sèvres Treaty (1920) had even included promises of an independent Kurdistan. When the Kurds revolted against Ankara in 1925, this certainly did not improve the young government's attitude towards other minorities. The government in effect declared various social and ethnic groups nonexistent.[564] This approach to minorities could hardly be combined with some sort of special treatment of Armenians. Everybody was a Turk now.

The succeeding governments have ever since been extremely reluctant to enter into any kind of process that might at some point involve reparations, or worse, relinquishing of territory. Suggesting that the government should look into what actually happened in 1915 and the following years could end you in jail. But towards the end of the 1990s, things started to happen. The Cold War was over, Turkey was trying to look better in the eyes of the European Union, and a few courageous Turkish scholars actually did research the fate of the Armenians. An American scholar with Armenian heritage, Ronald Suny, was approached in 1998 by a former student, by then a professor at an Istanbul university, and asked if he would like to come and speak about the Armenians. Suny recounts:

> Given the official position of the Turkish government that no genocide had taken place, and with laws in place prescribing that insults to the Turkish state were punishable by imprisonment, this seemed a bizarre and even dangerous suggestion. Yet it also was an opportunity that I could not turn down. I consulted with friends, some of whom suggested that I was taking an unnecessary risk. One Turkish colleague encouraged the trip: "Don't worry, if anything happens, we can get you out!" That was not the kind of assurance I wanted to hear, but as someone who has long advocated intellectual exchange between Turks, Armenians, and others on the issue of genocide, I decided to fly to Istanbul.[565]

Suny gave a lecture at Koç University in Istanbul for an hour. Several people walked out during the lecture, but many remained and applauded when it was over. The first step had been taken towards opening up a scholarly, collaborative conversation between Turkish and non-Turkish scholars on the Armenian genocide. Not long after, Suny decided to invite scholars "to present work on the non-Turkish peoples in the last years of Ottoman rule."[566] The initiative was met with hostility by both Armenian and Turkish diaspora, and prominent scholars on genocide declined their invitations. "Articles appeared in English-language Armenian newspapers warning that 'the Turks are coming' to Chicago and asserting that 'Suny is worse than a Turk!'"[567] Nevertheless, enough scholars were willing to attend for a workshop to take place, and it was held at the University of Michigan in March, 2000.

The fledgling dialogue between scholars within Turkey and without was met with increased efforts by the Turkish government to deny the genocide. Turkish scholars were threatened, and the Turkish ambassador to the US tried to make the Microsoft Encarta Encyclopedia remove the word "genocide" from its entry regarding the 1915 events. Both in 2000 and 2007, Turkey was able to stop a resolution in the US Congress labeling the mass killings of Armenians as genocide. In 2007, Turkey's leverage was to threaten American supply lines to Iraq.[568] But Suny and his group of scholars did not stop a process they saw bearing real fruit; the distance between the opposite sides of the issue grew smaller. They knew how politicized the issue was, and decided to focus their conversation on what scholars exist for: "[E]stablish the documentary evidence, review the various interpretations, and make judgments about the most convincing arguments."[569] In the beginning of the 2000s they met annually at different universities in the US and Europe. There was more agreement than disagreement. The mass killings, the responsibility of the Young Turks, these things were not in dispute.

> Yet many blank spots remained; archival access in Turkey remained restricted; and disagreements about the timing of events, the motivations of the Young Turk leaders, and, most important, the question of whether to call the mass killings genocide remained yet to be resolved.[570]

In May 2005, Turkish scholars invited the group to Istanbul. The organizers received threats, and the minister of justice, Cemil Çiçek, said that organizing such a conference was tantamount to stabbing Turkey in the back, adding that he wished he had not renounced his authority to open criminal cases as justice minister.[571] The conference was postponed for a few months, and then held in September at Bilgi University despite a (fairly limited) group of protesters throwing eggs and tomatoes outside. The conference contributed to a broadening of the dialogue within Turkey, including civil society, the media and scholars. This also led to a backlash from nationalists and the authorities. Writers and publishers, including the famous writer Orhan Pamuk, were either prosecuted or threatened with prosecution for "insulting Turkishness." An important Armenian figure, Hrant Dink, was given a suspended sentence.

The response of the Turkish government to claims that a genocide took place tend to be logically inconsistent and frequently characterized by "whataboutism" - that is, pointing to something another country has done at some point, saying "What about that? That's just as bad!" For instance, when the French parliament in 1998 passed a bill recognizing the 1915 events as genocide, the Turkish foreign minister, İsmail Cem, said, among other things:

> France would also have to explain past conduct in its colonies as well as the atrocities committed more recently by the French Army in Algeria, before saddling modern Turkey with the shame imposed by this bill . . . Turks did not commit this horrible crime they are accused of.[572]

Part of Turkey's argument has usually been that the Armenians were joining enemy forces, and what happened between the Ottoman government and the Armenians should rather be characterized as civil war; people were killed on both sides. Suny has described the Turkish response like this: "There was no genocide, and the Armenians are to blame for it."[573] Although it is true that thousands of Ottoman Armenians did join Russian forces against Ottoman forces, and that Armenians did massacre many Muslims, this in no way justifies the indiscriminate extermination of the Anatolian Armenians undertaken by the Ottoman government.

What Suny and his circle of scholars discovered through their conferences, was that their academic approach enabled a conversation free of accusations and political rhetoric. The scholars were able to alter the way some Turks and Armenians looked at the issue, making it more difficult to view "the other" as an enemy. Unfortunately, the staunchest antagonists were not swayed. On January 19, 2007, on a street in Istanbul, a seventeen-year-old nationalist from Trabzon shot the aforementioned Hrant Dink in the head from behind and killed him, just like Talat had been killed 86 years earlier. Dink had emerged as a leading voice among the Armenians in Turkey, but he had always spoken in a reconciliatory manner. He was very clear that his cause was not Armenian nationalism or any form of separatism. He was aiming for reconciliation between the Armenians and the Turks and did not embrace the untimely meddling by foreign parliaments trying to establish once and for all, through parliamentary resolutions, that genocide had taken place. In fact, "he described such resolutions as a pact between those who wanted to isolate Turkey and Turks who basked in that isolation."[574] When the French parliament started a legislative process to make the denial of the Armenian genocide a crime, Dink said that if the bill was passed, he would challenge the law by travelling to France and deny the genocide himself.

The killing of Hrant Dink did not in any way end the work to thaw the relationship between Armenians and Turks; in fact, it had the opposite effect. An American journalist who covered the murder described how the people in Istanbul had reacted immediately, in support of Dink and the cause:

> [I]n the immediate aftermath of the shooting I stood in front of a CNN camera in the street in which Hrant's *Argos* newspaper had its office. I became apprehensive as I saw a crowd gathering behind me. The newspaper is only a few blocks from the criminal court where in previous months I had seen Hrant confront jeering demonstrators at his own trial, and my first shocked reaction was that this, too, was a shameful assembly of bully-boy rightists come to gloat at his death. It was only slowly that I realized how very wrong I was, and that these were people who came to pay their respects to a man who had touched their lives. By the time I finished my work, the trickle of faces had grown into a sea.[575]

In relation to his funeral, tens of thousands of *Istanbullus*[576] marched in the streets with signs saying, "We are all Hrant" and "We are all Armenians." After his assassination, a foundation was established bearing his name, the Hrant Dink Foundation, working to further improve the relationship between Armenians and Turkey. But there was also a backlash from Turkish nationalists, celebrating Dink's murderer as a national hero.[577] In addition, the government was harshly criticized for its actions both before and after the murder. Shortly before the murder, the justice minister had spoken of Dink as "a target," and the police was accused of not having done enough to protect him. Although the police did arrest the murderer after a few weeks, photographs were leaked of policemen posing with him while he waved a Turkish flag.[578] Ten years later, a former officer in a leadership position in the security police stated that the authorities had "deliberately refrained from stopping the killer."[579]

Current Status

Turkey's project of shaping the minds of its citizens through their childhood education[580] must be said to have been quite successful. Those who - for four or five generations - have not looked into the matter after high school, have mainly been taught that Armenians were fighting alongside the Russians during the First World War, and that they killed a lot of Muslim Turks. Not untrue, but it leaves out a huge chunk of truth. The rest of the story has largely been ignored in the schoolbooks.[581] To the extent that Turkish schoolchildren have been told about what happened to the Armenians, they are told that the deportations were in response to the Armenian treachery; that the fact that several Armenian communities, such as those in Izmir and Aleppo, were spared, proves that there was no plan of total annihilation; and that the number of 1.5 million Armenians killed has been hugely inflated in order to demand money and territory[582].

It is therefore quite understandable that so many people in Turkey agree with their government's claim that no genocide occurred. The aforementioned Fethiye Çetin, who wrote the book about her grandmother, stated:

> I would never have believed any of this, unless it was my grandmother telling me. What she told me did not fit with anything I knew. It turned the known world on its head, smashing my values into a thousand pieces. (...) Because I was one of the best students in the class, my teachers would ask me to read out heroic poems on every national holiday. I would recite these poems about our 'glorious past' at the top of my voice, and with such passion.[583]

On one side were the schoolchildren of Turkey not learning about what had happened with the Armenians, taking this lack of knowledge into adulthood. On the other side were all the surviving Armenians in Turkey who were too traumatized and fearful to speak openly about what they had experienced. The combination has led to mass ignorance.

The Armenian fear of speaking out was well founded. Having been reduced to a tiny minority, Armenians had little to gain in their social contexts by speaking openly about the past. In some places the non-Armenians would openly refer to the children who had been taken in by non-Armenian families as "leftovers of the sword."[584] In other words, growing up they were repeatedly reminded that they were supposed to have been killed. In 1928, it became illegal to speak a minority language in public. Decades later, adult Armenians in Istanbul who were interviewed by researchers shared how traumatizing it had been, when they were children, to fear making the mistake of speaking Armenian to their parents when out of the house.[585] Then came the 1942 Wealth Tax which financially punished non-Muslims, and then the Istanbul pogrom in September 1955, when "gangs organized by state institutions attacked minority businesses, homes and churches."[586]

An Istanbul Armenian who was interviewed by researchers told a story from the 1960s. When she was ten years old, she used to play with a Turkish girl next-door every day:

> One day I went over as usual to her house, the little girl stood at the door and said 'My grandmother does not want us to be friends anymore because you are Armenian.' I didn't understand what this meant and went home crying, 'what does being Armenian mean?'[587]

The discrimination could sometimes be subtle, sometimes not so subtle. An Ankara Armenian interviewed by the Hrant Dink Foundation recounted how his religion exam in primary school had gone:

> My family presented a petition for me to take the [religion] class, so I could learn about Islam as well. I attended religion class in the fourth and fifth years of primary school; I learned prayers; I still remember some of them. I entered an oral exam in religion as part of the primary school graduation exams. The jury formed of three teachers first asked me my name. When they realized I was Christian they whispered to each other, and asked me to leave the room without asking any questions. Although I had always earned the highest grades from that course during the educational year, a straight line stood opposite the religion class section in my primary school graduation report; in other words, they hadn't marked me. Yet I had studied for the exam, and wanted to get a good grade.[588]

The same man explained that although he was accepted to different faculties at university, he chose faculty based on his access to the job market. Being Armenian, he would not be allowed to become a bureaucrat or diplomat, so he opted for the Academy of Press and Publishing at Ankara University.[589] Numerous similar stories have been, and are still being, collected by the Hrant Dink

Foundation from Armenians from various cities and towns across Turkey. One known case is that of a young military conscript who wanted to become a fighter pilot but was told by the military that he was marked as Armenian in their registers. He could therefore not become a pilot. Despairing at his situation, the young man killed himself.[590]

Today Armenian schools must teach the one government-approved curriculum in full, but they can teach Armenian language in addition. The schools are not allowed to hire teachers from outside Turkey, however. This affects the quality of the language education, since the teachers have not been able to study Armenian at university level, as this is not taught in Turkey. Furthermore, all minority schools are required to employ a vice-principal appointed by the government, acting as an inspector on behalf of the Turkish state.[591]

Armenians today have different approaches to the fact that they are Armenians in Turkey. Some have distinct Armenian and Turkish sets of friends. Some have experienced that when they reveal to their Turkish friends that they are Armenian, the Turks end the friendship. Navigating in the professional life, some have two versions of their business card; one with the Armenian name and one Turkish version.[592]

The fact that the Armenian issue is international has made the problem bigger and more difficult to solve. As we have seen in chapter 4, the way Turkey relates to the Armenian question has affected its relation to other countries, especially Armenia (naturally), Russia, Azerbaijan, Iran, and Israel, but also more than twenty countries in which parliaments have passed "Armenian genocide" resolutions.[593]

Generally, one can say that how the countries in the region relate to each other can be explained, at least partially, by their minorities. In 1993, Turkey closed its border with Armenia because of the latter's occupation of the disputed Nagornoh Karabakh region in its war with Azerbaijan (Armenia claims the region because of its large Armenian population). There have occasionally been attempts at normalizing the relationship between Turkey and Armenia, where the latest attempt resulted in agreement in 2022 to partially open the border. As of the beginning of 2024, this has yet to happen.

Azerbaijan, on its side, has played a role in putting the breaks on the Turkey-Armenia rapprochement, because it has wanted to keep up the pressure on Armenia. With its ability to withhold oil and gas from going to Turkey, Azerbaijan has some leverage. Then there is Iran, which has a large Azeri minority, and Iran is not interested in too strong of an Azerbaijan. Shiite Iran has therefore supported Christian Armenia. So has Russia, which has military bases in the country. The Turkish relationship with Israel has also been affected by the Armenian issue. In 1992, Turkey marked the 500th anniversary of welcoming the Jews who were expelled from Spain. This became part of an effort to convince the Jewish and Israeli lobby in Washington to work against the lobby efforts of Armenians.[594]

In other words: Foreign policy in this region of the world is usually about much more than what meets the eye. There is usually a good explanation for a country's behavior that ostensibly has nothing to do with the matter at hand.

Where Do We Go from Here?

Although the acts that can be characterized as genocide against the Armenians happened a century ago, the injustice suffered by the Armenians did not end in the Mesopotamian desert during World War I. At different points during the following decades the Armenians became targets - together with other minorities - of very discriminatory policies by the Turkish government. This continuing discrimination contributed to keeping the wounds from the "deportations" open. The official denial that genocide had taken place similarly prevented healing.

Does it all matter now, more than a hundred years later? How about simply ignoring the past, and getting on with life? Experience from elsewhere in the world indicates that that is not a good idea. The global track record of simply burying the past is generally not good, especially when very large numbers of people have been murdered. People who have suffered injustice on a large scale tend to hold on to their grudges - collectively - until the opportunity arises to "restore balance." In the Armenian case, we saw one attempt at righting a past wrong during the 1970s and 1980s when Turkish embassy staff were killed around the world. Not surprisingly, this only made matters worse, and since then there has been no proper process to come to terms with the underlying causes of the killings. Why? It has simply not been politically or personally rewarding to go in that direction in Turkey. Quite the opposite, it has been punitive.

Among those requesting a proper process to deal with the past is Fethiye Çetin. Since the book about her grandmother first came out in 2004, she has been involved in several initiatives to address the Armenian-Turkish relationship. She sees such a process as a prerequisite to being able to deal with the violence that is still ongoing in the Turkish society, for instance against the Kurds, against women and against children. "The government can't just ignore the past," she explains to me while we sit in the pleasant living room of her apartment in Ataşehir in Istanbul. "We are the grandchildren of a generation who participated in mass violence. One part of my family massacred another part of my family. We have to get to the truth."

After her book came out, much attention was given to the suffering experienced by the Armenian girls who were taken from their families around 1915, who became grandmothers and great-grandmothers in Turkish families. "But we have to confront what our [non-Armenian] grandfathers and great-grandfathers did, too. We have to ask what they did. Then we will hear answers that we don't want to hear," she explains with her resolute voice and serious but friendly, grandmotherly face. She goes on to explain that part of the heritage from them is the raping and other forms of violence taking place in the Turkish society today, referring to research showing how trauma is passed on from one generation to the next. "We all carry the trauma from the massacres that have taken place ever since the Ottomans," she continues. "It is not possible for us to create a different life, a different society, if we don't boldly confront the truth about our past."

The obstacles to dealing properly and sufficiently with the injustice that has been suffered by the Armenians are in some ways similar to the obstacles that prevent a solution to the Kurdish-Turkish conflict. Those that have been mentioned in this chapter are: Legal obstacles, specifically the crime of "insulting Turkishness"; the inadequate education of generations of school children in Turkey; lack of freedom of speech, so that the public is kept in the dark about what actually happened; perpetuated violence and injustice against Armenians in Turkey and the violence that was perpetrated against Turkish diplomats, exacerbating mutual resentment. All this contributes to yet another obstacle, namely the Turkish fear of opening Pandora's box. If Turkey starts some sort of truth process relating to the Armenian issue, where will it end? What will be the consequences with regard to the Armenian issue, but also with regard to any other perception of injustice that a minority in Turkey may have experienced?

Scholars have suggested that in order to truly deal with the Armenian issue, Turkey has to become an actual democracy where it is safe to make historical or political claims.[595] Dealing properly with what has happened to the Armenians, and taking steps towards becoming a liberal democracy, would be two sides of the same coin. This argument has merit. If free speech and freedom of the press became a reality in Turkey, it would be a good point of departure for dealing with several of the underlying issues that still keep resulting in violence.

Even without those prerequisites, fruitful steps are already being taken outside of official channels to build consensus and spread awareness about the Armenian issue. After Hrant Dink was killed in 2007 a foundation bearing his name was established. The Hrant Dink Foundation is now the most important institution articulating the position of Armenians in Turkey.[596] The establishment of such an institution must be considered to be an important step. Although the Agos newspaper has a similar purpose, the mandate of the foundation is wider. The efforts done by Armenians outside of Turkey are not always adequately considerate of the vulnerable position of the Armenians within Turkey, and therefore not always perceived to be helpful. This includes the work to convince foreign parliaments to pass genocide resolutions, or, as in France, make genocide denial a crime.

What works, then? What has been done so far that has actually had a positive effect on how Armenians view Turkey and how Turkey views the "deportations"? It seems that small steps are what work. But as we saw with the academic conferences organized by Professor Suny, even small steps can be perceived as too radical and even treacherous. Once the small steps are seen to be nonthreatening, however, they seem to be accepted and even seen as useful in some circles. The response to the Hrant Dink murder was not violent riots, but a small step: The establishment of a foundation. The Turkish government has also taken a few small steps. One of them is the restoration of the famous Armenian Church of the Holy Cross, on the Aktamar Island on Lake Van in the east of Turkey. The restoration started in 2005 and the church was opened as a museum in 2007. Although this drew criticism for being a half-hearted effort on the side of the government for a number of reasons, including the fact that it was turned into a museum and not a place of worship, at least the restoration happened. In 2011 the government took another small step, allowing for a church service to take place inside the church. Armenians from Istanbul, Armenia and the diaspora came to take part in the service.[597] The latest restoration of an Armenian church was completed in Kayseri in January 2020, though it was turned into a library. The authorities, and the media covering the opening, made sure not to mention that it had been an Armenian church.[598]

Fethiye Çetin's experience is that one of the things that enable people to have meaningful conversations about the Armenian-Turkish relationship is telling and listening to stories of what people have experienced. She worked as a lawyer for Hrant Dink, and for his family after he was assassinated, and in her role as a lawyer she was the target of much negative criticism. But she has never been criticized for her book.

"How do you explain that?" I ask her.

"It's because the book tells a story of human life. People easily relate to that," she explains. "Also, my grandmother was not alone. There were so many like her." In any large family in Turkey, she explains, there will be an Armenian grandmother who was forced to become Muslim. Çetin's phone was constantly ringing after the book was published, and her inbox filled up with e-mails from people eager to tell her their own stories. The first printing of the book sold out in a week, journalists wrote about it, and a newspaper column was created called "She is my grandmother, too." The stories that people shared were collected in a second book, The Grandchildren, that came out in 2009.

Çetin's experience with these books taught her how powerful stories are. "For example, I was at a book fair in Italy once, and even Italians who don't have any connection to Armenians had been strongly affected by my book." In Turkey she has been stopped in the street by people telling her that her book inspired them to look into their own family background, discovering that their grandmother mysteriously had no relatives. "People have been made aware that maybe Armenians aren't our enemies; they may even have discovered that they themselves - having Armenian grandmothers - are part Armenian."

The Armenian issue is still the source of pain in people's lives, within Turkey and without. Outside of Turkey it is mainly the collective trauma that lives on among Armenians, causing resentment towards Turkey and/or Turks. Inside Turkey it is not only Armenians who suffer injustice, but anybody who is brave enough to speak up against the government's policy, facing the risk of harassment and violence with impunity from nationalists or the government itself. But the Armenian issue is also, like other difficult issues in Turkey, an issue that can show the way for Turkey and its citizens to become a proper democracy.

8. Kumbaya?

Places mentioned in this chapter.

The story of the Republic of Turkey is similar to that of a cold and failing marriage where one side has more power than the other. When the weaker side has believed in the use of resistance, like the Kurds or the Armenians, resistance has taken place, but at a high cost. When resisting has seemed futile, the weaker side has either stayed and been controlled, shaped, and forced to let go of parts of its identity, or left.

In addition to the Turkish Sunni majority, Turkey has 51 ethnic elements or religious communities.[599] In this chapter we will look at how the biggest or most well-known groups have been treated by the republic, and how these groups have responded. They are the Greeks, the Jews, and the Alevis. We will then have a brief look at how gender and sexuality shape one's life in Turkey. Finally, we will look at what is possible with regards to a more democratic, less violent future.

The Greeks - "We Fear Renewed Persecution."

"I saw this beautiful quayside full of members of a race which was our sworn enemy, and I concluded that Izmir had slipped away from the hands of its true and noble Turkish inhabitants."[600] Mustafa Kemal Atatürk said this in 1924, referring to his first visit to Izmir in 1905. It does not leave much room for the inclusive interpretation of "Turk" of which he would later try to convince Turkey's minorities. Greeks were the "sworn enemy" of Turks, and although most of them disappeared during the big population exchange between Greece and Turkey in the 1920s, some remained, especially in Istanbul where Greeks were exempt from the exchange. The cost of remaining was high, peaking in 1955 with the Istanbul pogrom. The number of Greeks have dwindled. In 1918, 30% of the inhabitants of Istanbul were Greeks.[601] Today there are only around 2000 of them.

The history of how the Greeks have been treated in Turkey cannot be understood without some basic knowledge of the Cyprus conflict. Cyprus was given by the Sultan to the British in 1878 in return for British intervention in the Ottoman-Russian conflict. The island had eighty percent Greek speaking inhabitants, mainly in the south, whereas the remaining twenty percent were Turkish speakers, mainly in the north. The Greek Cypriots started pushing for independence from Great Britain after World War II. In 1954 it escalated into riots and terrorist attacks against the British presence. Greece supported independence for Cyprus, aiming for Cypriot unification with Greece. For Turkey, that would mean an enlargement of the Greek-Turkish border. Independence for Cyprus was seen as a big threat.[602]

As a result of the Cyprus related polarization, ultra-nationalist organizations were formed. The media joined in and spread dehumanizing propaganda against non-Muslim communities by describing them in pathological terms like "microbe" and "abscess". They also spread unsubstantiated rumors about plans of a massacre of Turkish Cypriots, and falsely reported that the Greek Orthodox patriarchate was financially supporting Greek Cypriot insurgents. This was repeated so many times that it came to be perceived as facts. On August 24, 1955, Prime Minister Menderes referred to the alleged massacre in a speech, adding further credibility to the rumor.[603] This coincided with negotiations between Turkey, Greece and Great Britain regarding the future of Cyprus.[604] While the Turkish press was stirring up nationalist flames, the negotiations did not lead to any conclusive results.

Two weeks later, what has been called a pogrom started in Istanbul, after a bomb had been placed in the Turkish consulate in Thessaloniki by a Greek citizen of Turkish origin in order to provoke a reaction in Turkey.[605] On the night of September 6, 1955, a mob of 100,000 Turkish nationalists started attacking Greek, Jewish and Armenian communities in Istanbul.

> Mass violence rapidly spread all over the city and had also repercussions in Izmir. During the night, the mob killed up to 15 people, tortured, forcibly circumcised and converted them to Islam, raped women and children, and exhumed and defiled dead bodies from their burial places. First and foremost the mob pillaged and destroyed 10,000 shops, residential houses, schools and sport clubs, but it also desecrated churches, synagogues and cemeteries belonging to the targeted groups. The pogrom left the non-Muslim communities of Istanbul economically ruined and psychologically strained. With their confidence in the Turkish state fundamentally shaken and without any prospect of obtaining adequate compensation, the Armenian, Jewish and Greek Orthodox communities left Turkey in a major wave of emigration.[606]

The Turkish government enabled the pogrom.[607] The police had been instructed not to intervene,[608] and lists of people and places to attack had been prepared in advance.[609]

The pogrom has since been described as an attack on the Greeks, although the mob did not seem to discriminate much between the non-Muslim groups. The reason why it looked mainly like an attack on the Greeks, was the anti-Greek rhetoric and the fact that the Greek population was substantially larger than that of the Jews and Armenians.

"We haven't forgotten how we were suddenly attacked, so we fear renewed persecution," a young Greek man in Istanbul told a journalist in 2018.[610] He was born more than three decades after the 1955 pogrom, but when he refers to how "we" were attacked, it is a sign of collective trauma. Little has been done by the government to heal it. Although the interior minister in 1955 had to leave office because of the pogrom, and some compensation was paid to the victims, the state was clearly moving in the direction of removing its Greek inhabitants.

In 1964, there were still around 80,000 Greeks living in Istanbul. Some were citizens of Greece who had lived in Istanbul all their lives, and a Turkish-Greek agreement from 1930 gave them the right to keep residing in Turkey. But as the Cyprus situation remained tense, the Turkish government decided to annul the 1930 agreement and expelled around 12,500 Greeks. Many of these had spouses and other family members who were Turkish citizens, and who would follow them to Greece. This, coupled with other repressive measures, caused the Greek population in Istanbul to shrink from 80,000 to 30,000 in 1964. The migration to Greece continued for years thereafter, so that there are only 2,000 left today.[611]

The Jews - "One Day I'd Go to Israel"

In 1942 the Turkish government introduced the so-called Wealth Tax. It had as its stated purpose to tax people who benefited from the difficult economic situation without paying their fair share of taxes. In practice, it was the last of several attempts to skew wealth and power from non-Muslims and non-Turks to Muslim Turks. The tax was calculated based on people's entire wealth, not on their income. Taxpayers were at first divided into Muslims and non-Muslims, but then Muslims of Jewish descent, *dönme*, became their own category. The information gathered regarding the people's wealth was inaccurate and frequently grossly exaggerated, and the rules were enforced in a discriminatory manner. Dönmes were required to pay around twice as much as Muslims, and non-Muslims were required to pay up to ten times as much.[612]

All non-Muslims suffered from it, but the Wealth Tax - coupled with the general anti-Semitism that was so prevalent in many places at the time - caused more emigration of Jews than of other non-Muslim groups. Those who were unable to pay the taxes would have their property confiscated before being sent off to labor camps. Aşkale in Erzurum was the first one of these camps. The number of people who could not pay the tax was so high that more camps had to be established. Only non-Muslims were sent to the labor camps, where they would stay until they had "paid off" their tax. By the end of it all, 21 people had died in the camps.[613]

"During the Wealth Tax, they took my father to the military; they took all the men in my family to Aşkale... We remained with no food, no money - these things really scared me. I put it in my mind that one day I'd go to Israel."[614] This narrator, Beki, was seven years old in 1942 when the Wealth Tax was implemented. Many Jews in Turkey suffered a similar fate as that of Beki, and the yearning for a place, a country, that would be safe for Jews grew stronger.

Four and a half centuries earlier, the Ottoman Empire had been that place. When the Jews were expelled from Spain in 1492, the Ottomans were the ones to provide them refuge. A rather large group of Spanish speaking Jews settled in Istanbul. There they were able to go about their lives in peace, but Istanbul was not a singular harmonious community. The different ethnic and religious communities tended to stay with "their own." The Jews would say "Ni a fuego, ni a pleto" - "Don't go to a fire or to a fight" - to remind themselves to mind their own business and keep their heads down.[615] Other towns in what is today Turkey also had a substantial Jewish population until the mid-1900s.

Around 30,000 Jews left Istanbul because of the Wealth Tax.[616] It came only eight years after what has been called the 1934 Thrace Pogrom, which included the forcible transfer of 7,000-8,000 Jews from Thrace to Istanbul.[617] The anti-Semitism continued, sometimes violently, causing waves of migration of Jews to what in 1948 became Israel.

The anti-Semitism continues to this day. The Hrant Dink Foundation (see Chapter 7) recorded 427 instances of hate speech targeting Jews in the course of four months in 2018.[618] One of the founding members of Erdoğan's AKP tweeted that year that Jewish families were "managing the world" and that Zionists were behind political assassinations in the US.[619] This does not, however, translate into government measures to make life harder for the Jews. The estimated 18,000[620] Jews who remain in Turkey seem intent on staying. It is not a matter of happenstance who have stayed and who have left. Those who have stayed are usually affluent, and staying has seemed like the best option. "We are born here, and we were raised here, and leaving would only be a last resort," explained a Jewish columnist in Istanbul to a journalist.[621]

The Jews in Turkey are mainly located in Istanbul. I have met one Jew who lives in Ankara, whose family has not been actively participating in the Jewish community. He was therefore not aware of other Jews in town. He told me that his ancestors were expelled from Portugal centuries ago,[622] and that Portugal, like Spain, in recent years had made it possible for descendants of those Jews to apply for Portuguese citizenship. He had no plans of moving to Portugal, but he had obtained his Portuguese citizenship as a precaution, and also as a means of being able to freely travel to Europe. So has thousands of other Jews in Turkey.

The Alevis - Not Quite Muslims

The "problem" with the Alevis is that they are too non-Sunni, too liberal and left leaning politically, and too many. They have therefore been perceived as a threat both to the Sunni Muslim establishment and the conservative, Kemalist politicians and military officers.

Explaining who the Alevis are can be a little challenging, because they do not fit easily into ready-made boxes like Sunni/Shiite or Turkish/Kurdish. If one asks an Alevi *dede* (elder, or literally grandfather) directly, like I did at one of the many Alevi tombs in Turkey, one may hear something like this: When Turks first entered Anatolia from Iran, they were Alevis. It was the Arabs who brought their Sunni Islam and forced that upon the Alevi Turks. That is why most people in Turkey are now Sunnis. But the Alevis survived, and under the Ottomans the Alevis were respected as their own group. Then the Republic of Turkey refused to recognize the Alevis as a separate group and considered them simply Muslim. Sunni Muslim, that is.

This portrayal does not harmonize frictionlessly with historical facts about the Alevis and their origin. It is not true, for instance, that Alevis generally were treated fairly by the Ottoman Sultans, although it may be convenient now to compare the "bad Turkey" with some imagined, harmonious past. The Alevis have been the victims of social and religious discrimination and oppression for centuries, from Ottoman times until today.[623] This oppression has kept Alevis socially underprivileged, pushing them towards the political left. As we have seen, that is a dangerous place to be in Turkey.

The Alevi religious tradition mainly derives from Shia Islam, "Alevi" meaning "follower of Ali" - the prophet Mohammad's cousin, whom the Shiites also follow. There are, however, few similarities between Alevis and today's Iranian Shiites. The Alevis do not base their moral code on the Koran, they do not fast during Ramadan but during Muharram[624] and only for a few days, and they do not make the pilgrimage to Mecca. Nature worship (sun, moon, rivers, trees) is part of the tradition . And (scandalously!) women take part in religious rituals, which include singing and dancing. This has caused Alevis to be labeled as promiscuous by the Sunni majority. The religious teachings are divided into four levels, with only a few select individuals reaching the highest level.[625]

The exact number of Alevis in Turkey is unknown because they have always been counted as simply Muslims by the authorities. The estimates are between 10 million and 25 million,[626] spanning different ethnicities. Being counted as Muslims, Alevi children are unable to be exempt from the Sunni Muslim religious classes in school. Their places of worship have not been recognized as such by the authorities, but in 2018 the Supreme Court ruled that they should be.

Alevis are known to be politically active leftists, which they have been and still are at their own peril. The worst single incident of a later date happened in Kahramanmaraş in 1978 (mentioned in chapters 3 and 4) where more than a hundred Alevis were murdered in the course of a week by the Grey Wolves, aided by the military. Another important incident is the 1993 Sivas massacre. An Alevi conference was attacked by a local mob and 37 intellectuals, poets and writers were killed. During the 2013 Gezi protests, the majority of those who lost their lives or were arrested were Alevis.[627]

Suppression and violence do not seem to work, however. The Alevis simply will not acquiesce. They are certainly a nuisance to President Erdoğan, who knows that they will be part of any political movement to get him out of office. In 2013, he named a new bridge over the Bosporus after Sultan Selim I (1470-1520). Selim I was responsible for mass killings of Alevis, an operation that has been referred to as a genocide.[628] When Erdoğan named the bridge after the Alevi slayer, he was not exactly extending his hand out to Turkey's Alevis.

Because of their sheer size in numbers, the Alevis are going to remain a substantial social force in Turkey. The effect of their presence is that Turkish society is pulled in a more secular direction and towards the political left.

Gender and Sexuality - "I Don't Want to Die!"

In January 2019, Emine Dirican let her abusive husband in to her parents' apartment in Istanbul. She had recently left him because of his violent behavior. Now, he was full of remorse and wanted to mend ties. In the kitchen, he pulled out his gun and shot her. He went out into the living room, pointed the gun at Emine's mother and pulled the trigger, but the gun malfunctioned. He used it to hit her in the head. Emine lay bleeding on the kitchen floor with her father bent over her. She said: "Daddy, please, I don't want to die!"[629]

In August of the same year, another Emine, Emine Bulut, was at a café in Kırıkkale in central Turkey. She was there with her ten-year-old daughter to meet her ex-husband. While talking about custody of the child, he pulled out a knife, stabbed Emine and slit her throat. In the videos posted on social media, one can hear Emine scream "I don't want to die!" and her daughter screaming "Mom, don't die!"[630]

The Bulut case became well known because of the video footage, and Turkey was outraged. In the demonstrations that erupted, women were chanting "We don't want to die!" holding up the picture of Emine Bulut. Even the president came out and said he would support the restoring of the death penalty for the murder of a woman.[631]

And then, nothing. More murders of women, no systematic response from the government to reduce the violence. A year after Bulut's murder, women were protesting the government's intention of pulling out of the Council of Europe Convention on Preventing and Combating Violence Against Women and Domestic Violence. The government saw the convention as a threat to "family values" and traditional gender roles and as the importation of "Western values." Furthermore, the government claimed the convention promoted LGBT lifestyles and normalized homosexuality. Activists were less than understanding towards their government: "Because they aren't able to openly say they want women as their domestic slaves and the freedom to beat women at will, they latch on to LGBTI+ rights as a more 'socially acceptable' pretext to attack the convention, hoping rampant homophobia will do the trick."[632] The protests did not succeed. In March 2021, President Erdoğan withdrew Turkey from the convention, a move many saw as an attempt to remain popular among religious groups. His outraged words about introducing the death penalty a year and a half before rang ever hollower.

What is the relevance of violence against women for explaining why Turkey is the way Turkey is? Well, the problem is enormous. In 2015, four in ten women in Turkey said that they had experienced physical or sexual violence from their intimate partner. That is almost half of the women. One in ten women said they had experienced that type of violence during the last twelve months.[633] What makes this relevant is that the violence - in addition to being a clear language in its own right - is just the most visible symptom of a much broader problem: An attitude towards women's autonomy, their role in society, and their right to influence important decisions.

Of course, this is not unique to Turkey. Europe has its own major problems with violence against women, and 25% of women there say they have experienced physical or sexual violence from their intimate partner.[634] But the way it looks is unique to each culture. In Turkey, it is not uncommon for women to be told that their main aim should be to have a family and become a mother. The president said in 2016 that women who are not mothers are incomplete. Two years earlier he had said that it would be against nature to treat women and men equally.[635]

In 2011, a young woman had her hip broken in a clash with police during a protest against hydropower plants. The prime minister questioned the legitimacy of her participation in the protest.

> 'I can't know if she is a girl or a woman,' he said. In Turkish, 'a girl' used this way means 'a virgin.' A sexually active and unmarried young woman, he wanted Turks to infer, could not possibly have political beliefs that should be taken seriously. What is more, she deserved her violent treatment at the hands of the authorities.[636]

This attitude, that women's sexuality somehow disqualifies them from autonomy or physical integrity, is widespread, including in the justice system. Several hundred women are killed by their partners, former partners, or families in Turkey every year. The courts are generally lenient, meting out "light punishments that lend credence to the moral logic of the crimes."[637] If the killer in court claims to be religious and dresses well, it is so common for him to receive a reduced sentence that it is referred to as "tie reduction."[638]

The problems start during the women's first encounter with the justice system and persist throughout the court case. During the 2013 Gezi protests, several women reported sexual harassment by the police upon getting arrested. "The big picture shows that the state is more likely to perpetrate crimes against women's bodies than to prevent them. Murder, rape and harassment are used as a means of sanctioning the nation's wayward women."[639] These problems became worse after the purges following the attempted coup in 2016.[640]

Women activists have grown in numbers and become louder during the past decades. Conservative women have also become more vocal about their rights in recent years, including the youngest daughter of President Erdoğan. She is the deputy head of a newly founded organization that came out in support of the Council of Europe Convention. This increase in women activists unfortunately does not mean that violence against women has been reduced, because the opposition has also grown stronger. "In the last 20 years society has changed a lot: more women are demanding their right to work and go to university. The more choices we have, the more intense the backlash gets," explained the head of an organization working to stop the killing of women.[641] It seems reasonable to assume that the backlash will begin to fade as the women activists persist and keep growing in numbers, and the old perceptions of gender norms will die with the people holding on to them. A Turkish woman told me that she sometimes, when she knows she will encounter people with conservative attitudes, dresses in a mini skirt to normalize it and to force them, in a way, to accept it.

Sometimes men decide to perceive women's behavior as "provocative." When they do, it is the women who pay the price. The government does not want to know exactly how high that price is. During the first decade of the 2000s, the numbers of women killed rose every year until 2009, when 953 murders of women were recorded.[642] That year, the government decided that these numbers were not useful and stopped recording them. A government consisting of mainly men, that is. Had more women been represented in government and parliament, that decision might not have been made. Turkey ranks very low on how well women are represented in parliament. Out of 193 countries, Turkey was ranked as number 129 with only 17% women in parliament in January 2021.[643] In other words, Turkish politics has a big blind spot when it comes to gender related issues.

This is in spite of the fact that Turkey was relatively early in introducing suffrage for women, in 1934. Atatürk was convinced that letting women have more influence in society would be beneficial for the country. But his reasoning would probably not sit very well with feminists. In his early writings he wrote that the liberation of women would "have a good effect on men's morals, thoughts and feelings."[644] In other words, women should have freedom and autonomy not because they are half of humanity, of inherently equal value, and with the same right to dignity as men, but because it would improve the world of men.

Despite Atatürk's questionable reasoning for improving women's rights, it is a widely held belief that "Turkish women owe their rights to Atatürk."[645] This view is not only held by (male) historians but also by many women in Turkey. It is a strange view to hold. It seems to disregard that while the women's movement in Europe has been progressively able to thrive, civil society and the women's movement in Turkey have been held back. In those countries where women's rights have progressed substantially, the conditions for civil society have been gradually improving. This has enabled women themselves to fight tooth and nail to increase their own rights and liberties. No man has "given" women their rights. The women have taken them. As civil society in Europe has had an ever freer playing ground, the women's movement has been able to win its victories. In Turkey, women have similarly fought tooth and nail, but civil society has been restricted and sometimes shut down, much thanks to Atatürk and his governmental universe. The structures and authoritarian political culture that he established proved very difficult to change. The limitations on civil society's space has thus held back progress for women's rights.

This point often falls flat among secular Turkish women who regard Atatürk as a liberator from the Ottoman or Muslim oppression of women. It is true that Atatürk forced great and rapid progress for women: the right to vote, the right to divorce and to inherit, schooling for girls and higher education for women. Gender segregation was abolished in many public places, and women were encouraged to get involved in society. That these were major upheavals that had major positive consequences for women is something for which Atatürk should rightfully be given credit. This is what the Turkish school system has been eager to inculcate in the minds of young Turkish citizens. The problem is that at the same time that Atatürk increased the abilities of women to shape their own lives, the restrictions on civil society functioned as a ceiling for women's rights and opportunities. Women suddenly gained many new rights, earlier than several of their European sisters, but were not given the opportunity to continue to work systematically for a constant strengthening and expansion of those rights.

In fact, Atatürk was personally involved in this restriction. In 1923, he persuaded a group of feminists not to establish a political party.[646] In 1927, the candidate of the Turkish Women's Association withdrew his candidacy in a political election after a meeting with Atatürk.[647]

Women were encouraged to get involved in the public debate and in politics, but only as long as it was in support of the state-authorized ideology. The Women's Association of Turkey was allowed to host the Twelfth Congress of the International Alliance of Women in Istanbul in 1935, but the association was banned two weeks later due to some feminist speeches that had been made by its members.[648] That Atatürk's structures put a ceiling on women's political participation is well illustrated by the proportion of women in the National Assembly: In 1935 it was 4.5%, and it did not become higher than this until 2007.[649]

A central argument against placing much of the responsibility for the current rights situation for women on Atatürk is that the alternative would have been worse. Greater freedom for civil society would also have meant greater freedom for political Islam, and since such a large proportion of the population is Muslim, the Muslims would have voted for worse conditions for women. It is possible that this would be true, but we will never get a definitive answer regarding what *might* have happened. What we know is what *did* happen. That there is an alternative that would have been worse does not mean that Atatürk's authoritarian legacy has no explanatory power for the situation of Turkish women today. If one is to explain the women's rights situation in Turkey, one cannot escape the fact that civil society has had poor conditions - compared to many of the countries in, for example, Europe - ever since the republic was founded in 1923.

Being a woman in Turkey may in certain circumstances be dangerous, but no one will deny that there is such a thing as women. For those who do not identify with the heterosexual gender norms, however, it is fairly common that one's gender and sexual identity is simply not acknowledged. In February 2021, President Erdoğan talked about the unwanted elements in society, saying that the mountains Judi and Gabar in Southeast Turkey had been turned into graveyards for "terrorists," referring to PKK casualties. "From now on we will do the same everywhere," he continued. "LGBT, there is no such thing."[650]

It was a specific response to the weeks of protesting that had recently taken place at Boğaziçi University in Istanbul, spreading to other cities across the country. The protests broke out after Erdoğan had appointed an academic closely aligned with his AKP party as rector of the university. Students and academic staff protested this, demanding to elect their own rector to protect the university's academic autonomy. After a few weeks of protests accompanied by police crackdown, students set up an artwork on campus depicting the Kaaba[651] together with LGBT symbols. This was apparently intolerable, and police raided the LGBT student club office and confiscated flags and books. The new rector then closed down the club, although the artwork had been put up by students who were not members of the club.[652] "Are you students, or are you terrorists?" asked Erdoğan,[653] implicitly threatening them with extrajudicial, violent sanctions by calling them terrorists. The leader of the co-governing party joined in, referring to the protesters as poisonous snakes, vandals, and barbarians. "Turkey has no such children!" he thundered.[654] Even the spokesperson of the opposition CHP party came out against the artwork: "We can never accept an attack or insult against humanity's sacred values. We strongly condemn this heinous provocation. We expect all those responsible to be revealed," he tweeted.[655]

Globally, the ability of people outside of the heterosexual norm to be themselves seems to increase, although with local setbacks. Turkey is one of the many countries where the fight is still going on, both culturally and legally. Although LGBT organizations are legally allowed to exist and organize events, the government frequently stops the events, citing the risk of "disorder" because of anti-LGBT protests. Sometimes, however, it becomes a little too obvious that "order" has nothing to do with it. When local authorities banned the movie festival Kuir Fest (kuir = queer) in Ankara in 2017 (and any other LGBT event), the German Embassy said it would host the film screenings on embassy grounds. Turkish authorities then responded by threatening to sit outside the embassy and record everybody who came for the screenings. For fear of putting the festival participants in danger, the embassy decided to cancel the screenings.

The ban on LGBT events in Ankara was only lifted in 2019, after a court found it to be unlawful. It was the LGBT organization KaosGL that had challenged the ban by opening a lawsuit. "So, the system seems to somehow be working?" I asked Damla Umut Uzun who works for KaosGL. "In that case, apparently," she said. "But it's rare."[656]

KaosGL started its activities in the 1990s by publishing a magazine. Gays and lesbians were encouraged to send in letters sharing their stories. Gradually, KaosGL became more institutionalized and was registered as an organization in 2005, the first LGBT organization to successfully do so. It was able to operate relatively normally until the Gezi protests of 2013. After those protests the government became aggressive in going after civil society organizations focusing on human rights. Organizations working on the Kurdish issue were especially targeted, and some were closed down. Other organizations were allowed to continue, but they are still closely monitored. The authorities frequently audit them, looking for mistakes that can be used as pretexts for closing them down. In late 2020, the Turkish parliament passed a law under the guise of counterterrorism which gave the government wide powers. In reality, it let the government "curtail and restrict the legitimate activities of any nongovernmental group it doesn't like," according to Human Rights Watch.[657] Damla Umut Uzun explained that KaosGL is constantly preparing for crisis, either of being closed down by the authorities or being violently attacked.

When I asked her about the future, she thought it looked mixed. "When I look at everything the current government is doing, the future doesn't look bright. But," she continued, "globalization and digitalization is making information more accessible. When the government says something, people can look up the facts for themselves." Especially young people do this, she explained. "Generation Z is more concerned with tolerance, although I don't like that word. Generation Z will change society."

I asked her what was wrong with the word "tolerance." "Well, when we are equal there's no need to be tolerant. Tolerance sounds like a gift. I don't want that gift. You should respect and accept me for who I am." Would Turkey get there, I wondered. "I don't think I will see a gay marriage in my lifetime," she replied, only 30 years old herself. "But one day it will happen. It's Turkey. We will see. Suddenly something can change."

Hope

Something can indeed change. There is hope for Turkey. And when I refer to hope it is from a normative standpoint, the norm being democracy and universal human rights. This hope is not based on wishful thinking. It is based on specific actions that have been taken by thousands, sometimes millions of citizens of Turkey, ever since the founding of the republic. Such actions have been taken by journalists, lawyers, activists, poets, and politicians to fight power abuse and corruption, and to show the public and those in power that there is a better way. There is a way that affords more dignity to those who are not part of the majority and to those who do not agree with the men in power. Many of the people taking these actions have been put in jail, expelled from the country, tortured, and sometimes killed. Despite this, courageous individuals keep believing that it matters that they object to the injustice and the power abuse. And sometimes their passion for improving their country has spilled over into the masses.

It is when the masses participate that there truly is reason to hope. We will get back to why below. First, we will look at the most recent example of the masses in Turkey coming together and telling the government in no uncertain terms that they were not happy about the direction the country was taking. That example is the Gezi protests of 2013.

The Gezi Park protests started on May 27, 2013, with a small group of environmental activists attempting to block government plans to replace a park in Istanbul's Taksim Square with a complex of hotels, a shopping mall, and restaurants.[658] The green lungs in Istanbul are few and far between. Mainly, they are cemeteries. It should come as no surprise that *Istanbullus* would want to defend their parks. Soon after the environmentalists had established themselves, hundreds joined in to protect the park. On May 29 and 30, police started using tear gas and water cannons against the activists. If the intention was to keep people away from the park, it did not go according to plan. Tens of thousands, appalled by the police brutality, joined the protesters in Taksim Square (where Gezi Park is). Before long, people were protesting in almost every province in the country. As many as 7.5 million may have joined in the protests, although the government set the number at 3.5 million.[659]

There has been a number of protests in Turkey over the decades, but Gezi brought out an enormous amount of people into the streets. For the first time, the middle class of Turkey participated on a massive scale. Even the most apolitical students participated, and middle-aged people who would otherwise discourage their children from participating, joined them.[660] This came as a surprise to most observers.[661] People were dissatisfied with the ever-increasing power of then Prime Minister Erdoğan, and Gezi became a pretext for venting resistance towards his power ambitions. The protests provided a space for freely expressing one's opinions. Anybody could participate without being affiliated with any one organization or political issue. In combination with this, many groups that did have clear affiliations with specific political issues participated. In Gezi Park, there were areas where the different groups gathered in specific areas: Anarchists, communists, socialists, nationalists, LGBT activists, environmentalists, Muslims, and Kurds. There was also an area allocated for football.[662]

The government response to the protests was brutal. The police arbitrarily detained large numbers of people, frequently keeping them on buses for hours without recording their detention and without bringing them to appropriate detention facilities. Police used tear gas and water cannons in a way that was deemed exaggerated and unnecessary by human rights monitors, including firing tear gas canisters directly at fleeing protesters as they entered hospitals seeking medical aid. In the streets, volunteer medical personnel who helped injured protesters were arrested. In the three largest cities, Istanbul, Ankara and Izmir, battles between protesters and police could be fierce, and many protesters and some police officers were injured. When the dust finally settled, eight people had lost their lives and 8,000 had been injured, of which 104 had incurred serious head injuries.[663]

The protests grew from the local intention of protecting Gezi Park into widespread demands for Prime Minister Erdoğan to resign. In the end, the demands regarding Gezi Park were met. On June 13, the government suspended the construction plans for the park and demanded in return that the protesters go home. The protesters discussed this amongst themselves but could not agree by the short deadline the government had set. On June 15, the police gave the protesters in Gezi Park a warning to leave the park. Twenty minutes later they started firing tear gas canisters and rubber bullets at people in the park, including at families with children. The park was emptied of people, and the protests spread to other parts of town.

The protesting began to diminish but did not end completely. In some places the protesters kept up their activities, sometimes as a response to a specific case of police brutality. In Antakya in the southeast, protesters gathered every Monday for months after the death of a protester in early June. When another Antakya protester died in September it set off large protests in Istanbul, Ankara, and elsewhere.

Some initiatives were taken to systematize and organize the mass civic engagement that Gezi had set off, but most of these initiatives were unable to attract large numbers on a national level. They were mainly local initiatives focusing on city planning, or more narrow political issues like local environmental protection. On a local level, for years after the Gezi protests, environmentalists were able to gather large crowds to protest specific, local government projects that would damage the environment.[664]

The post-Gezi initiatives also included an attempt to start a political party, but it was unable to establish the number of provincial level branches required to participate in elections. Other initiatives were about less confrontational events or gatherings like film screenings or camping trips. Such events have attracted people who might have tacitly supported a protest, but who would not risk the trouble it might entail to participate.

One initiative that has drawn a fairly large number of active citizens is the organization Vote and Beyond (*Oy ve Ötesi*) which has mainly focused on election monitoring. This may at first sound uninteresting, but there have been elections almost every year since Gezi. The organization has around 50,000 members, which means tens of thousands of people are mobilized every year to monitor their government's organizing of elections. This has a substantial potential for building nationwide consensus on what Turkish democracy should look like. It is already happening on a local level, where Vote and Beyond is assisting local communities deal with local problems together with municipalities.[665]

The Gezi protests did die down, but Gezi taught several lessons about nonviolent struggle to those who were willing to learn. One lesson was the discovery of possibilities that seemingly had not been there before. A space was discovered where one could come together across political divides. Staunch Kemalists were sharing the space with communists and Kurdish activists.[666] One of the things that made this possible was the combined emphasis on freedom of expression and tolerance for the views of others. This shared emphasis united people, and it has become one of the main legacies of Gezi.[667]

Another lesson was that the media could not be trusted. Although this may not have come as a surprise to the most attentive part of the population, the acknowledgment of misinformation and lack of accuracy in the media became more widespread. Those who could follow both international and Turkish news could clearly see the right and wrong way to do journalism. On June 1, 2013, while CNN International continuously showed protest coverage, CNN Türk showed a documentary about penguins. The penguin was to become a symbol of media cowardice.[668]

Not least with regard to the Kurdish issue people realized, shamefully, that they had been fooled for years by the media. One Twitter user wrote: "Friends, apologies to you all. We have been following the Kurdish problem through the media for years. We were idiots to do so. Sorry."[669]

Although the media in general were under-performing, some journalists and editors did have the courage to bring actual news to the public. They faced consequences. The main opposition party put together a list of 77 journalists who had lost their jobs because of their reporting from the protests. Other sources reported far higher numbers of fired journalists.[670]

A third lesson to be learned from the protests was that the lack of direction and organization was an important cause of the demise of the protests. Gezi had no explicit long-term goals that the different activist groups gathered around, no strategy, and no leaders.[671] The majority of the protesters where (young) people with little to no experience with civic engagement. They had not signed up for a sustained, systematic effort, and did not pursue such a path. An important element of this was that there was no ready-made path for them to pursue.

The question, then, is what could be done differently next time to achieve lasting, systemic change. This does not have a simple answer, but we know much more about resisting power abuse now than we did only fifty years ago. One major contribution to this knowledge was a study published in 2011 which took all major violent and nonviolent domestic conflicts between 1900 and 2006 into consideration.[672] The data set included a total of 323 campaigns of resistance. The scientists behind the study were looking for explanations to two aspects of their data. Firstly, they wanted to explain why nonviolent campaigns seemed to be more effective than violent campaigns. Secondly, they wanted to explain under which conditions nonviolent campaigns succeeded or failed.

The 2011 study was groundbreaking because it was the first one to systematically compare all known major violent and nonviolent struggles in such a manner. The findings were striking: In the 20th century, a nonviolent campaign was twice as likely as a violent campaign to reach its political goals fully or partially. It did matter, however, what the objective of the campaign was. Nonviolence was more efficient than violence to achieve regime change and self-determination. For secession, violent campaigns were more efficient than nonviolent ones, although the overall success rate for secession was very low.[673] It seems that a reasonable conclusion to draw from this is that if Turkey is to become a country ruled democratically, the most efficient way to achieve this is through nonviolent means.

A key factor for a nonviolent campaign to achieve its goal is mass participation. If the campaign can attract a large number of participants from different parts of the society, that will increase its likelihood of success. There are several reasons for this.[674] Firstly, the more people who participate and the more diverse the participants are, the more the protests look like a credible force for change. This affects the way regime supporters assess their own situation. Members of the security forces and key members of the business world are more likely to shift their loyalty towards the protesters when there is mass, diverse participation. Most people want to be on the winning team.

Secondly, the larger the protest, the larger the odds that the government's repressive measures will backfire. A brutal government crackdown on nonviolent protesters may cause backfiring through international sanctions or increased protest participation. As we saw, this was exactly what happened when tens of thousands of protesters came to Taksim Square when they saw the police brutality in Gezi Park. Also, the European Parliament on June 13, 2013, approved a resolution expressing "deep concern" at the excessive use of force by the police against "the peaceful and legitimate protests." The European Parliament also "deplored" the "reactions of the Turkish Government and of Prime Minister Erdoğan."[675]

Thirdly, the larger the participation, the larger the odds of receiving international support. In South Africa, for instance, it was only after the struggle against the apartheid regime drew large masses of nonviolent participants that international sanctions came about.[676]

Finally, the larger and more diversified the participation, the more resilient the protest. When the security forces are grossly outnumbered, there is only so many protesters they can arrest. The resilience also comes from the fact that more people means more new ideas about tactics, new ways of pressuring the regime, and the regime will constantly have to spend resources on handling the protest's new moves.

Gezi showed that mass participation in Turkey is possible. In fact, the government's official number of 3.5 million protest participants is higher than that of any of the nonviolent protests that took place globally between 1900 and 2006.[677] So why did the protest achieve so little?

The protest succeeded at protecting Gezi Park, but the protesters outside of Istanbul did not protest to protect a park. They protested police brutality and their government's increasingly authoritarian behavior. They did not, however, fight *for* any shared cause. This was the main weakness of Gezi, and one that will have to be rectified for future mass protests to be able to change Turkey. It is a very challenging weakness to rectify because of the polarized divide in Turkish society between the secularist and the Muslims. The secularists frequently show their love and admiration for Atatürk, while the Muslims fear that secularism will take away their freedom to be Muslims.

Acting Prime Minister Erdoğan knew that he had the support of around half the population and could call on them to become a counterforce against the Gezi protesters. Some of his comments have been perceived as threatening with civil war, and it is possible that many of his followers would have gone out in the streets with sticks and guns had he asked them to.[678]

It seems that those who want to see a democratic Turkey will have to make an effort to find common ground that the Muslim and secular population can agree on. They will have to find a platform, a number of issues that they can agree to fight *for*. The aforementioned election monitoring organization Vote and Beyond seems to be on the right track. Presumably elections without fraud is something the majority of both Muslims and secularists can agree on. But they will only want that if they trust that regardless of the outcome of the election, they will be free to live according to their religious or non-religious conviction. If they cannot trust that their freedoms will not be taken away, it may be tempting to cheat in the elections.

But if the aim is to turn Turkey into a democratic country where human rights are upheld, it is not enough to ensure free and fair elections. Those free and fair elections are namely dependent on the principles we went through in chapter 3, including free speech, freedom of the press, freedom of assembly, and rule of law. Without these, it is impossible to find out what the will of the people is.

There is another important element that is crucial for how pleasant it will be to be a citizen of Turkey, and that is the question of identity. Which aspects of identity should the state emphasize when defining a "proper" citizen of Turkey? The political scientist Francis Fukuyama (mentioned in chapter 3) suggests that the way governments and political parties define "identity" must be widened to encompass a larger "us," large enough to have room for all the minorities. The identity must also emphasize what brings the different groups together.[679] For Turkey, there really is no alternative. Or rather, the alternative is perpetual violence. The first century of Turkey's existence has proved that trying to force people into a narrow understanding of Turkish identity has been the cause of recurring violence that seemingly never stops.

So, a shared national identity that people can believe in is key for becoming a peaceful, strong, and thriving country. When nationalism grew stronger and stronger in Europe during the beginning of the 1900s, the problem was not national identity itself, but "the narrow, ethnically based, intolerant, aggressive, and deeply illiberal form that national identity took."[680] Unfortunately, the state structures that were set up in the Republic of Turkey did not allow the country to let go of that form of national identity. Instead, those politicians who promoted it thrived - and still thrive. Those who criticized it were jailed.

The advantages of including all the citizens in the national identity are many, according to Fukuyama. One is that the country's physical security will be strengthened. When all groups feel included in the national identity, they will contribute to the shared security of the country. When groups do not feel included, they will rather focus on the security of their group. That frequently leads to bloodshed. A second advantage is that the quality of government increases, because the government officials will more frequently place the public's interests above their own narrow interests. A third advantage is that a wider national identity better facilitates economic development. "The strong national identities in Japan, South Korea and China produced elites that were intensely focused on their countries' economic development rather than on their personal enrichment."[681] When more people are included in the "in-group," more people will be encouraged to pull in the same direction. A fourth advantage of an inclusive national identity is that the level of trust between people increases. This increases the so-called social capital, which is a crucial lubricant for social and economic interaction. Finally, a widely shared national identity usually strengthens social safety nets which increase economic equality. When people feel that "we are all in this together" they are more accepting of the idea of taxes being spent on fellow citizens who need it.[682]

All people have numerous parts that make up their identities. A random citizen of Turkey can be a doctor, woman, sister, heavy metal fan, friend, wife, Kurd, and Alevi, all at the same time. There is no objective reason why any of these identity markers should disqualify her from being a first-rate citizen of Turkey. Yet, she is very likely to be discriminated against because of her Kurdish ethnicity. This discrimination may typically cause her to emphasize her Kurdish-ness in an exaggerated, confrontational way in an attempt to create space and freedom to be herself.

This is normal, predictable human behavior. When a person feels attacked for one part of his or her identity, that part will become much more important to him or her than the other parts. He or she will typically either succumb to the social or violent pressure to assimilate (like a gay man who marries a woman to please his surroundings), flee (like a gay man who leaves his conservative small town to find freedom in the big city), or fight back (like a gay man who participates in the pride parade). None of this should be necessary for any citizen of any country.

The question of whether Turkey will ever become a democracy is really a question of what the people of Turkey will choose. Some, like Fethiye Çetin (chapter 7), are optimistic: "When we were young, even the most progressive were whispering. Now we talk openly. It's not enough, still, but it's coming from below, from the grassroots."[683] An Armenian man who was interviewed by the Hrant Dink Foundation shared the following about his views on the future:

> I believe that we can play an active role in this country becoming a more democratic, more modern country where basic rights and freedoms are respected and the views of people are deemed important. Our faiths, our cultures of living may be different, it matters not. The choice to coexist is completely in our hands.[684]

What will the people of Turkey choose? A story comes to mind: In a village there was a very wise, old man to whom people came to seek advice. People would travel from far away to hear what he had to say about this and that. In the same village there was a boy who found this man's popularity annoying. "Who does that old fellow think he is?" the boy thought. "Surely, he doesn't know everything." He caught a small bird and went to test the old, wise man. The plan was to ask him whether the bird in his hands was alive or dead. If the old man said it was alive, the boy would quickly and unnoticeably squeeze it to death. If the old man said it was dead, the boy would open his hands and let the bird fly. It was a foolproof plan.

The boy went to where the old man lived and asked him: "This bird that I'm holding in my hands, is it dead or alive?" With his friendly eyes the old man looked at the boy and smiled. "My child," he said, "only you know."

Tables

Governing Periods of Ottoman Sultans

1299–1326	Osman 1
1326–1360	Orhan
1360–1389	Murat 1
1389–1402	Bayezid 1
1402-1413	Ottoman Civil War/Interregnum
1413–1421	Mehmet 1
1421–1444	Murat 2 (abdicated)
1444–1446	Mehmet 2
1446–1451	Murat 2
1451–1481	Mehmet 2
1481–1512	Bayezid 2 (forced to abdicate)
1512–1520	Selim 1
1520–1566	Süleyman 1
1566–1574	Selim 2
1574–1595	Murat 3
1595–1603	Mehmet 3
1603–1617	Ahmet 1
1617–1618	Mustafa 1 (deposed)
1618–1622	Osman 2 (murdered)
1622–1623	Mustafa 1 (deposed)
1623–1640	Murat 4
1640–1648	Ibrahim (executed)
1648–1687	Mehmet 4 (deposed)
1687–1691	Suleyman 2
1691–1695	Ahmet 2
1695–1703	Mustafa 2 (deposed)
1703–1730	Ahmet 3 (deposed)
1730–1754	Mahmut 1
1754–1757	Osman 3

1757–7174	Mustafa 3
1774–1789	Abdülhamid 1
1789–1807	Selim 3 (deposed, then assassinated)
1807–1808	Mustafa 4 (deposed, then executed)
1808–1839	Mahmut 2
1839–1861	Abdülmecit 1
1861–1876	Abdülaziz (deposed)
1876	Murat 5 (deposed)
1876–1909	Abdülhamid 2 (deposed)
1909–1918	Mehmet 5
1918–1922	Mehmet 6 (abdicated)
1922–1924	Abdülmecid 2 (caliph only)

Presidents of Turkey

1923–1938	Mustafa Kemal (Atatürk)
1938–1950	Ismet Inönü
1950–1960	Celal Bayar
1960–1961	Cemal Gürsel (acting)
1961–1966	Cemal Gürsel
1966–1973	Cevdet Sunay
1973–1980	Fahri Korutürk
1980	Ihsan Sabri Çaglayangil (acting)
1980–1982	Kenan Evren (acting)
1982–1989	Kenan Evren
1989–1993	Turgut Özal
1993–2000	Süleyman Demirel
2000–2007	Ahmed Necdet Sezer
2007–2014	Abdullah Gül
2014–	Recep Tayyip Erdoğan

Prime Ministers of Turkey

1923–1924	Mustafa İsmet (İsmet İnönü from 1934)

1924–1925	Ali Fethi Bey
1925–1937	İsmet İnönü
1937–1939	Celal Bayar
1939–1942	Refik Saydam
1942–1946	Sükrü Saracoglu
1946–1947	Recep Peker
1947–1949	Hasan Saka
1949–1950	Semsettin Günaltay
1950–1960	Adnan Menderes
1960–1961	Cemal Gürsel
1961–1965	İsmet İnönü
1965	Ali Suat Hayri Ürgüplü
1965–1971	Süleyman Demirel
1971–1972	Nihat Erim
1972–1973	Ferit Melen
1973–1974	Naim Talu
1974	Bülent Ecevit
1974–1975	Sadi Irmak
1975–1977	Süleyman Demirel
1977	Bülent Ecevit
1977–1978	Süleyman Demirel
1978–1979	Bülent Ecevit
1979–1980	Süleyman Demirel
1980–1983	Bülent Ülüsü
1983–1989	Turgut Özal
1989–1991	Yıldırım Akbulut
1991	Mesut Yılmaz
1991–1993	Süleyman Demirel
1993–1996	Tansu Çiller
1996	Mesut Yilmaz
1996–1997	Necmettin Erbakan
1997–1999	Mesut Yılmaz
1999–2002	Bülent Ecevit
2002–2003	Abdullah Gül
2003–2014	Recep Tayyip Erdoğan
2014–2016	Ahmet Davutoğlu
2016–2018	Binali Yıldırım
2018	Office of prime minister abolished

Bibliography

Acemoglu, D., 2015. *Why Turkish growth ended.* Retrieved November 16, 2020, from https://www.weforum.org/agenda/2015/11/why-turkish-growth-ended.

Ahmad, F., 2014. Turkey: A quest for identity. Oneworld Books [Kindle version].

Akan, A. A Critical Analysis of the Turkish Press Discourse against Non-Muslims: A Case Analysis of the Newspaper Coverage of the 1942 Wealth Tax in Middle Eastern Studies, July 2011, Vol. 47, No. 4 (July 2011), pp. 605-621.

Al Jazeera Staff, 2017. *What is the Muslim Brotherhood?* Retrieved July 15, 2020, from https://www.aljazeera.com/features/2017/6/18/what-is-the-muslim-brotherhood.

Alonso, C. R., 2015. *Gezi Park: A Revindication of Public Space.* In David, I., & K. F. Toktamış (Eds.), Everywhere Taksim: Sowing the Seeds for a New Turkey at Gezi. Amsterdam University Press.

Altayli, B., C. Caglayan, 2019. *Turkish cities could become 'graveyards' with building amnesty.* Retrieved March 5, 2020, from https://www.reuters.com/article/us-turkey-construction-idUSKCN1QF1VU.

Alver, A. (2009, March 24). *Tsjerkessere [Circassians].* In Store norske leksikon. Retrieved May 9, 2019, from https://snl.no/tsjerkessere.

American Committee for Armenian and Syrian Relief, n.d. *The Most Terrible Winter the World Has Ever Known.* Retrieved January 17, 2020, from https://archive.org/details/ldpd_11077593_000.

Amnesty International, n.d. *Turkey 2017/2018: Annual report.* Retrieved February 20, 2020, from https://www.refworld.org/docid/5a9938470.html.

Amnesty International, 2019. *Turkey: 'Judicial Reform' Package Is A Lost Opportunity to Address Deep Flaws in the Justice System.* Retrieved February 19, 2020, from https://www.amnesty.org/en/documents/eur44/1161/2019/en/.

Associated Press, 2020. *Second member of banned Turkish folk group dies after hunger strike.* Retrieved July 10, 2020, from https://www.theguardian.com/world/2020/may/07/second-member-banned-turkish-folk-group-grup-yorum-dies-hunger-strike--ibrahim-gokcek.

Astourian, S. *The Armenian Genocide: An Interpretation.* In The History Teacher, Vol. 23, No. 2 (Feb., 1990), pp. 111-160.

Ayata, S. *Patronage, Party, and State: The Politicization of Islam in Turkey.* In Middle East Journal, Vol. 50, No. 1 (Winter, 1996), pp. 40-56.

Aydogan, A., 2018. *Why the results of Turkey's election are surprising.* Retrieved August 26, 2023, from https://www.washingtonpost.com/news/monkey-cage/wp/2018/07/31/why-the-results-of-turkeys-election-are-surprising/

Balancar, F. (red.), 2013. The Sound of Silence II: Diyarbakır's Armenians Speak. Hrant Dink Foundation Publications.

Balancar, F. (red.), 2015. The Sound of Silence III: Ankara's Armenians Speak. Hrant Dink Foundation Publications.

Bakeer, A. H., 2020. *Coronavirus: Why conspiracy theories have taken root in Turkey,* retrieved December 3, 2020, from https://www.middleeasteye.net/opinion/coronavirus-turkey-why-conspiracy-theories-have-taken-root

Baran, Z., 2000. *Corruption: The Turkish Challenge,* in Journal of International Affairs, Fall 2000, Vol. 54, No. 1, Turkey: A Struggle between Nation and State (Fall 2000), pp. 127-146.

Barlow, D., 2006. *Ezogelin Çorbası - Turkish Red Lentil, Bulgur, and Mint Soup,* retrieved September 13, 2020, from https://cmes.fas.harvard.edu/news/ezogelin-çorbası-turkish-red-lentil-bulgur-and-mint-soup

Başaran, E., 2017. Frontline Turkey: The conflict at the heart of the Middle East. I.B. Tauris.

BBC, 2013. *Profile: Fethullah Gulen's Hizmet movement,* retrieved March 13, 2020, from https://www.bbc.com/news/world-13503361

BBC, 2017. *Turkey referendum: The numbers that tell the story,* retrieved August 26, 2023, from https://www.bbc.com/news/world-europe-39619354

BBC News, 2019. *Emine Bulut: Anger in Turkey over mother's murder,* retrieved January 15, 2020, from https://www.bbc.com/news/world-europe-49446389

Bekdil, B. *Erdoğan's Mission Impossible: Sustainable Turkish-Arab Solidarity,* in BESA Center Perspectives Paper, No. 535, (July 2017).

Bell-Fialkoff, A. *A Brief History of Ethnic Cleansing,* in Foreign Affairs, Vol. 72, No. 3 (Summer, 1993), pp. 110-121.

Bergum, V., 2018. Hummus og granateple: Mat fra Tyrkia og Midtøsten [Humus and Pomegranate: Food from Turkey and the Middle East]. Cappelen Damm.

Berkowitz, R. *"The Angry Jew Has Gotten His Revenge": Hannah Arendt on Revenge and Reconciliation,* in Philosophical Topics, Vol. 39, No. 2, Hannah Arendt (FALL 2011), pp. 1-20.

Bild, 2016. *Erdogans schillernder Clan,* retrieved December 14, 2020, from https://www.bild.de/politik/ausland/recep-tayyip-erdogan/wer-gehoert-zu-den-vertrauten-des-tuerkischen-praesidenten-45692482.bild.html

BirGün, 2019. *Tek adama koruma düşünceye pranga,* retrieved April 7, 2020, from https://www.birgun.net/haber/tek-adama-koruma-dusunceye-pranga-257653

BirGün, 2021. Bahçeli'den Boğaziçi eylemcilerine: Evlat değil başı ezilmesi gereken zehirli yılanlardır! [From Bahçeli to Boğaziçi activists: They are not our children, they are venomous snakes whose heads should be crushed!], retrieved February 23, 2021, from https://www.birgun.net/haber/bahceli-den-bogazici-eylemcilerine-evlat-degil-basi-ezilmesi-gereken-zehirli-yilanlardir-332892

Bora, A. and Çalışkan, K. *What is Under a Headscarf? Neo-Islamist vs. Kemalist Conservatism in Turkey,* in The Arab Studies Journal, Vol. 15/16, No. 2/1 (Fall 2007/Spring 2008), pp. 140-155.

Britannica, n.d. *Muslim Brotherhood,* retrieved July 15, 2020, from https://www.britannica.com/topic/Muslim-Brotherhood/Uprising-and-electoral-success

Butt, A. I., 2017. *The Ottoman Empire's Escalation from Reforms to the Armenian Genocide, 1908–1915,* in Secession and Security: Explaining State Strategy against Separatists. Cornell University Press.

Cagaptay, S. Race, *Assimilation and Kemalism: Turkish Nationalism and the Minorities in the 1930s,* in Middle Eastern Studies, Vol. 40, No. 3 (May, 2004), pp. 86-101.

Cagaptay, S., 2017. The new sultan: Erdogan and the crisis of modern Turkey. I. B. Tauris.

CBC News, air date March 12, 1985. *Deadly embassy attack in Ottawa by Armenian terrorists.* Accessed November 12, 2019, at https://youtu.be/kMxl9e3YsbE

Celasun, M. and D. Rodrik, 1989. *Turkish Economic Development: An Overview,* in J. D. Sachs and S. M. Collins (eds.), Developing Country Debt and Economic Performance, Volume 3: Country Studies - Indonesia, Korea, Philippines, Turkey. University of Chicago Press.

Chenoweth, E. and M. J. Stephan, 2011. Why Civil Resistance Works: The Strategic Logic of Nonviolent Conflict. Columbia University Press.

Cohen, J. P. B*etween civic and Islamic Ottomanism: Jewish imperial citizenship in the Hamidian era,* in International Journal of Middle East Studies, Vol. 44, No. 2 (May 2012), pp. 237-255.

Committee to Protect Journalists, n.d. *25 Journalists Killed in Turkey,* retrieved April 7, 2020, from https://cpj.org/data/killed/2016/turkey?status=Killed&motiveConfirmed%5B%5D=Confirmed&type%5B%5D=Journalist&cc_fips%5B%5D=TU&start_year=1992&end_year=2016&group_by=location

Constitution of October 4, 1958, of France. Retrieved April 22, 2020, from https://www.conseil-constitutionnel.fr/sites/default/files/as/root/bank_mm/anglais/constiution_anglais_oct2009.pdf

Constitution of the United States of America, retrieved April 22, 2020, from https://constitutioncenter.org/media/files/constitution.pdf

Constitution of Turkey, retrieved April 22, 2020, from https://global.tbmm.gov.tr/docs/constitution_en.pdf?TSPD_101_R0=08ffcef486ab200056748f6e9e8f67f7611d7299ccbb343212cea6a6c0f9dacbcaf7e5ba7db9fe65084f3f9ca41430009c980ed63fb7afb574c01c89a7fe7213df619ea2273047c67444fcdc36f79fb0fddb43373349d4aba235ac96481259b8

Convention on the Prevention and Punishment of the Crime of Genocide, adopted December 9, 1948, by United Nations General Assembly resolution 260 A (III), retrieved January 20, 2024, from https://www.ohchr.org/en/instruments-mechanisms/instruments/convention-prevention-and-punishment-crime-genocide

Cook, S. A., 2016. *How Happy Is the One Who Says, I Am a Turk!* retrieved March 17, 2020, from https://foreignpolicy.com/2016/03/28/how-happy-is-the-one-who-says-i-am-a-turk/

Cooper, B., T. Akçam. *Turks, Armenians, and the "G-Word",* in World Policy Journal, Vol. 22, No. 3 (Fall, 2005), pp. 81-93.

Corke, S., A. Finkel, D. J. Kramer, C. A. Robbins, N. Schenkkan, 2014. *Democracy in Crisis: Corruption, Media, and Power in Turkey,* retrieved April 2, 2021, from https://freedomhouse.org/sites/default/files/2020-02/SR_Corruption_Media_Power_Turkey_PDF.pdf

Çatalhöyük Research Project, n.d., *The Rise and Fall of a Neolithic Town.* Retrieved March 20, 2019, from http://www.catalhoyuk.com/site/rise_and_fall_of_a_neolithic_town

Çelebi, S., 2009. *1971-1972: Last Days of Young Revolutionaries Before Execution,* retrieved April 19, 2020, from https://bianet.org/english/people/114342-1971-1972-last-days-of-young-revolutionaries-before-execution

Çetin, F., 2008. My grandmother: An Armenian-Turkish memoir. Verso.

Çetin, R., 2023. *Brain drain: As Turkey's youth looks abroad, some mothers are encouraging them,* retrieved August 27, 2023, from https://turkeyrecap.substack.com/p/brain-drain-as-turkeys-youth-looks

Danforth, N., 2014. *Notes on a Turkish Conspiracy,* retrieved December 3, 2020, from https://foreignpolicy.com/2014/10/02/notes-on-a-turkish-conspiracy/

Daily Sabah, 2020. *Turkey-Russia S-400 deal delayed due to coronavirus pandemic,* retrieved May 2, 2020, from https://www.dailysabah.com/politics/turkey-russia-s-400-deal-delayed-due-to-coronavirus-pandemic/news

Dashdondog, B., 2011. *A brief historical background of the Armenians and Mongols,* in The Mongols and the Armenians (1220-1335). Brill.

Davis, P. K., E. V. Larson, Z. Haldeman, M. Oguz, Y. Rana, 2012. *Public Support for the Kurdistan Workers' Party (PKK) in Turkey,* in Understanding and Influencing Public Support for Insurgency and Terrorism. RAND Corporation.

de Bernières, L., 2005. Birds without wings. Vintage.

Ercan, H. Talking to the ontological other: armed struggle and the negotiations between the Turkish state and the PKK, in Dialectical Anthropology, Vol. 37, No. 1 (March 2013), pp. 113-122.

Esen, B. Nation-building, party-strength, and regime consolidation: Kemalism in comparative perspective, in Turkish Studies, 15:4 (2014), pp. 600-620.

European Commission, 2019. *Commission staff working document. Turkey 2019 report,* retrieved April 30, 2020, from https://www.avrupa.info.tr/sites/default/files/2019-05/20190529-turkey-report.pdf

European Commission, 2020a. *Turkey,* retrieved April 30, 2020, from https://ec.europa.eu/trade/policy/countries-and-regions/countries/turkey/

European Commission, 2020b. *Turkey: Customs Unions and Preferential Arrangements,* retrieved April 30, 2020, from https://ec.europa.eu/taxation_customs/business/calculation-customs-duties/rules-origin/customs-unions/turkey-customs-unions-preferential-arrangements_en

European Federation of Journalists, 2019, *Monitoring jailed journalists in Turkey.* Retrieved on April 7, 2020, from https://europeanjournalists.org/turkey-journalists-in-jail/

European Parliament, 1997. *Luxembourg European Council 12 and 13 December 1997 Presidency Conclusions,* retrieved April 30, 2020, from https://www.europarl.europa.eu/summits/lux1_en.htm

European Parliament, 2013. *European Parliament resolution of 13 June 2013 on the situation in Turkey (2013/2664(RSP)),* retrieved January 11, 2022, from https://www.europarl.europa.eu/doceo/document/TA-7-2013-0277_EN.pdf

Farber, H. S., D. Herbst, I. Kuziemko, S. Naidu, 2018. *Working paper # 620: Unions and Inequality Over the Twentieth Century: New Evidence from Survey Data.* Princeton University, Industrial Relations Section.

Finkel, A., 2012. Turkey: What everyone needs to know. Oxford University Press [Kindle version].

Finkel, C., 2005. Osman's dream: The history of the Ottoman Empire. Basic Books [Kindle version].

Forensic Architecture, 2019. *The Killing of Tahir Elçi,* retrieved April 9, 2020, at https://forensic-architecture.org/investigation/the-killing-of-tahir-elci

Fradkin, H. and L. Libby. *Erdogan's Grand Vision,* in World Affairs, MARCH / APRIL 2013, Vol. 175, No. 6 (MARCH / APRIL 2013), pp. 41-50.

Frazer, S., 2020. *Member of Turkish band dies on 288th day of hunger strike,* retrieved April 6, 2020, from https://abcnews.go.com/Entertainment/wireStory/member-turkish-folk-band-dies-288th-hunger-strike-69956509

Fukuyama, F., 2018. Identity: Contemporary identity politics and the struggle for recognition. Profile Books [Kindle version].

GAP Southeastern Regional Development Administration, 2015. *What is GAP?*, retrieved April 29, 2020, from http://www.gap.gov.tr/en/

Georg, S., P. A. Michalove, A. M. Ramer, P. J. Sidwell. *Telling General Linguists about Altaic,* in Journal of Linguistics, Vol. 35, No. 1 (Mar., 1999), pp. 65-98.

Göçek, F. M. *Through a Glass Darkly: Consequences of a Politicized Past in Contemporary Turkey,* in The Annals of the American Academy of Political and Social Science, Vol. 617, ThePolitics of History in Comparative Perspective (May, 2008), pp. 88-106.

Guiness World Records, 2020. *Most trees planted in one hour by a team of unlimited size (single location),* retrieved November 23, 2020, from https://www.guinnessworldrecords.com/world-records/most-trees-planted-simultaneously?fb_comment_id=732983423461511_843856505707535

Gürbüz, M., 2016. *Kurdish Movements in the Southeast,* in Rival Kurdish Movements in Turkey: Transforming Ethnic Conflict. Amsterdam University Press.

HalkTV, 2021. *Erdoğan: Siz öğrenci misiniz yoksa terörist mi? [Erdoğan: Are you students or terrorists?]*, retrieved February 22, 2021, from https://halktv.com.tr/erdogan-akp-il-kongresinde-konusuyor-446488h

hanggliding.org, 2016. *A Comparison of Hang Gliding to Paragliding,* retrieved September 17, 2019, from https://www.hanggliding.org/wiki/A_Comparison_of_Hang_Gliding_to_Paragliding

Hanioğlu, M. S., 2011. Atatürk: An intellectual biography. Princeton University Press.

Hansen, S., 2019. *'The Era of People Like You Is Over': How Turkey Purged Its Intellectuals,* retrieved November 11, 2020, from https://www.nytimes.com/2019/07/24/magazine/the-era-of-people-like-you-is-over-how-turkey-purged-its-intellectuals.html

Hashim, A. S., 2012. *The Return of the Partiya Karkaren Kurdistan: Terrorism and Political Violence in Turkey in 2012,* in Counter Terrorist Trends and Analyses , Vol. 4, No. 11 (November 2012), pp. 2-6.

Harris, G. S., *The Causes of the 1960 Revolution in Turkey,* in The Middle East Journal, Vol. 24, No. 4 (Autumn 1970), pp. 438-454.

Helliwell, J. F., R. Layard, J. D. Sachs, 2019. *World Happiness Report 2019.* New York: Sustainable Development Solutions Network.

Heper, M. *Islam and Democracy in Turkey: Toward a Reconciliation?* in Middle East Journal, Vol. 51, No. 1 (Winter, 1997), pp. 32-45.

Human Rights Watch, 1996. *Turkey's failed policy to aid the forcibly displaced in the southeast,* retrieved November 30, 2018, from https://www.hrw.org/legacy/reports/1996/Turkey2.htm

Human Rights Watch, 2013. *Turkey: A weekend of police abuse,* downloaded April 1, 2021, from https://www.hrw.org/news/2013/06/18/turkey-weekend-police-abuse

Human Rights Watch, 2019. *Lawyers on trial: Abusive prosecutions and erosion of fair trial rights in Turkey,* retrieved February 19, 2020, from https://www.hrw.org/report/2019/04/10/lawyers-trial/abusive-prosecutions-and-erosion-fair-trial-rights-turkey

Human Rights Watch, 2020. *Turkey: Events of 2019,* retrieved February 24, 2020, from https://www.hrw.org/world-report/2020/country-chapters/turkey#

Human Rights Watch, 2021. *Turkey: Draft Law Threatens Civil Society,* retrieved May 5, 2021, from https://www.hrw.org/news/2020/12/24/turkey-draft-law-threatens-civil-society

Hürriyet Daily News, 2015. *20 dogs killed by poison in western Turkey,* retrieved January 9, 2020, from https://www.hurriyetdailynews.com/20-dogs-killed-by-poison-in-western-turkey-93114

Hürriyet Daily News, 2019a. *Erdoğan says he supports restoring death penalty amid nationwide outrage over femicides,* retrieved March 4, 2021, from https://www.hurriyetdailynews.com/erdogan-says-wont-allow-us-stalling-in-syria-deal-146147

Hürriyet Daily News, 2019b. *Student killed by stray dogs in Turkey's Kayseri,* retrieved January 9, 2020, from https://www.hurriyetdailynews.com/student-killed-by-stray-dogs-in-turkeys-kayseri-140273

Hürriyet Daily News, 2020. *Historic Virgin Mary Church reopens as library,* retrieved February 27, 2020, from https://www.hurriyetdailynews.com/historic-virgin-mary-church-reopens-as-library-151050

Hussein, M., 2018. V*ision 2023: Turkey and the post-Ottoman anniversary,* retrieved March 5, 2020, from https://www.middleeastmonitor.com/20180212-vision-2023-turkey-and-the-post-ottoman-anniversary/

International Crisis Group, 2011. *Turkey: Ending the PKK insurgency.* Europe Report N°213 – 20 September 2011.

International Crisis Group, 2012. *Turkey's Kurdish impasse: The view from Diyarbakir.* Europe Report N°222 – 30 November 2012.

International Crisis Group, 2013. *Turkey's Protests: The Politics of an Unexpected Movement.* Commentary / Europe & Central Asia - 4 June 2013.

Inter-Parliamentary Union, 2021. *Monthly ranking of women in national parliaments,* retrieved March 9, 2021, from https://data.ipu.org/women-ranking?month=1&year=2021

İdil N., 2021. *Turkish gov't uses protests at Boğaziçi University to attack LGBT rights with Islamist discourse,* retrieved January 12, 2022, from https://www.duvarenglish.com/turkish-govt-uses-protests-at-bogazici-university-to-attack-lgbt-rights-with-islamist-discourse-news-56071

Johnsen, N., 2018. *Tyrkias siste kristne: Vi frykter forfølgelse [Turkey's last Christians: We fear persecution],* retrieved January 15, 2020, from https://www.vg.no/nyheter/utenriks/i/A2n8ME/tyrkias-siste-kristne-vi-frykter-forfoelgelse

Johnsen, N., 2019. Erdogan - Tyrkias nye sultan [Erdogan - Turkey's new sultan]. Aschehoug.

Kadercan, B., Strong Armies, Slow Adaptation: Civil-Military Relations and the Diffusion of Military Power, in International Security, Vol. 38, No. 3 (WINTER 2013/14), pp. 117-152.

Kalaycioglu, E., *Turkish Democracy: Patronage versus Governance,* in Turkish Studies, Vol. 2, No.1 (Spring 2001), pp. 54-70.

Kaliber, A., Re-engaging the Self/Other Problematic in Post-Positivist International Relations: The 1964 Expulsion of Greeks from Istanbul Revisited, in Journal of Southeast European and Black Sea Studies 19 (4) 2019, pp. 365-386.

Kakissis, J., 2019, *'We Don't Want To Die': Women In Turkey Decry Rise In Violence And Killings,* retrieved January 19, 2020, from https://www.npr.org/2019/09/15/760135010/we-dont-want-to-die-women-in-turkey-decry-rise-in-violence-and-killings

Karakaş, B., 2019. *Femicide in Turkey: What's lacking is political will,* retrieved June 6, 2021, from https://www.mei.edu/publications/femicide-turkey-whats-lacking-political-will

Karaveli, H., 2018. Why Turkey is authoritarian. Pluto Press.

Kasbarian, S., 2016. *The Istanbul Armenians: Negotiating Coexistence,* in Bryant, R. (red.), Post-Ottoman Coexistence: Sharing Space in the Shadow of Conflict. Berghahn Books.

Kent, S., 2020. *Most of 11m trees planted in Turkish project 'may be dead',* retrieved November 24, 2020, from https://www.theguardian.com/world/2020/jan/30/most-of-11m-trees-planted-in-turkish-project-may-be-dead

Kevorkian, R. H. *Earth, fire, water: or how to make the Armenian corpses disappear,* in Anstett, É. and J.-M. Dreyfus (red.), Destruction and Human Remains: Disposal and Concealment in Genocide and Mass Violence. Manchester University Press, 2014.

Kevorkian, R. H. *A few historical notes on the Armenian presence,* in Ankara, in Balancar, F. (red.), The Sound of Silence III: Ankara's Armenians Speak. Hrant Dink Foundation Publications, 2015.

Kili, S. *Kemalism in Contemporary Turkey,* in International Political Science Review, Vol. 1, No. 3, Political Ideology: Its Impact on Contemporary Political Transformations (1980), pp. 381-404.

King, C., 2014. Midnight at the Pera Palace: The birth of modern Istanbul. W.W. Norton & Company, Inc [Kindle version].

Knaus, K. *Turkish women: A century of change,* in Turkish Policy Quarterly, Vol. 6, No. 5 (2007), pp. 47-59.

Lehtinen, A., 2012. *Cleaning up the Bosphorus,* retrieved October 28, 2020, from https://theecologist.org/2012/oct/22/cleaning-bosphorus

Leiser, G,. 2016. Review of Peacock, A.C.S, 2015. The Great Seljuk Empire. Edinburgh University Press, in Journal of the American Oriental Society 136.4 (2016).

Lewis, B. *The Mongols, the Turks and the Muslim Polity,* in Transactions of the Royal Historical Society, Vol. 18 (1968), pp. 49-68. Cambridge University Press.

Luban, D. *Folktales of International Justice,* in Proceedings of the Annual Meeting (American Society of International Law), Vol.98 (MARCH 31-APRIL 3, 2004), pp. 182-185.

Maltz, 2016. *Why Jews in Terror-stricken Turkey Aren't Fleeing to Israel – Yet,* retrieved January 10, 2020, from https://www.haaretz.com/israel-news/.premium-why-jews-in-terror-stricken-turkey- arent-fleeing-to-israel-yet-1.5433261

Mango, A., 1999. Ataturk: The biography of the founder of modern Turkey. John Murray.

Marcus, A., 2007. Blood and belief: The PKK and the Kurdish fight for independence. New York University Press [Kindle version].

McKernan, B., 2020. *Murder in Turkey sparks outrage over rising violence against women in Istanbul,* retrieved March 9, 2021, from https://www.theguardian.com/world/2020/jul/23/turkey-outrage-rising-violence-against-women

McTighe, K., 2019. *Turkish scientist gets 15-month sentence for publishing environmental study,* retrieved March 9, 2020, from https://www.sciencemag.org/news/2019/09/turkishscientist-gets-15-month-sentence-publishing-environmental-study

Mengü, N., 2020. *What happened in Gezi did not stay in Gezi,* retrieved March 21, 2021, from https://www.duvarenglish.com/columns/2020/02/19/what-happened-in-gezi-did-not-stay-in-gezi

Mendelsohn, O., 2017. *Den armensk-ortodokse kirke [The Armenian Orthodox Church],* in Store norske leksikon, retrieved October 23, 2019, from https://snl.no/den_armensk-ortodokse_kirke

Miller, D. E. and L. T. Miller. *Armenian Survivors: A Typological Analysis of Victim Response,* in The Oral History Review, Vol. 10 (1982), pp. 47-72.

Mills, A. *The Place of Locality for Identity in the Nation: Minority Narratives of Cosmopolitan Istanbul,* in International Journal of Middle East Studies, Aug., 2008, Vol. 40, No. 3 (Aug., 2008), pp. 383-401

Moody, B., 2020. *Women leaders in Turkey stand up to gender based violence,* retrieved March 3, 2021, from https://www.ndi.org/our-stories/women-leaders-turkey-stand-gender-based-violence

Nachmani, A., 2003. Turkey: Facing a new millennium: Coping with intertwined conflicts. Manchester University Press.

New Zealand Ministry for Culture and Heritage, 2016. *Gallipoli casualties by country,* retrieved July 24, 2019, from https://nzhistory.govt.nz/media/interactive/gallipoli-casualties-country

Ochsenwald, W. L. *The Jidda Massacre of 1858*, in Middle Eastern Studies, Vol. 13, No. 3 (Oct., 1977), pp. 314-326.

OECD, n.d. *Better Life Index. Turkey,* retrieved November 21, 2020, from http://www.oecdbetterlifeindex.org/countries/turkey/

OECD, n.d. *Labour force,* retrieved November 17, 2020, from https://data.oecd.org/emp/labour-force.htm#indicator-chart

OECD, 2018. *OECD Economic Surveys: Turkey: July 2018 Overview,* retrieved November 19, 2020, from www.oecd.org/eco/surveys/economic-survey-turkey.htm

OECD, 2020, *OECD Tourism Trends and Policies 2020*, retrieved on November 16, 2020, from https://www.oecd-ilibrary.org/sites/f3b16239-en/index.html?itemId=/content/component/f3b16239-en

Olson, R. *The Remains of Talat: A Dialectic between Republic and Empire,* in Die Welt des Islams, New Series, Bd. 26, Nr. 1/4 (1986), pp. 46-56.

Osterlund, P. B., 2020. *Members of popular Turkish folk collective approach death on hunger strike,* retrieved April 6, 2020, from https://www.al-monitor.com/originals/2020/03/members-of-popular-turkish-folk-collective-approach-death-on.html

Pamuk, O., 1994. Svart bok [Black book]. Gyldendal.

Parker, E. H. *The Origin of the Turks*, in The English Historical Review, Vol. 11, No. 43 (Jul., 1896), pp. 431-445.

Peacock, A. C. S., 2015. The Great Seljuk Empire. Edinburgh University Press [Kindle version].

Pitel, L., 2018. *Erdogan takes control of Turkey's sovereign wealth fund,* retrieved December 15, 2020, from https://www.ft.com/content/8fe07c16-b693-11e8-bbc3-ccd7de085ffe

Pring, C. and J. Vrushi, 2019. *Tackling the crisis of democracy, promoting rule of law and fighting corruption,* retrieved December 13, 2020, from https://www.transparency.org/en/news/tackling-crisis-of-democracy-promoting-rule-of-law-and-fighting-corruption

Reuters Institute for the Study of Journalism, 2018. Reuters Institute Digital News Report 2018 - Turkey Supplementary Report.

Reuters Staff, 2017. *German spy agency chief says does not believe Gulen behind Turkey coup attempt,* retrieved April 25, 2020, from https://www.reuters.com/article/us-turkey-security-germany-idUSKBN16P0LQ

Republic of Turkey, Ministry of Foreign Affairs, n.d. Lausanne Peace Treaty VI. Convention Concerning the Exchange of Greek and Turkish Populations Signed at Lausanne, January 30, 1923. Retrieved January 9, 2022, from http://www.mfa.gov.tr/lausanne-peace-treaty-vi_-convention-concerning-the-exchange-of-greek-and-turkish-populations-signed-at-lausanne_.en.mfa

Robins, P., 2008. *Back from the Brink: Turkey's Ambivalent Approaches to the Hard Drugs Issue,* in Middle East Journal, Autumn, 2008, Vol. 62, No. 4 (Autumn, 2008), pp. 630-650.

Roche, J. T. In the Wake of Mantzikert: The First Crusade and the Alexian Reconquest of Western Anatolia, in History, Vol. 94, No. 2 (314) (April 2009), pp. 135-153.

Rousseau, J.-J., 1762. The Social Contract. Barnes & Noble Publishing.

Sande, S. (2018, October 8). *Troja [Troy],* in Store norske leksikon. Retrieved March 20, 2019, from https://snl.no/Troja

Schenkkan, N., 2018. *The Remarkable Scale of Turkey's "Global Purge": How It Became a Threat to the Rule of Law Everywhere,* retrieved March 6, 2020, from https://www.foreignaffairs.com/articles/turkey/2018-01-29/remarkable-scale-turkeys-global-purge

Schønhardt, A., Smith-Meyer, T., Filseth, G., 2019. *Armenias historie [Armenia's history],* in Store norske leksikon at snl.no. Retrieved October 23, 2019, from https://snl.no/Armenias_historie

Sen, N. *Turkey's Woman in the Red Dress,* in Middle East Report, No. 268, GENDER FRONT LINES: EGYPT, SYRIA, TUNISIA, TURKEY (Fall 2013), pp. 38-39, 48.

Seim, J., and G. Lurås. *Bulgarias historie [Bulgaria's history],* in Store norske leksikon at snl.no, retrieved July 17, 2020, from https://snl.no/Bulgarias_historie

Shepard, F. D. *Personal Experience in Turkish Massacres and Relief Work,* in The Journal of Race Development, Vol. 1, No. 3 (Jan., 1911), pp. 316-339.

Shields, S. *The Greek-Turkish Population Exchange: Internationally Administered Ethnic Cleansing,* in Middle East Report, No. 267, CHRISTIANS: EGYPT, IRAQ, LEBANON, PALESTINE (Summer 2013), pp. 2-6.

Silverman, R., 2015. *The Şükrü Kaya Problem,* retrieved January 11, 2022, from https://reubensilverman.wordpress.com/2015/04/19/the-sukru-kaya-problem/#_ftn14

SIPRI Arms Transfers Database, http://armstrade.sipri.org/armstrade/page/values.php

Smith, O., 2017. *Which country drinks the most tea? The answer might surprise you,* retrieved September 13, 2020, from https://www.telegraph.co.uk/travel/maps-and-graphics/tea-consumption-per-capita/

Starostin, G., 2016. *Altaic Languages,* in Oxford Research Encyclopedia of Linguistics, retrieved September 18, 2020, from https://oxfordre.com/linguistics/linguistics/view/10.1093/acrefor

e/9780199384655.001.0001/acrefore-9780199384655-e-35; Georg et al. 1999.

Store norske leksikon. *Gallipolifelttoget [Gallipoli Campaign],* retrieved January 9, 2022, from https://snl.no/Gallipolifelttoget

Store norske leksikon. *Lilleasia [Asia Minor],* retrieved December 28, 2021, from https://snl.no/Lilleasia

Store norske leksikon. *Lilleasias historie [History of Asia Minor],* retrieved March 20, 2019, from https://snl.no/Lilleasias_historie

Store norske leksikon. *Normannere [Normans],* retrieved April 4, 2019, from https://snl.no/normannere

Shaw, S. J. *Resettlement of Refugees in Anatolia, 1918-1923,* in Turkish Studies Association Bulletin, Vol. 22, No. 1 (Spring 1998), pp. 58-90.

Statista, 2020. *Gross Domestic Product of G20 Countries in 2019, with a Projection for 2025 (in Billion U.S. Dollars),* retrieved November 16, 2020, from https://www.statista.com/statistics/722944/g20-country-gdp-levels/

Suny, R. G. *Truth in Telling: Reconciling Realities in the Genocide of the Ottoman Armenians,* in The American Historical Review, Vol. 114, No. 4 (OCTOBER 2009), pp. 930-946.

The Constantinopolitan Society, 2017. OSCE Human Dimension Implementation Meeting, retrieved July 18, 2020, from https://www.osce.org/files/f/documents/d/7/341036.pdf

Thiesen, F., and C. Kaveh, 2020. *Kurdisk [Kurdish],* in Store norske leksikon at snl.no. Retrieved January 10, 2022, from https://snl.no/kurdisk

Törne, A. *Recent Studies on the September Pogrom in Istanbul 1955,* in Iran & the Caucasus, 2015, Vol. 19, No. 4 (2015), pp. 403-417.

TRT World/Saad Hasan, 2017. *The New York Librarian who Nearly Ruled the Ottoman Empire.* Retrieved June 10, 2019, from https://www.trtworld.com/magazine/the-new-york-librarian-who-could-have-ruled-the-ottoman-empire-317001

Turkish Minute, 2019. *1,477 Killed in Work-related Accidents in Turkey in First 10 Months of 2019,* retrieved November 20, 2020, from https://www.turkishminute.com/2019/11/04/1477-killed-in-work-related-accidents-in-turkey-in-first-10-months-of-2019/

Turkish Statistical Institute, 2020. Front page of website, retrieved November 16, 2020, from https://www.tuik.gov.tr/

Tuysuz, G., 2020. *Turkish Women Rally Against Domestic Violence as Ruling Party Contemplates Leaving Key Rights Treaty,* retrieved March 8, 2021, from https://edition.cnn.com/2020/08/05/europe/turkey-gender-protests-istanbul-convention-intl/index.html

Ueno, M. *For the Fatherland and the State: Armenians Negotiate the Tanzimat Reforms,* in International Journal of Middle East Studies, Vol. 45, No. 1 (February 2013), pp. 93-109.

UN Women, 2016. *Global Database on Violence Against Women. Turkey,* retrieved March 3, 2021, from https://evaw-global-database.unwomen.org/es/countries/asia/turkey#2

United States Commission on International Religious Freedom, 2019. *Annual Report of the U.S. Commission on International Religious Freedom,* retrieved April 25, 2020, from https://www.uscirf.gov/sites/default/files/2019USCIRFAnnualReport.pdf

U.S. News and World Report, 2019. *The 10 Countries With the Most Religious Freedom, Ranked by Perception.* Retrieved March 17, 2020, from https://www.usnews.com/news/best-countries/slideshows/the-10-countries-with-the-most-religious-freedom-ranked-by-perception

van Bruinessen, M. *Religion in Kurdistan,* in Kurdish Times (New York) vol. 4 nos. 1-2 (1991), pp. 5-27.

World Bank, 2014. *2013 Turkey Enterprise Survey: Country Highlights,* retrieved November 16, 2020, from https://www.enterprisesurveys.org/content/dam/enterprisesurveys/documents/country-highlights/Turkey-2013.pdf

World Bank, 2020. *Gini Index (World Bank Estimate),* retrieved November 19, 2020, from https://data.worldbank.org/indicator/SI.POV.GINI

Vogt, K. *Alevitter [Alevis],* in Store norske leksikon at snl.no. Retrieved February 19, 2021, from https://snl.no/alevitter

Wilkinson, P. *Armenian Terrorism,* in The World Today, Vol. 39, No. 9 (Sep., 1983), pp. 344-350.

Wikipedia. (2018, September 24). *Sevim Tanürek.* From Wikipedia, The Free Encyclopedia. Retrieved December 15, 2020, from https://en.wikipedia.org/w/index.php?title=Sevim_Tan%C3%BCrek&oldid=861009557

Wikipedia. (2019, August 24). *Hezârfen Ahmed Çelebi.* From Wikipedia, The Free Encyclopedia. Retrieved September 17, 2019, from https://en.m.wikipedia.org/wiki/Hezârfen_Ahmed_Çelebi

Wikipedia. (2020, August 3). *List of Countries by Tea Consumption Per Capita.* From Wikipedia, The Free Encyclopedia. Retrieved September 13, 2020, from https://en.wikipedia.org/w/index.php?title=List_of_countries_by_tea_consumption_per_capita&oldid=971010802

Wikipedia. (2020, March 24). *List of Russian Military Bases Abroad,* retrieved April 29, 2020, from https://en.wikipedia.org/wiki/List_of_Russian_military_bases_abroad

Wikipedia. (2020, April 1). *List of Journalists Killed in Turkey.* From Wikipedia, The Free Encyclopedia. Retrieved April 7, 2020, from https://en.wikipedia.org/wiki/List_of_journalists_killed_in_Turkey

Wikipedia. (2020, June 16). *List of Earthquakes in Turkey.* From Wikipedia, The Free Encyclopedia. Retrieved September 29, 2020, from https://en.wikipedia.org/w/index.php?title=List_of_earthquakes_in_Turkey&oldid=962838505

Wikipedia. (2020, September 12). *İmam Bayıldı.* From Wikipedia, The Free Encyclopedia. Retrieved September 13, 2020, from https://en.wikipedia.org/w/index.php?title=%C4%B0mam_bay%C4%B1ld%C4%B1&oldid=978109302

Wikipedia. (2021, January 4). *Roussel de Bailleul.* From Wikipedia, The Free Encyclopedia. Retrieved January 25, 2021, from https://en.wikipedia.org/w/index.php?title=Roussel_de_Bailleul&oldid=998196856

World Inequality Database, n.d. *Turkey. Inequality in Turkey, 1990-2019,* retrieved January 24, 2021, from https://wid.world/country/turkey/

Yackley, A. J., 2016. *Ottoman Prince Visits Former Realm to Spread Laughter.* Retrieved June 8, 2019, from https://www.reuters.com/article/us-turkey-comedy-ottoman/ottoman-prince-visits-former-realm-to-spread-laughter-idUSKCN12P1PW

Zihnioğlu, Ö., 2019. *The Legacy of the Gezi Protests in Turkey, i*n Youngs, R. (ed.), After Protest: Pathways Beyond Mass Mobilization. Carnegie Endowment for International Peace.

Zürcher, E. J., 2004. Turkey: A Modern History. I. B. Tauris [Kindle version].

Zürcher, E. J., 2010. The Young Turk Legacy and Nation Building: From the Ottoman Empire to Atatürk's Turkey. I. B. Tauris.

Notes

[1] It was common for the chief of the servants in harem to be black. He also had to be a eunuch, like the other male servants of the harem, so as not to be a "threat" to the women of the harem. Arab slave traders made sure that the demand for black eunuchs by powerful officials in Istanbul was met.

[2] Store norske leksikon, *Lilleasias historie*; Çatalhöyük Research Project, n.d.

[3] One of (at least) three museums that are particularly worth visiting in Turkey for people interested in early civilization. The other two are the Museum of Ancient Orient in Istanbul and the Antalya Museum.

[4] Store norske leksikon, *Lilleasia.*

[5] Sande, 2018.

[6] The Galatians were descendants of a people who lived in Gaul, which included much of today's France, Belgium, the Netherlands, parts of Switzerland and Germany and northern Italy. One of the letters in the Bible from the Apostle Paul was sent to the Galatians in Asia Minor (Anatolia).

[7] King, 2014, p. 273.

[8] King, 2014, p. 273.

[9] Venice, which today is a city in Italy, was a duchy - established in the late 600s - which evolved into an important center of power and commerce. The plan for the fourth crusade was initially that it would go by sea from Venice to Palestine, but the Venetian Duke persuaded the crusaders to go to Constantinople instead. The crusade thus lost its religious motive, and the Venetian Duke ended up with dominance over vast areas of the Balkan Peninsula and many Greek islands.

[10] Especially known for its famous church meeting in the year 325.

[11] In today's western China.

[12] Parker, 1896. The Huns became known in Europe as powerful warriors at the end of the fourth century. They came from Asia, fought on horseback and subjugated much of Europe. When the famous Hun King Attila died in 453, the kingdom disintegrated.

[13] But possibly still within modern Gansu in China.

[14] Today called Syr Darya, flowing through several countries in Central Asia.

[15] A vassal state was a state that had been defeated by another state, had limited autonomy, and regularly had to pay taxes to its superior.

[16] Peacock, 2015; Leiser, 2016.

[17] Leiser, 2016.

[18] Current Malazgirt north of the Van lake in eastern Turkey.

[19] Finkel, C., 2005, p. 3. It is unclear what the different authors think was the difference between Turkmen and Turks in Anatolia at that time. The terms appear to be used interchangeably, and no effort is made to highlight the differences. Today, however, Turkmen and Turkish are considered as two different languages that are mutually understandable, more or less in the same way as the Scandinavian languages.

[20] Store norske leksikon, *Normannere*; Wikipedia, *Roussel de Bailleul*.

[21] Lindner, 1983, as cited in Finkel, C., 2005, p. 2.

[22] I do not here go into detail of how Islam in reality greatly influenced many of the decisions taken in the Ottoman Empire. There was a continuous interplay between religious and political considerations, which, in my opinion, is of limited use for understanding the Turkey of today. Knowing that Islam was a central part of the Ottoman Empire is important, but the current role of Islam in Turkey is of a different nature, to a large extent because of the forced secularization that followed the establishment of the Turkish Republic. I write more about the secularization in later chapters.

[23] 500 years later, the historic battle became the motif for a famous painting by Adam Stefanovic in 1870, and another 100 years after this the event - and the painting - was used by Serbian nationalists during the war in the 1990s to "prove" that the Muslims (the Bosnians) had always wanted to get rid of them. According to

the warmongers, the Serbs had to take the Bosnians before the Bosnians took them.

[24] Lewis, 1968, p. 67.

[25] "Harem" comes from the word for "forbidden" in Arabic and refers to the part of a house where guests did not have access. The guests were met in the part of the house meant for this, called the *selamlık*. (The word "selam" means "hello" or "regards" in today's Turkey.) In daily life the harem was the place where the women stayed, where only the men of the closest family had access. For a sultan, this would mean wife(s), concubines and their children, and often the sultan's mother. Concubines were women taken into the harem without the sultan marrying them. They could be slaves or abducted from the enemy's family during war (and thereby turned into what we today would call sex slaves).

[26] Ruthenia is the Latin name of Rus, a large area in Eastern Europe. Ruthenia could be used to refer to the area of the entire former Kievan Rus' federation, which, at its largest, stretched from the Baltic Sea almost to the Black Sea.

[27] Peirce, 1993, as quoted in C. Finkel, p. 132.

[28] Peirce, 1993, as quoted in C. Finkel, p. 133.

[29] Finkel, C., 2005, p. 339.

[30] In today's western Turkey, south of Izmir.

[31] Although to a much lesser extent in the Ottoman Empire than in many European countries. For example, when the Jews were banned from Spain in 1492, it was with the Ottomans they sought refuge.

[32] Finkel, C., 2005, p. 355-6.

[33] An insignia is an object showing that the owner holds a particular high rank, such as a flag, a crown, or a seal.

[34] Finkel, C., 2005, p. 11-12.

[35] The Mamluks ruled Egypt from approx. 1250 to 1517.

[36] Finkel, C., 2005, pp. 111, 114-115.

[37] Tsar Nicholas I is to have been the first to do this. King, 2014, p. 31.

[38] The data and arguments in the following paragraphs are mainly those of Kadercan, 2013-14.

[39] See, for instance, an example in Kadercan, 2013-14, p. 134, and several in Finkel, C., 2005.

[40] Finkel, C., 2005, p. 224.

[41] Zürcher, 2004, 22.

[42] Both Hezarfen, meaning "having a thousand techniques," and Çelebi, meaning "gentleman" or "well-mannered," are titles.

[43] Wikipedia, 2019, Hezârfen Ahmed Çelebi.

[44] Wikipedia, 2019, Hezârfen Ahmed Çelebi; hanggliding.org, 2016.

[45] Zürcher, 2004, pp. 13-14, 47-48.

[46] Zürcher, 2010, p. 63.

[47] Zürcher, 2010, p. 66.

[48] Zürcher, 2004, pp. 26, 41.

[49] Zürcher, 2004, p. 45.

[50] Reform minister Mithat Pasha was sent into exile in February 1877, incarcerated in Hijaz in 1881 and strangled to death in 1884, "most likely on the orders of the sultan." Karaveli, 2018, p. 81.

[51] TRT World, 2017.

[52] TRT World, 2017.

[53] Yackley, 2016.

[54] Yackley, 2016.

[55] The data regarding the Jeddah Massacre is retrieved from Ochsenwald, 1977.

[56] Zürcher, 2004, p. 71

[57] Zürcher, 2004, p. 80.

[58] An example from recent history is the reaction that came in Nepal in 2004 after a group associated with al-Qaeda killed twelve Nepalis in Iraq. People in Kathmandu and other cities in Nepal took to the streets, and there were several incidents of attacks on Muslims, mosques, and employment and travel agencies from the Middle East.

[59] de Bernières, 2005, p. 565.

[60] The information used for describing the situation of the Jews is retrieved from Cohen, 2012.

61 The information in this section is mainly retrieved from Zürcher, 2004.

[62] The Circassians come from the steppe country north of the Caucasus and the east coast of the Black Sea. After a long war against the Russians, the Circassians suffered defeat in 1864, with most of them migrating to the Ottoman Empire. Circassian is still spoken by around. 150,000 people in Turkey. Alver, 2009.

[63] Zürcher, 2004, p. 88.

[64] Zürcher, 2004, pp. 88-90.

[65] Zürcher, 2004, pp. 95-99.

[66] Thrace is the southeastern "tip" of the Balkan Peninsula, where Istanbul is at the very end of the tip.

[67] Store norske leksikon, Gallipolifelttoget; Zürcher 2004, pp. 118-119.

[68] King, 2014, p. 36.

[69] Zürcher, 2004, p. 118; New Zealand n.d.

[70] Reproduced several places, including on the website of the Australian embassy in Turkey. During the war, Europeans were referred to as "Johnnies" and Turks were referred to as "Mehmets."

[71] The information in this section is mainly retrieved from Finkel, C., 2005, unless otherwise noted.

[72] Finkel, C., 2005, p. 529.

[73] Antep was named Gaziantep ("gazi" means "veteran" or "war hero") in 1921 by the nationalists in Ankara, in recognition of the city's war efforts against the French. Maraş was able to convince the parliament to add *kahraman* (hero/heroic) to its name in 1973.

Urfa could not simply observe this without needing some cosmetic changes itself, and convinced parliament in 1984 to rename it Şanlıurfa ("Urfa the Glorious").

[74] See Chapter 7 on the Armenians regarding these legal procedures.

[75] A census done in 1927, when Ankara had been the capital of Turkey for four years, counted only 74,500 inhabitants in the town. Although the city now has five million inhabitants, the growth has happened mainly after World War II. "The Turkish capital had been willed into existence," and in the mid-1940s, "it still took an act of imagination to see it as a real city." King, 2014, pp. 193, 327.

[76] Finkel, C. pp.541-2.

[77] Mango, 1999, p. 275.

[78] Zürcher, 2004, p. 152.

[79] Ahmad, 2014, loc. 1544; Mango, 1999, p. 275.

[80] Finkel, C., 2005, pp.. 542-543; Schønhardt et al,2019.

[81] Karavelli, 2018, p. 35.

[82] Karavelli, 2018, p. 35; Mango, 1999, 345.

[83] Finkel, C., 2005, pp. 543-44.

[84] King, 2014, p. 51.

[85] Bell-Fialkoff, 1993.

[86] Shaw, 1998.

[87] Shaw, 1998, pp. 59-60.

[88] Shaw, 1998.

[89] Shaw, 1998, p. 74.

[90] King, 2014, p. 64.

[91] Shaw, 1998, p. 76.

[92] Shaw, 1998, p. 77.

[93] In present-day Georgia.

[94] Eastern provinces of present-day Turkey.

[95] The majority population in Azerbaijan.

[96] Shaw, 1998.

[97] Musbah Haidar, 1945, as quoted in King, 2014, p. 40.

[98] King, 2014, p. 71.

[99] Republic of Turkey, Ministry of Foreign Affairs, n.d.

[100] Shields, 2013, p. 5.

[101] Johnsen, 2019, p. 38.

[102] Zürcher, 2004, p. 160.

[103] King, 2014, pp. 85-87.

[104] Zürcher, 2004, p. 160-62.

[105] Finkel, C., 2005, p. 545.

[106] Mango, 1999, p. 406.

[107] Mango, 1999, p. 406.

[108] Mango, 1999, p. 406.

[109] King, 2014, p. 180-81.

[110] Finkel, C., 2005, pp. 552-53; Zürcher, 2004, pp. 158-59; Ahmad, 2014, loc. 1560.

111 Zürcher, 2004, p. 158.

112 Finkel, C., 2005, p. 545; Karaveli, 2018, p. 37

113 Finkel, C., 2005, p. 550; Mango, 1999, pp. 424-5.

114 Finkel, C., 2005, pp. 551-2; Zürcher, 2010, pp. 6-7.

115 C Finkel, 2005, p. 554

116 Zürcher, 2010, pp. 10-11.

117 Zürcher, 2010, p. 15.

118 Zürcher, 2010, pp. 17-25.

119 Johnsen, 2019, p. 32.

120 "Islamist" refers to political Islam, i.e. the use of (one's interpretation of) Islam in politics, and the use of Islam to justify politics.

121 Ayata, 1996, p. 41.

122 As quoted in Ellison, Grace, Turkey Today, Hutchinson, London, 1928, p. 24, reproduced in Mango, 1999, p. 463.

123 Mango, 1999, p. 437.

124 Ayata, 1996, p. 42.

125 Mango, 1999, p. 499; Heper, 1997, p. 34.

126 Sufism, the mystic approach to Islam, plays a large role in Turkish religious life.

127 Çağaptay, 2017, p. 23-24; Heper, 1997, p. 34.

128 Gürbüz, 2016, p. 43.

129 Nachmani 2003, p. 88-89.

130 Fukuyama, 2018, p. 6.

131 Nachmani, 2003, p. 90.

132 Cağaptay, 2017, p. 79.

133 More on this under the "Military Coups" headline below.

134 Johnsen, 2019, p. 84

135 Bora and Caliskan, 2007/8, p. 140.

136 The series is called Ethos outside of Turkey.

137 Cagaptay, 2017, p. 8.

[138] United States Commission on International Religious Freedom, 2019, p. 216.

[139] United States Commission on International Religious Freedom, 2019, p. 217.

[140] United States Commission on International Religious Freedom, 2019, p. 216.

[141] A substantial number of the population in Turkey are Alevis and do not identify as Muslims. The Alevis are further described in Chapter 8.

[142] United States Commission on International Religious Freedom, 2019, p. 218.

[143] Kasbarian, 2016, p. 209.

[144] United States Commission on International Religious Freedom, 2019, p. 220.

[145] U.S. News and World Report, 2019, "The 10 Countries With the Most Religious Freedom, Ranked by Perception," accessed on March 17, 2020, at https://www.usnews.com/news/best-countries/slideshows/the-10-countries-with-the-most-religious-freedom-ranked-by-perception

[146] Cook, 2016.

[147] C. Finkel, p. 548-49.

[148] The members of an ethnic groups almost always subscribed to the same religion, at least if one can count Alevism as a branch of Islam. The non-Turkish Muslims groups included Kurds, Arabs, Lazes, Muslim Georgians, Greek-speaking Muslims, Albanians, Macedonian Muslims, Pomaks, Serb Muslims, Bosnians, Tartars, Circassians, Abkhazes, and Daghestanis. Cagaptay, 2004, p. 86-7.

[149] C. Finkel, p. 546-7.

[150] Fukuyama, 2018, p. 55.

[151] Fukuyama, 2018, p. 56.

[152] Cagaptay, 2004, p. 93.

[153] As quoted in Cagaptay, 2004, p. 89.

[154] Cagaptay, 2004, p. 91.

[155] Mango, 1999, p. 495. The words were written on a blackboard by the dining table, and then discussed back and forth.

[156] Cagaptay, 2004, p. 88.

[157] Mango, 1999, p. 496.

[158] "The name Rio Amazonas was given after native warriors attacked a 16th-century expedition by Francisco de Orellana. The warriors were led by women, reminding de Orellana of the Amazon warriors, a tribe of women warriors (...) mentioned in Greek mythology." Wikipedia, 2020, "Amazon River," accessed March 19, 2020, at https://en.wikipedia.org/wiki/Amazon_River.

[159] Mango, 1999, p. 517.

[160] Cagaptay, 2004, p. 88.

[161] Quoted in Karaveli, 2018, p. 94.

[162] Cagaptay, 2004, p. 89.

[163] Ruşen Eşref Ünaydın as quoted in Cagaptay, 2004, p. 94.

[164] C. Finkel, p. 520.

[165] Quoted in Kili, 1980, p. 388.

[166] As quoted in Kili, 1980, p. 388.

[167] Kili, 1980, p. 388.

[168] Fukuyama, 2018, p. 166.

[169] Fukuyama, 2018, p. 183-4.

[170] Mango, 1999, p. 496.

[171] Gürbüz, 2016, p. 32.

[172] Quoted in Hussein, 2018.

[173] Bora and Caliskan, 2007/8, p. 146.

[174] Esen, 2014, p. 602.

[175] Kili, 1980, p. 391.

[176] Kili, 1980, p. 392.

[177] As quoted in Kili, 1980, p. 389.

[178] Karaveli, 2018, p. 40, 102.

[179] Nachmani, 2003, p. 96-7.

[180] Quoted in Karaveli, 2018, p. 128.

[181] This is of course also explained by the amount of resources spent on science.

[182] Bora and Caliskan, 2007/8, p. 146.

[183] Quoted in Marcus, p. 84.

[184] Roussau, 1762, Book III, Chapter XV.

[185] Kili, 1980, p. 393-4.

[186] Kili, 1980, p. 397.

[187] Kalaycioglu, 2001, p. 57.

[188] Heper, 1997, p. 32.

[189] Karaveli, 2018, p. 105.

[190] Nachmani, 2003, p. 93.

[191] In 2022 it was reduced to 7%.

[192] Cagaptay, 2017, p. 87-9; Johnsen, 2019, p. 81.

[193] Amnesty International, n.d., "Background" section.

[194] Finkel, C., 2005, p. 515.

[195] Göçek, 2008, p. 104.

[196] Göçek, 2008, p. 104.

[197] Karaveli, 2018, p. 116.

[198] Amnesty International, 2019, p. 2.

[199] The Kurdish armed group with which we will acquaint ourselves in chapter 6.

[200] Quoted in Marcus, p. 192. The sentence "I think, therefore I am." was formulated by the French philosopher Descartes.

[201] Amnesty International, 2019, p. 2-3.

[202] After the latest revision in 2008, article 301 in the penal code now reads:

"The person who denigrates openly the Turkish Nation, the State of the Turkish Republic or the Grand Assembly of Turkey and the judicial institutions of the State shall be punishable by imprisonment from 6 months to 2 years.

The persons who denigrate the military and police organizations of the State will too receive the same punishment.

Expressions of thought with the intention to critique shall not constitute a crime.

The prosecution under this article will require the approval of the Ministry of Justice."

Retrieved on April 7, 2020, from http://bianet.org/english/english/106668-parliament-passes-the-revised-article-301-with-250-votes-against-65

203 Cagaptay, 2017, p. 107.

204 Bir Gün, 2019.

205 As quoted in Mango, 1999, p. 364.

206 Mango, 1999, p. 473.

207 Mango, 1999, p. 303.

208 Karaveli, 2018, p. 16, 30-31.

209 Mango, 1999, provides 1920 as the year (p. 303), but most other sources set the year at 1921, including Karaveli, 2018.

210 Mango, 1999, pp. 303-4.

211 Mango, 1999, p. 365.

212 Mango, 1999, p. 448.

213 Mango, 1999, p. 450.

214 Karaveli, 2018, p. 33.

215 Karaveli, 2018, p. 32.

216 Karaveli, 2018, pp. 118-9.

217 Karaveli, 2018, pp. 11-12.

218 Karaveli, 2018, pp. 177-80.

219 Schenkkan, 2018.

220 The Kurdish armed group.

221 Başaran, 2017, pp. 77-81.

222 Osterlund, 2020.

223 Osterlund, 2020; Frazer, 2020.

224 Associated Press, 2020.

[225] Mango, 1999, p. 427.

[226] Committee to Protect Journalists, n.d.

[227] Wikipedia, 2020 "List of journalists killed in Turkey."

[228] European Federation of Journalists, 2019.

[229] Corke et al., 2014, p. 8.

[230] Corke et al., 2014, p. 4.

[231] Corke et al., 2014, p. 7.

[232] Corke et al., 2014, p. 7.

[233] Corke et al., 2014, p. 12.

[234] Corke et al., 2014, p. 7.

[235] Karaveli, 2018, p. 56.

[236] Corke et al., 2014, p. 6.

[237] Forensic Architecture, 2019; Human Rights Watch, 2020, "HR defenders" section.

[238] Amnesty International, 2019, p. 1.

[239] Quoted in Human Rights Watch, 2019, "III. Undermining the Right to a Legal Defense" section.

[240] Human Rights Watch, 2019, "Summary" section.

[241] Nachmani, 2003, p. 153.

[242] Nachmani, 2003, p. 153.

[243] Amnesty International, n.d., "Torture and other ill-treatment" section.

[244] Johnsen, 2019, p. 54.

[245] Johnsen, 2019, p. 34. The biography was written by H.C. Armstrong and the full title is "Grey Wolf, Mustafa Kemal. An intimate study of a dictator."

[246] Mango, 1999, p. 396.

[247] A slight revision of the famous Lord Acton quote "Power tends to corrupt and absolute power corrupts absolutely," which Acton wrote in a 1887 letter.

[248] Johnsen, 2019, p. 85.

[249] Quoted in Johnsen, 2019, p. 70.

[250] Not his real name. Engin's story has been altered to anonymize him.

[251] Harris, 1970, p. 441.

[252] Harris, 1970.

[253] As quoted in Ahmad, 2014, Loc 2032.

[254] Harris, 1970.

[255] Harris, 1970, p. 451.

[256] Zürcher, 2004, p. 248.

[257] Mehmet Ali Bayar, interview, December 16, 2019.

[258] Zürcher, 2004, p. 248.

[259] Marcus, 2007, p. 19.

[260] Marcus, 2007, p. 19.

[261] Zürcher, 2004, p. 251.

[262] Zürcher, 2004, p. 257.

[263] Zürcher, 2004, p. 256.

[264] Zürcher, 2004, p. 258.

[265] Zürcher, 2004, p. 258.

[266] Zürcher, 2004, p. 258.

[267] Marcus, 2007, p. 21.

[268] Çelebi, 2009.

[269] Senem Deniz, interview, Ankara, December 19, 2019.

[270] Karaveli, 2018, p. 170-1.

[271] Marcus, 2007, p. 49-50.

[272] Kalaycioglu, 2001, p. 55.

[273] Karaveli, 2018, p. 178.

[274] Karaveli, 2018, p. 178.

[275] Karaveli, 2018, p. 185.

[276] Johnsen, p. 56.

[277] Cagaptay, 2017, p. 55.

[278] Cagaptay, 2017, p. 55.

[279] van Bruinessen, 1991, p. 19.

[280] Marcus, 2007, pp. 83-4.

[281] Kalaycioglu, 2001, p. 55.

[282] Constitution of the Republic of Turkey.

[283] The Constitution of the United States of America.

[284] Constitution of October 4, 1958 (France).

[285] Although the constitution has been amended a few times through referenda, a referendum in Turkey is rarely free and fair. There is also a problem related to the one-off referendum on a constitutional change, where the process of changing such a fundamental document is simply not thorough enough. Other models of changing a constitution involve a two-tiered process where two separate parliaments have to approve an amendment. This gives everybody more time to assess the change, and it gives the people the opportunity to change the distribution of parliament seats in the intermediate election.

[286] Johnsen, 2019, p. 233.

[287] Quoted in BBC, 2013.

[288] Information on Fethullah Gülen and his relationship with Erdoğan is gathered from Johnsen, 2019; Cagaptay, 2017; Schenkkan, 2018; BBC, 2013; Ayata, 1996.

[289] Cagaptay, 2017, p. 9.

[290] Johnsen, 2019, p. 9.

[291] Cagaptay, 2017, p. 9.

[292] Johnsen, 2019, p. 8-9.

[293] Johnsen, 2019, p. 9.

[294] Johnsen, 2019, p. 225.

[295] Human Rights Watch, 2020, "After the state of emergency" section.

[296] Human Rights Watch, 2020, "After the state of emergency" section.

[297] Johnsen, 2019, p. 239.

[298] Johnsen, 2019, p. 258.

[299] U.S. Commission on International Religious Freedom, 2019, p. 217.

[300] Amnesty International, 2019, p. 4.

[301] Johnsen, 2019, p. 266.

[302] Johnsen, 2019, p. 278.

[303] Quoted in Schenkkan, 2018.

[304] Schenkkan, 2018.

---

[305] Johnsen, 2019, p. 235.

[306] Johnsen, 2019, pp. 245-6.

[307] Johnsen, 2019, pp. 239-40, 247-8.

[308] Johnsen, 2019, pp. 254-5.

[309] Johnsen, 2019, pp. 259-60.

[310] Quoted in Reuters Staff, 2017.

[311] Nachmani, 2003, p. 46.

[312] Nachmani, 2003, p. 46.

[313] Nachmani, 2003, pp. 27-8.

[314] Nachmani, 2003, pp. 104-5, 211-2; Finkel, A., 2012, p. 85.

[315] Nachmani, 2003, p. 106.

[316] Nachmani, 2003, pp. 99-106.

[317] The Constantinopolitan Society, 2017.

[318] Göçek, 2008, p. 99.

[319] Zürcher, 2004, p. 326; Seim and Lurås, *Bulgarias historie.*

[320] Zürcher, 2004, p. 236.

[321] Schenkkan, 2018.

[322] GAP Regional Development Administration, n.d.

[323] Hussein, 2018.

[324] Nachmani, 2003, p. 10.

[325] According to the official website, "The call of the Muslim Brotherhood was based on two key pillars:

1-The introduction of the Islamic Shari`ah as the basis controlling the affairs of state and society.

2-Work to achieve unification among the Islamic countries and states, mainly among the Arab states, and liberating them from foreign imperialism." Retrieved on July 16, 2020, from https://www.ikhwanweb.com/article.php?id=813

[326] Al Jazeera Staff, 2017; Britannica, n.d.; Bekdil, 2017; Fradkin and Libby, 2013.

[327] Cagaptay, 2017, p. 169.

[328] Cagaptay, 2017, pp. 169-73.

[329] Nachmani, 2003, pp. 122.

[330] Currently, Russia only has a military base in Armenia, if one disregards its illegal presence in Abhkazia and South-Ossetia in Georgia after the 2008 conflict. Wikipedia, 2020, List of Russian military bases abroad.

[331] Nachmani, 2003, p. 139.

[332] The European Economic Community became part of the European Union when the latter was founded in 1993.

[333] Nachmani, 2003, pp. 60-66; European Commission, 2020a; European Commission, 2020b.

[334] European Parliament, 1997.

[335] European Parliament, 1997.

[336] European Commission, 2019.

[337] Cagaptay, 2017, p. 98. None of the countries mentioned have become EU members.

[338] Nachmani, 2003, p. 57.

[339] Zürcher, 2004, p. 259.

[340] "McCarthyism" was the term used to describe the exaggerated hunt for communists in the US, led by Senator Joseph McCarthy (senator from 1947 until his death in 1957).

[341] Karaveli, 2018, p. 172.

[342] Karaveli, 2018, p. 175.

[343] Karaveli, 2018, p. 185.

[344] Karaveli, 2018, p. 180.

[345] Nachmani, 2003, p. 142.

[346] Nachmani, 2003, p. 143.

[347] Karaveli, 2018, p. 199.

[348] Daily Sabah, 2020.

[349] Nachmani, 2003, p. 7.

[350] Nachmani, 2003, p. 29.

[351] The preamble of the treaty states that the members of the alliance are "determined to safeguard the freedom, common heritage and civilisation of their peoples, founded on the principles of democracy, individual liberty and the rule of law."

[352] This faction is referred to as the Eurasians.

[353] Pamuk, 1994, p. 102.

---

[354] Wikipedia, 2020, *İmam bayıldı.*

[355] Bergum 2018, p. 57; Barlow, 2006.

[356] Bergum 2018, p. 9.

[357] Turkey is among the countries consuming the most tea in the world. According to Wikipedia, it is number one, but an article in the Telegraph from 2017 lists it as number eight, after Paraguay (no. 1), Uruguay, Argentina, Kenya, The Gambia, Djibouti and Kuwait. Smith, 2017; Wikipedia contributors, 2020, *List of countries by tea consumption per capita.*

[358] Bergum 2018, p. 18.

[359] Bergum 2018, p. 85.

[360] Johnsen 2019, p. 340.

[361] Mango 1999, p. 481.

[362] A suffix is the ending of a word that is added depending on, for instance, which time one is referring to (past, present, future) or whether an activity is done by one person or more than one person (he or they). In English one usually only uses one suffix per word. For instance, the suffix '-es' is added to the verb 'go' if one is talking about a single person going: "He goes." The sentence "They will go" has no suffixes in English, whereas in Turkish both 'will' (-ecek) and 'they' (-ler) are conveyed in the suffixes of the word, so the whole sentence can be said in one word: "Gidecekler."

[363] For an explanation of the pronunciation of Turkish letters, see the foreword.

[364] Starostin, George, 2016; Georg et al. 1999.

[365] Wikipedia contributors, 2020, *List of earthquakes in Turkey.*

[366] Altayli and Caglayan, 2019.

[367] Altayli and Caglayan, 2019.

[368] Altayli and Caglayan, 2019.

[369] King, 2014, p. 238.

[370] Hürriyet Daily News, 2019b.

[371] Hürriyet Daily News, 2015.

[372] McTighe, 2019.

[373] Nachmani, 2003, pp. 128-9.

[374] Lehtinen, 2012.

[375] Nachmani, 2003, p. 128.

[376] Nachmani, 2003, pp. 129-30.

[377] Karaveli, 2018, p. 19.

[378] Karaveli, 2018, p. 19.

[379] Karaveli 2018, pp. 135-6.

[380] Quoted in Karaveli, 2018, p. 136.

[381] Finkel, A., 2012, p. 10.

[382] Karaveli, 2018, p. 189. Notice that Erdoğan, from a working class family, does not know for sure that his father's side is Laz. Had his family been more prestigious or renowned, he would probably have known.

[383] Mango, 1999, p. 498.

[384] Mango, 1999, p. 499.

[385] Nachmani, 2003, p. 75.

[386] Celasun and Rodrik, 1989, p. 619.

[387] Karaveli, 2018, p. 83.

[388] Karaveli, 2018, p. 91.

[389] A cotton gin is a machine that separates the cotton fibres from the seed.

[390] Karaveli, 2018, p. 97.

[391] Karaveli, 2018, p.97.

[392] Celasun and Rodrik, 1989, p. 619.

[393] Mango, 1999, pp. 481-2.

[394] Celasun and Rodrik, 1989, p. 620.

[395] Acemoglu, 2015.

[396] OECD, 2018, p. 8-9. The growth was 7.4% in 2017 and projected to be 5.1% in 2018.

[397] Içduygu, 2005, p. 89.

[398] Turkish Statistical Institute, 2020.

[399] Statista, 2020.

[400] OECD, n.d., *Labour force.*

[401] Nachmani, 2003, p. 80.

[402] OECD, 2020, *Turkey* section.

[403] The Gini index, which measures inequality, is at 24.2 for Slovenia (2017), the most equal country in the World Bank data. For Turkey it is 41.9 (2018), slightly higher than the US at 41.1 (2016), China at 38.5 (2016) and Russia at 37.5 (2018). World Bank, 2020.

[404] Karaveli, 2018, p. 132.

[405] World Inequality Database, n.d.

[406] A recent study showing the significant impacts of unions on inequality is Farber et al, 2018.

[407] Karaveli, 2018, p. 132.

[408] Turkish Minute, 2019.

[409] Helliwell et al, 2019, p. 26.

[410] Helliwell et al, 2019, p. 36.

[411] Cagaptay, 2017, p. 5.

[412] OECD, n.d., Better Life Index. Turkey. How's Life.

[413] "Life satisfaction measures how people evaluate their life as a whole rather than their current feelings. When asked to rate their general satisfaction with life on a scale from 0 to 10, Turkish people on average gave it a 5.5 grade, much lower than the OECD average of 6.5." OECD, n.d., Better Life Index. Life Satisfaction. Turkey.

[414] OECD, n.d., Better Life Index. Jobs. Turkey.

[415] World Bank, 2014, p. 2.

[416] Hansen, 2019.

[417] Guiness World Records, 2020.

[418] Union head Şükrü Durmuş quoted in Kent, 2020.

[419] Johnsen, 2019, pp. 149-51; Freedom House, 2014, p. 7.

[420] Johnsen, 2019, pp. 151-56.

[421] Robins, 2008, p. 641.

[422] Baran, 2000, p. 138.

[423] Cagaptay, 2017, p. 109.

[424] Johnsen, 2019, p. 343.

[425] Johnsen, 2019, p. 176.

[426] Danforth, 2014.

[427] Bakeer, 2020; Reuters Institue for the Study of Journalism, 2018.

[428] Bakeer, 2020.

[429] Danforth, 2014.

[430] Karaveli, 2018, p. 135.

[431] Baran, 2000, p. 136.

[432] Nachmani, 2003, p. 95.

[433] Freedom House, 2014, p. 7.

[434] Johnsen, 2019, p. 152.

[435] Johnsen, 2019,

[436] Cagaptay, 2017, p. 137.

[437] Quoted in Cagaptay, 2017, p. 67.

[438] Examples of this behavioral pattern "range from Austria's Freedom Party, the Italian Lega Nord, Turkey's Erdogan, Hungary's Orban, Venezuela's Chavez, Guatemala's Morales and not least the United States' Trump." Pring and Vrushi, 2019.

[439] Freedom House, 2014, p. 13.

[440] Johnsen, 2019, pp. 103-4.

[441] Bild, 2016.

[442] Pitel, 2018.

[443] Johnsen, 2019, p. 331; Wikipedia contributors, 2018, *Sevim Tanürek.*

[444] The dark area is based on similar markings in CIA World Fact Book and the online encyclopedia *Store norske leksikon.*

[445] Norwegian and Swedish are mutually understandable.

[446] Not his real name. Some details about Mehmet have been changed in order to anonymize him.

[447] Finkel, A., 2012, p. 149.

448 van Bruinessen, 1991, p. 10.

449 See the section on nationalism in Chapter 3.

450 Literally "shit talk."

451 Although the government was technically civilian, the military had a lot of influence. For instance, it was the 1980 coup maker, General Kenan Evren, who was president until 1989.

452 Hashim, 2012, p. 3.

453 Quoted in Nachmani, 2003, p. 36.

454 Quoted in Human Rights Watch, 1996, p. 4.

455 Marcus, 2007, p. 96.

456 Quoted in Davis et al., 2012, p. 106.

457 Marcus, 2007, p. 144.

458 Marcus, 2007, p. 109.

459 Marcus, 2007, p. 263.

460 This was nothing new. Turkey had already received permission from Baghdad in 1986 to bomb the Kurds in northern Iraq. Of course, without such permission, the attacks themselves would have been in breach of international law. The fact that so many civilians were killed indicates that the way in which the attacks were carried out amounted to a war crime.

461 Cited in Marcus, 2007, p. 284.

462 Marcus, 2007, p. 284.

463 Oktay Eksi as cited in Marcus, 2007, p. 124.

464 As cited in Marcus, 2007, p. 249.

465 Çandar as cited in Marcus, 2007, p. 281.

466 The former leader of the HDP party, introduced in the PKK section of this chapter.

467 International Crisis Group, 2011, p. 22. BDP was the forerunner of the political party HDP, which has much support among Kurds.

468 Federalism is a way of structuring the government. The US is an example, where all its 50 states have a degree of autonomy, but the national parliament (the Congress) has the authority to make laws that govern the entire country. A ruling by the Supreme Court is valid in all the states.

469 As cited in International Crisis Group, 2011, p. 22.

[470] The discrimination takes several forms. For example, locally elected officials must fight much harder to get funds from the central government if they belong to a party other than that/those in government. Another example is the airport in Diyarbakır, which is the main hub in the area. It only has domestic flights, but in 2010 it was allowed to begin offering international flights. There are over half a million Kurds living in Germany, and tickets were sold for three months to Frankfurt and Stuttgart. The day before the first flight, the military withdrew the permission, canceled everything, and blamed the lack of security. International Crisis Group, 2011, pp.22-24.

[471] International Crisis Group, 2011, p. 24.

[472] The other NATO countries supplying Turkey with conventional weapons in the period 1990-2017 are (in descending order of value of exports) Spain, Italy, the Netherlands, Norway, Canada and Denmark. NATO has accounted for 91% of Turkey's arms imports during this period. SIPRI Arms Transfers Database.

[473] International Crisis Group, 2012b, p. 14.

[474] Nachmani, 2003, p. 175.

[475] According to the CIA World Fact Book, Turkey's 2017 national budget was USD 185 billion.

[476] Silverman, 2015; Zürcher, 2004, p. 113.

[477] Miller and Miller, 1982, p. 55.

[478] Lepsius, Johannes. Deutschland und Armenien. 1914-1918. Sammlung diplomatischer Aktenstücke. Tempelverlag zu Potsdam, 1919, p. 489-490, quoted in Miller and Miller, 1982, pp. 54-55.

[479] The estimates vary. According to Zürcher, 2004, "around 1,500,000 (...) is probably a reasonable estimate." (P. 113.) Wilkinson (1983) puts the number of Armenians in the Ottoman Empire before the First World War at 1,750,000 (p. 345). Silverman (2015) sets the number at 1.7 million, whereas Walker (1980) sites the Armenian Patriarchate which gave the figure 1,845,450 (quoted in Miller and Miller, 1983, p. 51).

[480] Zürcher, 2004, p. 113.

[481] Dashdondog 2011, p. 32.

[482] Dashdondog 2011, pp. 33-36; Mendelsohn, 2017; Schønhardt et al., 2019.

[483] Butt 2017; Schønhardt et al., 2019.

[484] Quoted in Ueno, 2013, p. 97.

[485] Ueno, 2013, p. 96.

[486] Göçek, 2008, p. 103.

[487] Butt, 2017, p. 130.

[488] Shepard, 1911, pp. 317-18.

[489] Cooper and Akçam, 2005, p. 82.

[490] Ueno, 2013, p. 93.

[491] Quoted in Ueno, 2013, p. 93.

[492] Quoted in Wilkinson, 1983, pp. 344-45.

[493] Butt, 2017, p. 134.

[494] Morgenthau, 1918, as quoted in Butt, 2017, p. 134.

[495] Butt, 2017, p. 136.

[496] Finkel, C., 2005, p. 516.

[497] Finkel, C., 2005, p. 517.

[498] Astourian, 1990, p. 130; Butt, 2017, p. 137.

[499] Astourian, 1990, p. 130.

[500] Astourian, 1990, p. 130; Finkel, C., 2005, p. 517.

[501] Hovanissian, 1987, as quoted in Butt, 2017, p. 138.

[502] Ziya Gökalp as quoted in Butt, 2017, p. 138.

[503] Quoted in Butt, 2017, p. 141.

[504] Butt, 2017, pp. 141-142.

[505] Butt, 2017, pp. 147, 152; Finkel, C., 2005, p. 533.

[506] Zürcher, 2004, p. 116.

[507] Quoted in Butt, 2017, p. 150.

[508] Quoted in Butt, 2017, p. 151.

[509] Quoted in Butt, 2017, p. 151.

[510] Butt, 2017, p. 159.

[511] Finkel, C., 2005, p. 534; Butt, 2017, p. 153-156; Cooper and Akçam, 2005, p. 82; Silverman, 2015.

[512] Zürcher, 2004, p. 115.

[513] Miller and Miller, p. 54. Also pointed out by Zürcher, 2004, p. 116.

[514] Ahmed Refik as cited in Finkel, C., 2005, p. 534.

[515] Zurcher, 2004, p. 109.

[516] Zürcher, 2004, p. 116.

[517] Çetin, 2008, pp. 52-53.

[518] Çetin, 2008, p. 63.

[519] Çetin, 2008, p. 64.

[520] Miller and Miller, 1982, p. 64.

[521] Kevorkian, 2015, p. 5; King, 2014, p. 193.

[522] As cited in Kevorkian, 2015, p. 8.

[523] Kevorkian, 2015, p. 10.

[524] Kevorkian, 2015, p. 11.

[525] Kevorkian, 2015, p. 14.

[526] As cited in Kevorkian, 2014, p. 94.

[527] As cited in Kevorkian, 2014, p. 94.

[528] Kevorkian, 2014, p. 95.

[529] Kevorkian, 2014, p. 98.

[530] As cited in Kevorkian, 2014, p. 98.

[531] As cited in Kevorkian, 2014, p. 102.

[532] Kevorkian, 2014, pp. 103-107.

[533] Kevorkian, 2014, p. 107.

[534] Kevorkian, 2014, p. 107.

[535] Walker, C. J., 1980, as cited in Miller and Miller, 1982, p. 51.

[536] Silverman, 2015: Finkel, A., 2012, pp. 177-8; Wilkinson, 1983, p. 345.

[537] Finkel, A., 2012, pp. 177-8.

[538] Dyer, G., 1976, as cited in Butt, 2017, p. 160.

[539] Zürcher, 2004, p. 116.

[540] As cited in Butt, 2017, p. 160.

[541] Mango, 1999, p. 190.

---

[542] Finkel, C., 2005, pp. 538-9.

[543] Finkel, A., 2012, p. 180.

[544] Olson, 1986, p. 47.

[545] Luban, 2004, p. 183-4.

[546] Miller and Miller, 1982, p. 68.

[547] Berkowitz, 2011, pp. 1-2.

[548] Berkowitz, 2011, p. 15.

[549] The spelling varies somewhat. The most common spelling is Tehlirian.

[550] As cited in Olson, 1986, p. 52.

[551] First Secretary D.L. Busk, as cited in Olson, 1986, p. 52.

[552] Miller and Miller, 1982, p. 69.

[553] Zürcher, 2004, p. 338.

[554] Wilkinson, 1983, p. 346.

[555] Wilkinson, 1983, p. 347.

[556] CBC News, 1985.

[557] Finkel, A., 2012, p. 176.

[558] Göçek, 2008, pp. 100-1.

[559] As cited in Cooper and Akçam, 2005, p. 84.

[560] Luban, 2004, p. 183.

[561] Cooper and Akçam, 2005, p. 84.

[562] Convention on the Prevention and Punishment of the Crime of Genocide, 1948.

[563] Cooper and Akçam, 2005, p. 83.

[564] Cooper and Akçam, 2005, p. 84.

[565] Suny, 2009, p. 936.

[566] Suny, 2009, p. 937.

[567] Suny, 2009, p. 937.

[568] Suny, 2009, p. 938.

[569] Suny, 2009, p. 939.

[570] Suny, 2009, p. 939.

[571] Suny, 2009, p. 942.

[572] As cited in Nachmani, 2003, p. 71.

[573] Suny, 2009, p. 932.

[574] Finkel, A., 2012, p. 184.

[575] Finkel, A., 2012, pp. 186-7.

[576] A person from Istanbul is referred to as an *Istanbullu* in Turkish. (Similarly, a person from Izmir is an *Izmirli*, a person from Ankara is an *Ankaralı*, etc.)

[577] Suny, 2009, p. 944.

[578] Cağaptay, 2017, p. 109.

[579] Johnsen, 2019, p. 286.

[580] Kadıoğlu, 2007, p. 289.

[581] Finkel, A., 2012, p. 179.

[582] Maureen Freely, in preface of Çetin, 2008; Finkel, A., 2012, pp. 175-6.

[583] Çetin, 2008, p. 65.

[584] Çetin, 2008, p. 102.

[585] Kasbarian, 2016, p. 209.

[586] Kasbarian, 2016, p. 210.

[587] As cited in Kasbarian, 2016, p. 223.

[588] Balancar (ed.), 2015, p. 24.

[589] Balancar (ed.), 2015, p. 26.

[590] Karaveli, 2018, p. 136-7.

[591] Kasbarian, 2016, p. 226.

[592] Kasbarian, 2016, p. 223.

[593] Finkel, A., 2012, pp. 175-6.

[594] Nachmani, 2003, pp. 104-5, 211-2; A. Finkel, 2012, p. 85.

[595] Cooper and Akçam, 2005, p. 89-92.

[596] Kasbarian, 2016, p. 217.

[597] Kasbarian, 2016, p. 218.

[598] Hürriyet Daily News, 2020.

599 Nachmani, 2003, p. 45.
600 Mustafa Kemal Atatürk as cited in Mango, 1999, pp. 217-18.
601 Mango, 1999, p. 198.
602 Göçek 2008, p. 104; Zürcher 2004, p. 237.
603 Törne, 2015, p. 412-14.
604 Zürcher, 2004, p. 237.
605 Zürcher, 2004, p. 230.
606 Törne, 2015, pp. 403-04.
607 Törne, 2015.
608 Zürcher, 2004, p. 231.
609 Törne, 2015, p. 411.
610 Johnsen, 2018.
611 Kaliber, 2019, pp. 1-2.
612 Akan, 2011, p. 608.
613 Akan, 2011, p. 609.
614 Mills, 2008, p. 394.
615 King, 2014, p. 61.
616 Akan, 2011, p. 606.
617 Törne, 2015, p. 409.
618 USCIRF, 2019, p. 219.
619 USCIRF, 2019, p. 219.
620 Malz, 2016.
621 Malz, 2016.
622 Jews were expelled from Portugal in 1496.
623 Karaveli, 2018, p. 12.
624 The first month of the Islamic calendar.
625 van Bruinessen, 1991, p. 10; Vogt, 2018.
626 USCIRF, 2019, p. 217; Vogt, 2018.
627 Johnsen, 2019, p. 173.
628 Karaveli, 2018, p. 21.
629 Kakissis, 2019.
630 Kakissis, 2019; BBC News, 2019.
631 Hürriyet Daily News, 2019.

[632] Feride Eralp, member of the Women are Stronger Together platform, quoted in Tuysuz, 2020.

[633] The exact numbers are 38 % and 11 %, respectively. UN Women, 2016.

[634] Moody, 2020.

[635] Karakaş, 2019.

[636] Sen, 2013, p. 39.

[637] Sen, 2013, p. 39.

[638] McKernan, 2020.

[639] Sen, 2013, p. 39.

[640] McKernan, 2020.

[641] Fidan Ataselim quoted in McKernan, 2020.

[642] Sen, 2013, p. 39.

[643] Inter-Parliamentary Union, 2021.

[644] As cited in Mango, 1999, p. 164.

[645] Mango, 1999, p. 535.

[646] Hanioğlu, 2011, p. 205.

[647] Knaus, 2007, p. 52.

[648] Hanioğlu, 2011, p. 205.

[649] Hanioğlu, 2011, p. 205.

[650] As cited in HalkTV, 2021.

[651] One of the most holy sites for Muslims, in Mecca. It is the destination of the pilgrimage.

[652] Damla Umut Uzun, interview.

[653] Quoted in HalkTV, 2021.

[654] BirGün, 2021.

[655] İdİl, 2021.

[656] Interview, March 5, 2021.

[657] Human Rights Watch, 2021.

[658] Corke et al., 2014, p. 8.

[659] Corke et al., 2014, p. 8; Johnsen, 2019, p. 170.

[660] Hansen, 2019.

[661] Mengü, 2020.

[662] Alonso, 2015, p. 244.

[663] Human Rights Watch, 2013; International Crisis Group, 2013; Başaran, 2017, p. 97.

[664] Zihnioğlu, 2019.

[665] Zihnioğlu, 2019, p. 14.

[666] Başaran, 2017, p. 96.

[667] Alonso, 2015, pp. 241-2.

[668] Corke et al., 2014, p. 8.

[669] As cited in Başaran, 2017, p. 96.

[670] Corke et al., 2014, p. 8.

[671] Başaran, 2017, p. 97.

[672] Chenoweth and Stephan, 2011.

[673] Chenoweth and Stephan, 2011, p. 7.

[674] The reasons are listed in Chenoweth and Stephan, 2011, pp. 220-21.

[675] European Parliament, 2013.

[676] Chenoweth and Stephan, 2011, p. 53

[677] Chenoweth and Stephan, 2011, p. 33. The largest protests during that period were the 1978-79 protest in Iran and the 1983-86 protest in the Philippines. Both had a peak membership of two million.

[678] Mengü, 2020.

[679] Fukuyama, 2018.

[680] Fukuyama, 2018, p. 128.

[681] Fukuyama, 2018, p. 129.

[682] Fukuyama, 2018, pp. 128-30.

[683] Fethiye Çetin, interview.

[684] As cited in Hrant Dink Foundation, 2013, p. 68.

About the Author

Tor K. Birkeland (b. 1981) has worked on peace and conflict related issues on behalf of Norwegian churches and organizations in Africa, the Middle East, Asia, and in the context of the United Nations. He has a Master of Arts in International Peace and Conflict Resolution from American University, Washington, D.C. From 2017 to 2020, he lived in Ankara, and during his stay he started writing the book Turkey - The Middle Kingdom. Drawing upon historical documents, academic literature, news articles and commentary, and interviews of people from various parts of Turkish society, the book provides an insight into Turkey's history, politics and society. The Norwegian hardback version of the book, *Tyrkia – hele historien kort fortalt,* was published in 2024 by the publishing company Vega Forlag.

Made in the USA
Las Vegas, NV
24 February 2026

42616250R00164